*To Mark and Anne*

## Acknowledgments

It is a pleasure to thank the Grant Founda-
tion for supporting the course at Swarthmore
College, which was a major stimulus for this
book; the Public Health Service, National In-
stitutes of Health (Grant MH-07615-03); Mr.
and Mrs. Nicholas Sclufer for their reading
of the manuscript and important suggestions;
and . . .
my parental family of the past and my marital family of the present for more than can be
expressed.

# LEON J. SAUL, M.D.

*with the editorial assistance of Kay Powell*

# FIDELITY
## and
# INFIDELITY

*and What Makes or Breaks a Marriage*

J. B. LIPPINCOTT COMPANY

*Philadelphia / New York*

# PREFACE

In this short volume I shall try to present something of the interplay of motivation and reaction in marriage, as seen by one practicing psychoanalyst and psychiatrist, by offering a few abbreviated and highly condensed samples of some clinical observations.

The stimulus for this book came from the usefulness of giving to men and women a professional perspective on their marital problems by recounting the pertinent experiences of others. It is my hope, therefore, that by relating some of these experiences—how they can be understood, and where they may lead—I can give the reader a degree of insight that will be of cultural, educational, and possibly even practical value. As in other branches of medicine, we learn about health by studying the deviations from it. For reasons of discretion and in order to have had time to follow up outcomes, the examples given are based upon my years in Chicago before World War II. Names and other identifiable features have been changed.

In selecting examples of marital problems from the first decade of my practice, I have chosen those that have recurred frequently enough since then to be recognized as typical. Details vary, of course, but it is remarkable how the basic patterns of marriage and the sources of these patterns in childhood repeat themselves. It is surprising how often in an initial interview, while hearing the story, I think, "Right out of the book," and feel that these types of problems and what underlies them should be common knowledge.

I have tried, then, to present the experiences of those couples through whom we are most likely to see aspects of ourselves. Insight into ourselves and others can help us become a little more mature and humane, and this can make life more gratifying for ourselves and our children, and ultimately for humanity.

The reader may think that some of the couples presented here show rather extreme emotional disturbances that would make them far from normal. However, most of these couples showed little evidence of their difficulties, even to close friends. Furthermore, it is in the extremes that we see most clearly the causes of problems and the nature of the mature and healthy; differences are mostly quantitative. The extremely disturbed reveal the kinds of emotional problems that exist in much lesser degree in the better balanced personalities and marriages.

Psychodynamics—or, for short, dynamics—means the interplay of motivations and reactions, which we experience as feelings. They might be called *emotional forces*. They make us think and fantasize, feel and behave as we do. In a sense they live our lives for us, at least to some degree. We need not—in fact, cannot—relinquish individual personal responsibility for ourselves and others—rather we must take responsibility for these forces in ourselves. It should be a primary task of education, from the earliest grades, to acquaint us with these forces and to teach us how to deal with them in order to create better lives for ourselves and for those whom we influence.

The detailed operations of these emotional forces often are very complex, but the basic forces themselves are strong and easily seen; so too are their interactions. A very simple formula, $e = mc^2$ (with a minor modification), expresses a fundamental relationship in physics. Perhaps the dynamics of some of the marriages to be presented will seem oversimplified, but this is true only to a limited extent. They are simple because I have omitted all peripheral psychological mechanisms and have focused on the central, major forces and their interplay. Our concern in this book is with the essentials, with the gross anatomy of the major forces in marriage and not with minutiae. Our concern is with what has been seen and described by the philosophers and writers and is plain to all who will look with an open mind, but which only recently has begun to be systematized as part of the new, still embryonic science of psychodynamics.

Should not "knowing ourselves," be the cornerstone of education? Self-knowledge, currently taking scientific form as psychodynamics, is central to history and literature, to the psychological and social sciences, and to the fruits and threats of the physical sciences. A great fact of our age is that we already know a good deal about what makes men of cruelty and men of good will. What is more important than that this knowledge be made general, and used for the prevention of the misery man brings upon his fellows and himself?

# CONTENTS

*To become a spouse and parent is all too easy*
*But to be one all too difficult.*

BUSCH (adapted)

# I    The Nature of Marriage

*Human beings, like all higher animals, multiply by the union of the two sexes. But neither conjugation, nor even the production of offspring, is as a rule sufficient for the maintenance of the species. The further advanced the animal in the order of evolution, the longer the immaturity and the helplessness of the young and the greater the need for prolonged parental care and training. It is thus the combination of mating with parenthood which constitutes marriage in higher animals, including man. Even in its biological aspect, "marriage is rooted in the family rather than the family in marriage."*

MALINOWSKI

# 1 ANIMAL MATING

The animal kingdom gives us a perspective on human marriage. True marriage is mating for life and involves an interchange of affection, understanding and shared responsibility. Not only do other forms of life establish marriages, but they often seem to be far more successful in doing so than most humans. Among these permanently monogamous creatures are beavers, wolves, coyotes, foxes, and chinchillas, avian couples such as Canada geese and probably hawks, and a few fish. Even after the mating season, pairs live together, raising the young and helping each other.

For most creatures there is gradual courtship. This is the case with porcupines, even though the female ovulates but once a year. Courtship is gentle and romantic with the ponderous elephant, who has a strong herding instinct. The female separates from the herd. A male comes into her proximity. Little by little he approaches. After a while they feed together. One day he brushes against her with his trunk; they come to brush foreheads, nibble each other's cheeks, murmur to each other. After weeks of such tenderness they come to petting—entwining trunks, putting the tips into each other's mouths. She becomes more provocative, the play more erotic. At the climax there is no coercion from the male.

In fact, below the primates, it is the female who controls coitus, because it must be timed to the point, sometimes very exact, of her ovulation. For the elephant, pregnancy is 22 months long, and after weeks of living with the male, with every sign of devotion and love, the female, now pregnant, returns to the herd. He finds that he

3

cannot hold her. Eventually he finds another female and again becomes involved in a deep relationship. This goes on until he is about 50 years old.

Certain female birds stake out an area as their own. A succession of males courts her, but the female accepts and chooses only one for her mate. The others become suitors for other females.

Knowledge of the lives and customs of our animal cousins is basic to the understanding of all aspects of human behavior. The best general survey I know about this expanding field of animal ethology, with special reference to human behavior, is Sally Carrighar's *Wild Heritage*. This book summarizes most of the recent studies in an attractive and readable form and provides a bridge to the technical literature and specialized research. I have relied upon it heavily for the observations given above. From it we learn not only about the courting, marriage and sex lives of various other members of the animal kingdom, but we also learn of their eating habits, their ways of dealing with hostility, their social habits, their play, their use of tools and their artistic creativity. Man does not come off very well by comparison. In speech, intellect, and art, man is far, far ahead, but morally, especially in his greed and in his brutality to his own kind, he stands as a partial biological failure, a disordered menace to his and other species, with his superior intellect resting on a pathological emotional base. Therefore, his capacity for responsible love toward spouse and children, toward friends and society, and toward the human race in general is far below that of many other animals; and now in an atomic holocaust man may well destroy his race, and with it many of the more socially successful species.

As Carrighar sees it, innocence may have been corrupted by intellect, at any rate by primate intellect, for it is in the rhesus monkeys of Asia that one first sees on the evolutionary scale the degradations that so permeate human life. Adult male bears and Norway rats are hostile to the young, who must be protected from them by the mother, but not until the rhesus monkeys does one see greed, laziness and obesity, selfishness and brutality, rape, hostility, and cruelty of male to female, even to his mates and young. To cope with this egocentric, hostile male domination, we see deviousness and prostitution on the part of the female, who uses sex to avoid attack and to gain such favors as a discarded bit of banana peel. Here too clearly is the human scene, except that humans, with far more intellect, carry it to far greater lengths. It is not the animals that are brutes—it is man.

But this is no justification for hopelessness. The monkeys of South America do not behave in this fashion. The gibbons (who incidentally seem truly to sing, in a half-tone octave) apparently live very affectionate family lives. The parents embrace on meeting each evening if the father has been away for part of the day, and the adolescents of different families date and go steady for a considerable period before finding their own area and settling down as mates. The great gorillas, even those with more than one wife (and the bachelors who take advantage of this fact), seem to be friendly and peaceful. The degradation and corruption of humans —rape, crime, cruelty, war and its unimaginable excesses—seem not to reflect true human nature, but the results of a warping in the development caused by grossly injurious influences on the young during their earliest, most formative period of life: from conception to about the age of six. How childhood influences operate in human marriage is evident in the following examples, which have been selected to illustrate certain of the components that must synchronize with maturity for a marriage to work with reasonable harmony.

*But neither heat, nor frost, nor thunder,*
*Shall wholly do away, I ween,*
*The marks of that which once hath been.*
COLERIDGE

# 2 LOVE, SEX, AND PSYCHODYNAMICS

General principles, however important, do not always make interesting reading, but we gain time and understanding from them. Hence we will first summarize very briefly some dynamics underlying marriage and some forces that make a marriage effective and happy. Thereafter we shall make our points by describing certain marriages and the forces we can discern behind them.

A great deal has been written, especially by Freud and later writers, on the interrelations of sex and personality, but it is not, I believe, a settled question. Without a summary of the extensive literature, the essentials, in oversimplified form, seem about as follows.

The young of animals, at least of the higher species, form attachments very soon after birth. Normally this attachment (which is roughly equivalent to what is technically called *imprinting*) is to the mother, but if she is not present the attachment forms to a substitute. For example, a baby bird in a cage was fed by hand and became attached to the hand. When it reached adolescence it mated sexually with the hand—not with other birds of its own kind. Konrad Lorenz, who introduced the term imprinting, tells of a crow that was in love with a vacuum cleaner. In a study of dogs, it was found that if newborn puppies were kept totally isolated from human beings for at least 14 weeks, they forever lost the capacity of forming the attachment to people that is so characteristic of our canine friends. Studies of many species show that sexual drives and social relations follow the path of the original imprinting— that is, the sexual and social attraction of the adult is toward the species, or even the inanimate object, to which the initial attachment was made. Hence monkeys have become attached to a cloth "mother" and not to other monkeys, sexually or socially.

Although attachments of the human young have only recently

been studied systematically, it seems clear from clinical observation that it occurs in babies and is of the greatest importance in their entire future emotional lives. In fact, since an outstanding feature of psychotic children is their inability to form emotional attachments to others, we may speculate that this inability is a result of the failure to form such an attachment normally in the first days, weeks and months because of the way they were treated; or that if they did imprint normally, later experiences soon disrupted this.

The first big step in developing feelings for other persons is achieving a healthy attachment at the proper time. The second step is how the child learns to react to the mother, or substitute, in order to keep this attachment. If the mother is loving and provides good care, the baby forms an image (*imago*) of her as loving and providing, and reacts with pleasure to the relationship. But if the mother is depriving, loveless and harsh, the baby forms this image of her and is in conflict. Because he must have her care and love to survive, his need for love is unquenchable, but if her presence brings psychic pain, he cowers and resents it (reacts with fight-or-flight impulses, or both). Once formed, these images and patterns of reacting last for life, however well the rest of the child's personality develops.

The development of this process of reacting is a different form of learning and is known as *conditioning*. To keep love and pleasure and to avoid rebuff and pain, the child unconsciously forms certain patterns of reacting that soon become permanent.

In normality and health, pregnancy is uneventful and desired, and the newborn baby is welcomed by loving parents into a loving home. The baby responds by attaching properly and is conditioned to enjoy the love of the parents and others who are close to him and responsible for him. Later his sexual desires follow this line and are directed toward a loving member of the opposite sex. From him or her, the postadolescent adult seeks the love he needed all through childhood, and also sexual gratification. Sex is normally part of mating, and we may say that his sexual urges and his whole mating mechanism follow the pattern of the original attachment and seek satisfaction with one of the opposite sex in a setting of love, such as he enjoyed all through childhood. With love and security during childhood, the child matures normally in his adult capacities for giving love to others and for relative independence, responsibility and productivity.

In general, the younger the child the more malleable he is. The complex of motivations and reactions at the core of the personality is mostly shaped by about the age of six. The first six years of a person's life—0 to 6 for short—is therefore critical. Love and security during that time provide a healthy base for whatever comes afterward. But lack of love and security, or actively injurious treatment, with disordered feelings toward others, fosters patterns of faulty feelings to others and to oneself for life, however well the rest of the personality matures. Disordered feelings toward oneself and others underlie all the problems and miseries of life, from headaches to murder—for life is almost entirely human relations.

One's personality involves such a complex interaction of violent feelings that one hesitates to identify the essentials in simple terms. But these essentials are themselves relatively few, although they produce so many combinations that every personality is unique. So, too, are the designs of snowflakes, each different although each one is six pointed; or the limitless number of chemical compounds, each made up from only 102 elements. Therefore we may hazard the observation that two forces underlie almost all emotional problems: the need to be loved and dependent, and hostility.

Loving others and being responsible for them is an attribute of maturity. If all humans were thus mature, divorce, crime, revolution and war would vanish. But when childhood dependent-love needs are frustrated they cause shame and anger; they cause competition and much else. Hostility is part of the fight-flight mechanism of adaptation. Any threat of frustration arouses impulses to eliminate it by fleeing from it or by destroying it. This is an invaluable reflex in the wild, but in society it threatens our existence, which depends upon a different mechanism of adaptation—social cooperation. Through social cooperation we defend ourselves against animals, forces of nature and even disease. It is the archaic fight-flight mechanism within us that is our greatest enemy, only now our fight response is with atomic bombs instead of with rocks.

Hostility is not only readily aroused by threats and frustrations that are external, but also by those within our own makeup (such as shame, inferiority feelings, hurt pride, and envy, stemming perhaps from too strong dependent-love needs). Hostility generates guilt and fear of retaliation, and often is turned against ourselves, making a person his own worst enemy (in current parlance, a loser). Thus one has a guide to any personality if he can see the two poles (something like magnetic poles)—dependent-love needs and all that underlies them and results from them, and the terrible hostility and what generates it and results from it.

Man has certain characteristics, mostly matters of degree, that make him different from the rest of the animal kingdom: upright posture, ability to touch his thumb to his other fingers, speech, writing and symbolic thinking, and individual and mass violence to his own kind—not only the perpetration of violence but the enjoyment of it, even to the extent of deriving sexual pleasure from it. Of course this is a mental and emotional disease, but it is widespread, a result in large part of how children are reared. And how children are reared depends in large part on the marriages they are born into.

Marriage is one kind of human relationship. The purpose of this book is to demonstrate what underlies typical problems of marriage in the hope that we may learn from these examples how better to prepare for family life and make it more gratifying. For family life shapes the child and is the base for the rest of his existence.

# 3 COMPONENTS OF MARRIAGE

The interrelation of humans with each other is an incredibly complex and sensitive matter. To live closely with another person, no matter what the age or sex, is extraordinarily difficult. Perhaps there are exceptions, but they must be rare. Even relatively loose, alterable relationships, such as those at work, in social groups, or among friends and acquaintances, are not noted for stability and easy harmony. What then of living with a person one has bound oneself to in closest intimacy for life? And what then of adding to this children who cannot be returned?

Why are emotional relations to others so taxing? They are, it seems, because of the differences in personality. We all are in some ways so similar, but in other ways so different—which stems from the fate of each of us in earliest childhood. Each child is born into a different family and circumstances and is subjected to different attitudes, feelings, behavior and treatment. The child's reactions to all these influences shape the core of his own personality for life, affecting how well and fully the forces of maturation operate. If all adults were adequately mature, relationships between them would not be so frustrating, painful and hostile. But the patterns of reacting to the *dramatis personae* of one's childhood live on in us all. Appropriate as these reactions may have been toward the persons of our earliest years, they are apt to be utterly unworkable when they emerge years later in the adult, and are directed toward co-workers, friends, spouse or children. It is these underlying forces that bring couples together in marriage, and then may drive them apart.

Thus, an emotionally deprived, lonely boy meets a girl who likewise is isolated and needful. Their common, underlying, lonesome hunger for closeness and acceptance enables them to understand each other. They can relate closely to each other because they can *identify* with each other. But if they are intimate for long, if they

11

marry, the boy's needs make him turn to the girl as an object; he craves more love, care and attention than she can give. And she, too, changes from identification with him to an *object relation,* in which she yearns for more than can be gratified in adult life. The mutual need that brought them together now generates the frustrations that bring hostility and flight in varying forms and degrees.

We speak of "love" but often mean much that is not love. True love means a responsible interest in another for his own sake, and not for ulterior, selfish reasons. This love is seen throughout the animal kingdom, most clearly perhaps in the devotion of parents to the young, and not only to their own young. It is seen in animals in forms that only the noblest of humans seem to achieve, or perhaps we should say that only the most *mature* of humans achieve.

But marriage requires more than love. It is also composed of sex, which should be an expression of love, but which often breaks loose from love and may become a thing apart or may even serve the most hostile, cruel impulses of which humans are capable—and these impulses far exceed anything in the so-called "lower" animals.

With love and sex there must also be an enduring sense of romance.

Marriage also requires responsibility—for breadwinning and for care of the home and the family members. Responsibility is a large word, and a large part of maturity.

In youth the pressure of sex is usually so strong that its relation to reproduction and parenthood may be forgotten or seem incidental. But this, after all, is what sex is all about. With prostitutes or in seductions and certain affairs, reproduction plays no part; the chances of conception are a nuisance and a threat. The goal is to have sex, romance, companionship, money, or whatever each seeks, while eliminating reproduction. In most marriages having children is a goal, but when they arrive they are a mixed blessing; they may be burdensome, interfering nuisances, and the irritation they cause the parents may reflect back upon the children and may impair their good feelings toward themselves and others for life.

Even if there are no problems with love, sex, children or daily responsibilities, there must be a "fit," a meshing, of the childhood patterns. Otherwise these patterns can generate tensions that may exceed what a person can stand.

Reasonable harmony in a marriage thus depends upon the adequacy in each partner of the following components:

1. Love—meaning a desire to be with and close to the partner, identification with the partner, and an interest in him or her for his or her own sake without ulterior, egocentric motives.

2. Sexual attractiveness, desire and healthy functioning and enjoyment, a physical relation to the partner with relative freedom from exaggerations, perversions and impairments.

3. A sense of romance. This is hard to define. Perhaps it is a part of whatever leads certain animals and birds to reject some suitors, but then mate for life with an acceptable one. Perhaps it is the end result of many elements, making what we call "being in love." Diminishing in quantity after marriage, in quality it may continue even into old age.

4. Parenthood. One of the deepest and most enduring satisfactions that life affords. But good child rearing is a long, trying, difficult job, because what is best for the child often clashes with the parents' own comforts and desires, and with the demands of life upon them.

5. Responsibility. This comprises personal responsibility for spouse and children, including the children's direct emotional need of the parents. These include their dependence and love needs and their requirements for models of mature adults on which to mold their own ideals and development. In addition there are the children's necessities for living, schooling and companionship.

Breadwinning is usually the primary nonpersonal responsibility of the husband. Perhaps all wives should be breadwinners for a year or two to gain some appreciation of the weight and pressure of this responsibility. And perhaps all husbands should stay home and take full responsibility for home, children, food, clothes, cleaning and the rest, to experience how the wife feels when he arrives home from work each day.

6. Maturity. This includes most of the foregoing. The essence of maturity is seen in the contrast between—on the one hand—the baby and small child's utter dependence upon the mother and father for physical necessities and personal love, and—on the other hand—the parents' responsibility for, and giving to, the child. The child is weak and helpless. He thus feels inferior, insecure and competitive, and therefore is readily afraid and hostile. The child is normally egocentric, because his chief task is growing up, that is, his own development. The parent, as an adult, should be, if his or her childhood attitudes are sufficiently outgrown, relatively

independent, giving and able, with minimal hostility and competitiveness, to live and let live as a responsible, productive, cooperative parent, spouse, friend and citizen.

7. Fit or mesh. The more adequate the capacities listed above and the more adequate the outgrowing of childhood patterns in favor of mature attitudes and feelings, the more easy, free and harmonious are the relationships in the family. But even if impairments and disturbances in development exist in any of these areas, a reasonably good home life is possible if the disorders in the couple *fit* each other sufficiently well. For example, a man who was deprived as a child developed emotional defenses against asking anything from anyone; he derived satisfaction from helping and giving to those dependent upon him. He married a girl who was herself deprived, which gave them a deep feeling in common. But in her the outcome was to remain dependent and needful, an orientation that just fitted the husband's emotional position of being the strong, giving, protective partner. The risk in such situations lies in the possibility of a breakdown of the defenses and of the mature attitudes—if the husband gave out beyond his emotional means or if the wife became less appreciative of him and demanded more than he could comfortably give.

In a first interview a wife complains with bitterness of her partner's preoccupation with other matters to the neglect and deprivation of herself, and feels that she can no longer go on with the marriage in her state of frustration. She recounts a history of disturbed relationships with her mother or father or both. This raises a vital diagnostic problem. This woman has had parental difficulties, but is the personality of her husband such that he would frustrate any woman, no matter how good her relationships, and drive her to this desperation?

If this turns out to be the case, then how did his wife come to marry him? Did she unconsciously select such a man to fit the disturbed relationships of her childhood, although she is now stable and no longer dominated by her infantile patterns? Or do these patterns continue the old feelings of deprivation even though the husband, though not perfect, is a basically good husband and father, with some warmth and consideration and not much internally generated hostility? If so, can it be that the wife feels deprived or restricted mostly because of her inner pattern, and unknowingly is provocative of her husband's feelings and behavior?

Usually it is a matter of the interplay, in varying degrees, of all these components—although sometimes one or another predominates.

Although harmony and satisfaction in marriage are primarily the effects of emotional fit, there are other elements that affect this, such as health, poverty, and intelligence. One partner with an intellect far superior to the other's may become bored or annoyed, and the one with the much lower I.Q. may feel inferior, unable to cope with his (or her) spouse. So, too, ill health can become tedious, as can poverty. Such factors can aggravate minor emotional incompatibilities and play up to emotional sensitivities until the limits of tolerance are passed.

The success of a marriage and a family is largely a function of the total score on the above points. Some factors compensate for others. For example, the wife in one of the best marriages I have ever seen was sexually frigid. Although she had never had an orgasm, she enjoyed sex, was faithful to her husband, bore five children, and was an excellent wife and mother. The husband was well aware of the situation but was entirely faithful to her and rejoiced in his good fortune in having a woman who was otherwise so excellent a wife and mother.

The seven points we have mentioned (and they could be differently organized and others added) show why marriage is such a difficult relationship. Within each marital partner, and between the partners, something can be wrong with each of these seven components, and certain of these components can be split off from the others.

Successful marriage means good relations, good feelings, and happiness for all members of the family. This is the soil from which children grow up to be mature, responsible, internally satisfied spouses, parents and citizens. Mature mating requires a harmonious fusion of a number of instincts. A man, for example, may have a strong, potent sexual interest in women, but be unable to concentrate it on his wife for any length of time; or he may do this very well, but have no patience with his children; or he may be a good husband and father, but a failure as a breadwinner. Some never get beyond adolescent adventuring and never mate permanently at all. Maturation and harmonious integration of all the component instincts (love, sex, parenthood, responsibility) are required for successful mating. Partial immaturities and fragmentations are common, and so too, therefore, are inadequacy and discord.

Marriage being so complex an interaction between the partners, relieved or exacerbated by children, it is small wonder that close to a third of all marriages end in divorce or separation. Probably the contention is very severe, even if bearable, in the next third, and perhaps it is optimistic to think that the remaining third of the families are easy and happy.

But marriage and family living are only special cases of all human relations. For the reasons we have listed (which boil down to a failure to mature adequately because of disturbed childhood patterns in reaction to improper treatment), all close relationships with other persons are demanding in the extreme. Marriage is simply more intimate and more difficult to dissolve. Even the power of the sex and mating drives cannot overbalance the hostilities if the childhood pattern of either partner is too disturbed, if the patterns too far impair the mature feelings, or if the fit of the patterns between the partners is poor.

# 4 LAWS OF NATURE AND MORAL LAW

For centuries, if not millennia, man has searched for guides to living and has suspected that natural law underlies human formulations of moral law.

The following are a few thoughts on the pertinent and ancient relationship of natural and moral law, a relationship that is poorly clarified but that has great theoretical and practical importance.

Newton described certain laws in the area of terrestrial mechanics. Einstein clarified some broader principles. Other physicists have made similar major contributions. These laws of nature in the physical world can be expressed with such precision in mathematical terms that a space craft can be sent to Mars and controlled from earth. Darwin discerned certain principles or laws in the behavior, not of the inanimate world, but of biological organisms. Since then ethologists, psychologists, psychiatrists and others interested in the various aspects of behavior, have provided certain guiding concepts.

One of these concepts is that each *individual* organism has a life cycle, which it strives from within to live out: birth, maturation, some form of mating, reproduction, provision for young, senescence, death. Another principle is that just as the individual organism strives for its own survival, so it also participates in the survival of its species. Elephants do not destroy elephants, nor do mosquitoes live on mosquitoes. Fights of males for females are not, as is now known, to the death: they are only to establish dominance. Fights to establish rights to a certain territory may be more serious, but members of a given species, say gorillas, use fighting to intimidate and bluff intruders to drive them off, and not to injure or kill and risk being injured and killed. Almost all animals within their own species cooperate with each other. Man's cooperation

17

with his kind to form societies is in accordance with natural law. Through cooperation we have developed our defenses against nature. Cooperation makes possible science, which gives us food, clothing, shelter and protection against hostile microorganisms. If every man had to hunt or till the soil, we would have no scientists and no science. As long as men cooperate they are reasonably secure; their only major threat is other humans. This destructiveness of man to man is contrary to the natural law of survival of the individual and the species. Our destructive behavior toward our own species is all but unknown elsewhere in the animal kingdom, with a few minor exceptions, usually under special circumstances.

Organized crime and war are uniquely human. In fact, as far as I am aware in only a single species is anything known to ethologists at present that is similar to human war—in the harvester ants, which store seeds. If one group runs out of food it may raid another group, kill the ants, and take their seeds.

The destruction of one's species and oneself on a mass scale is against moral law as well as natural law, for the bomb may eliminate us as an evolutionary failure. If war is a manifestation of fighting for property rights, as is seen throughout the animal kingdom, then it seems to be a pathological aberration of that instinct or its controls. I think it is at bottom a symptom of widespread emotional disorder, whatever other factors are involved. At least this element must be given due weight. Moral law against cruelty and killing expresses the natural process of maturation, reproduction and care of the young. Its standard is love, which means it is pro life. The breakdown of love, of moral law, is the sign of warped emotional development, of failure to mature adequately. The mature human conforms to the natural law of the other species; he is a responsible, loving spouse, parent and citizen in the community of his own species. He may feel hostility and fight, but he does not destroy his species and himself.

And warping, we now know, is chiefly the result of faulty child rearing in the earliest weeks, months and years (0 to 6), causing the reaction of egocentricity and hostility and impairment of love toward one's parents and siblings, which is transferred or displaced to others as a permanent pattern. A child badly treated by humans, by its own mother and father, may love horses or dogs better than humans and continue to do so for life, and hence a sadist may love animals.

The maturation of the individual, in accordance with natural law, into a responsible and loving spouse, parent and citizen is expressed in moral law. The need for moral law and secular law arises in large part from the faulty child rearing that makes the child form patterns of behavior that are against nature. Our laws proclaim the psychological pathology that makes them necessary. Canada geese, wolves, elephants, gorillas and most other species require no societies for the prevention of cruelty to their children, for their maturation into good parents is rarely interfered with, despite the dangers of life in the wilds. They regulate their sex lives and mating and territorial rights in reasonable ways, without recourse to anything like human warfare. Hostile aggression in animals may indeed be innate, as ethologists tell us. But in humans it goes as far as individual and mass murder. Whether this is innate or is a ready response of the fight–flight reaction, the practical conclusions are about the same. We still must study why some of us are brutal murderers and others are people of good will; and we must learn all we can about preventing, controlling, checking, sublimating, diverting, and weakening this destructiveness if we are to survive. To get children well reared is, of course, a vast task, dealing as we do with so many warped, immature, hostile parents.

Sex, mating and the rearing of the young involve the behavior of members of a society toward each other. Whatever disrupts the organization of the society, whether of gibbons or baboons or elephants or humans, is a threat to the survival of all its members. Their aggression must be used to help each other, to get food and to defend against dangers from the elements and from predators. Therefore society, by moral influence, if not by explicit laws, is concerned with protecting individuals from their own hostilities against themselves—from damaging themselves, for example, by tobacco, alcohol, drug addictions or even suicide. Danger to one social unit, whether from others or from self, is like a physiological disharmony of the body, such as indigestion; it impairs the internal harmony of the body politic and therefore weakens it in production, distribution and defense. Thus human laws and morality are rooted in the natural law of survival of the species.

We must be thankful for the new, expanding science of ethology, the scientific studies of animals in nature. It has already begun to cast new light on human behavior. Robert Ardrey, in his *The Territorial Imperative,* has some interesting discussions concerning morality in animals. Of course these observations cannot be applied immediately and directly to humans. They must be merged with what is known from psychological and sociological studies of all kinds. But that man is realizing that he has much to learn about his own nature from the rest of the animal kingdom is a new ray of hope in our efforts to bring happiness instead of misery and destruction to our lives on earth.

Here is part of a letter that expresses a mature kind of love, the genuine interest in another for the other's own sake, the kind of sturdy devotion to mate and young that assures stable homes in other animal species. This letter was written by a father to his daughter who was happily married and about to have her first child. She had just received an unjustified tirade from a difficult aunt for not being sufficiently hospitable to her parental family and relatives.

Lis dear:
Dora [the aunt] should have been ashamed of herself to take you to task under all the circumstances. I do not believe there is another member of the family who entertains any such idea about you. . . . There has never been a day since you were born that I would not have given my life for you and certainly by no manner of means do I regard you with any less love and affection than I have always entertained for you; your success in school and since you finished has been the pride and joy of my life, and if you think I would not divide, even give you all that I possess in this life, you let the occasion arise where your welfare makes it necessary. . . .

You hold on to the idea that the rest of the family are interested in you and love you; I do not think there is one who does not love and respect you and has the greatest admiration for you. You are and have been the joy of my life and I shall expect to enjoy you as long as I live. I have put the best of my life in preparing you for womanhood and motherhood. There has never been a moment that I have not loved you devotedly and enjoyed knowing that you were my child and daughter, so you erase the word "letdown" from your vocabulary. Of course there are a lot of things in your life and in Bill's [Lis's husband] life, that I do not understand, but I am not supposed to understand, but I do know that the main and most important thing in life for you is that you have married a fine boy . . . and that is the main thing that I am interested in. . . .

Your mother has for a long period of years been . . . [making] herself unhappy . . . because she cannot dominate me and make me over. . . . Hence at times she has been difficult to get along with, but my undying love for her holds me fast to her, notwithstanding. . . .

Such mature love precludes the infantile, egocentric destructiveness acted out against wife and children by husbands in affairs with other women.

Now and again I hear from Lis. She is now a grandmother several times over. Life has not been too kind to her, but she has done a fine job in her family; and she has been sustained through her stresses and trials by the internal support of her father's— and mother's—unconditional love.

We have mentioned seven components of marriage: love, sexual attractiveness, romance, parenthood, responsibility, maturity, fit or mesh; above all it is a personal, or interpersonal, emotional relationship between individuals. It takes considerable maturity to handle one's drives for loving and being loved, sex, and parenthood, and particularly to harmonize these drives with those of another person. Marriage can only succeed if the emotional maturation has been facilitated, not warped, by one's parents, especially during the earliest years. Here again the natural laws of proper childhood relationships, of adequate emotional development, of good human relations, lead to the capacity to be a good mate and parent; and this goal of development is expressed in human moral law.

Probably religious commandments and principles, moral law, social standards and secular laws all formulate the basic principles of natural law: the development of the young into good responsible mates, parents, citizens. In this they are more than agreed upon rules that are necessary for the existence of human societies; they are actually deeply grounded in the biological nature of man and of other species as well. It seems that those who go contrary to these laws are not simply being unconventional, but are manifesting disturbances in their maturing to the status of mate and parent. As we have said, it does require much maturity to handle the component drives that lead to the ability to make a happy home.

An example of modern studies of relations between natural and moral law is C. H. Waddington's *The Ethical Animal*. This fuses contributions from many fields, including biology, sociology, anthropology and psychology, and contains an extensive bibliography of relevant work in all these areas.

It is certainly incorrect and a half-truth to describe *Homo sapiens* as a fighting and warring animal or even as an adulterous one. It is true that humans behave in these ways, but this is only part of the picture; it ignores the other part—the men and women of good will and of family love and loyalty who loathe crime, violence, war, betrayal and suffering, especially of loved ones. There are these two sides and they seem, from the clinical evidence, to be manifestations respectively of warped infantile fixation and of healthy, adequate maturity. Love of parents for child and love between family members build up permanent patterns of love toward others and of checks on hostile feelings and behavior toward them.

Of course clinical studies of human beings cannot alone solve the problems involving natural law. This requires knowledge from other fields, especially from ethology, the growing science of the behavior of animals. Germane to our topic is *On Aggression,* by Konrad Lorenz. This book disregards the enormous effects of early influences on adult behavior; it assumes that aggression is a constant drive and not a reaction (fight or flight) to danger or frustration; and its applications to human behavior are rather superficial. (There are other limitations also.) But the descriptions of animal behavior are fascinating and afford insight into the nature and complexity of instincts, their component mechanisms, and the inhibitory activities that control them. It is these inhibitory patterns that protect the mate, young, society, and species from the fight instinct of hostile attack, keeping it channeled for useful purposes only, such as getting food and defense. The inhibitory forces are similar to human moral law. Here we have a picture of the animal organism as not homogeneous, not all loving to mate, young, and species, but motivated by a great variety of urges and responses, which are released or kept in check by other urges and responses. The actual behavior at any time is a result of the interaction of these forces. However complex the urges and reactions behind behavior are, instinctual, normal, healthy behavior serves the purposes of preservation of the individual, mate, young, society and species. If hostile aggression breaks loose and damages any of these, and if the aggression continues, the species will not survive.

Clinical experience with a single species, *Homo sapiens*, drives us to this question: Is what strains marriages and injures offspring and breaks out in crime and war a derangement of the normal, healthy interplay of instinct by mistreatment in the formative period? This period distinguishes man from other species, if only because of its unusual duration and the amount of learning that takes place—not only intellectual learning but the learning of emotional attitudes and responses as well. However complex the instinctual forces are, what we shall describe clinically of their outcome in human behavior fits with present findings of ethology. This must be so, because both fields are based, like all sciences, on factual observation of reality.

Probably it will turn out that all these instinctual patterns of animals are molded into over-all combinations, mostly during infancy. Human childhood is extremely prolonged compared with this period of growth to maturity in other animal forms. Therefore humans are so pliable and plastic during the long helpless dependence on the parents. Animals, too, vary enormously in their own personalities, no doubt for the same reasons.

Few of the fundamentals of courtship, reproduction, and rearing of young are absent from animal life, and few of the human variations in sexual behavior. Some people consider certain activities to be improper, but these occur in animals as well as humans. For example, most of the imaginative caresses of human foreplay are also indulged in by other animal species.

Sex, as we have noted, channels and drains all sorts of feelings—dependence, greed, hate, and hostility, as well as love, with which it is so commonly confused. These feelings and early sensual experiences, combined with the inevitable repressions and frustrations of the sexual impulses, result in all sorts of ways of seeking their gratification. The result is a wide variety of tastes and preferences in physical sexual behavior. However deviant and imaginative these may be, as long as culmination is in intromission of sperm in the female, reproduction ensues; the race is preserved and nature is satisfied. Leading up to this—that is, in the foreplay—anything goes that is to the mutual satisfaction of the couple. But if their tastes differ, then this becomes a problem of adjustment in marriage.

The same applies on a psychological level. A highly refined girl marries. Her husband at climax blurts out obscenities. This, for her, is an added thrill. To the beauty she finds in intercourse, this adds an earthy element which satisfies something in her animalistic nature. But another wife, subjected to this, feels only degraded and esthetically revolted. One likes sudden, surprising initiations of sex by her husband in all sorts of circumstances;

but another requires long wooing, gradually leading up, through dinner and after, to soft lights and bed. Some like lights on; others prefer total darkness; and there are many variations in between. Some relish the animalistic—but others are only satisfied if the act of intercourse is clearly, surely, and deeply an extension of intensifying feelings of love. Some have mutual orgasms even though one or both may have to indulge in mad fantasies during the act or think of another partner or several. Manual help may be needed and agreeable or desired. Thus the variations are endless. And this colorful variety is an advantage to those men and women who have all sorts of mixtures of these desires. For them, in their fortunate marriages, the sexual act expresses endlessly different moods at different times. But usually, if not always, greater or lesser adaptation is required by each partner to the urges of the other.

This variety and this adaptation seem to be the essentials in sexual relations. I sometimes wonder if sex education, in the usual sense, is desirable or, put more mildly, may not be overdone. Sex is a long-standing urge in the animal kingdom and is an instinct deep enough to take care of itself. Is not part of the charm of young love finding out about sex for oneself? Is not some of this lost by anatomical and physiological lectures? Should we not study carefully what is truly helpful and what is not? How much that helps is psychological rather than physical? How beneficial is it to know what others do, in order to gain a perspective on oneself? Perhaps the best sex education is still simply to answer your children's questions as soon as they are old enough to ask them.

# II Common Problems in Marriage and Their Causes

*In most instances, marital problems are fairly routine. But the people involved don't know this. They think this has happened only to them and no one will ever understand.*

WILLIAM T. ALBERTS,
Delaware County Daily Times

We will begin with a series of examples that reveal some common underlying dynamics and their effects on certain marriages.

The first is what might be called an *oscillation conflict*. Many a husband has no doubt felt, "I cannot live with her or without her," and wives have thought the same. This sentiment may be kept hidden or be expressed with humor or with despair. In our illustration, the feeling is so magnified that its existence is made dramatically clear. This magnification also reveals the emotional forces behind the conflict and how these forces can be traced back to their origins. They did not develop a month ago, or a year ago—their pattern was formed by reactions to treatment in childhood. This fact we shall see repeatedly.

In the man in the first example, attachment to his mother, intensified by her treatment of him, aroused hostility and efforts to escape. The consequence was the type of marital problem caused primarily by the emotional problem of one partner (in this case the husband). In the second example there is also conflict over continuing the marriage, this time primarily on the part of the wife. The source of the difficulty is within herself, and is not a rational response to neglect or mistreatment. Her hostility gives her husband a bad time and threatens to ruin her life as well as his. Why did he choose her? Why does he not protect himself? Why is she so destructive to him and to herself? Here the hostility and masochism are readily seen, and are traceable to their origins. The third marriage shows very directly the continuation into the marital home of the emotional patterns in the parental home, illustrated by the ubiquitous problem of which mate gives more and gets less. The dynamics, their source, and the outcome are all so frequently seen as to justify the contention that they may be typical of our society as a whole, or at least of one of its strata. The fourth series of marriages shows the continuation from childhood of a major tendency, or else a return to it, in one partner or the other. The child's normal drive and activity can be so dulled that he loses the taste and capacity for responsibility, which is clearly seen in husbands who cannot support their wives and children. Here is a different kind of marital problem—the couple may get on idyllically but the marriage fails, because the husband fails as a breadwinner.

We will thus see (1) attraction and repulsion, (2) hostility and masochism, (3) giving and getting, and (4) passivity. We will see these tendencies exaggerated by certain kinds of faulty treatment in childhood, especially domination, deprivation and overprotection; and we will see how the child tried to protect himself against this treatment by clinging and escape, by hostility and self-punishment, by demands and refusal to give, and by withdrawal into passivity.

*One was never married, and that's his hell;*
*Another is, and that's his plague.*

BURTON

*Marriage has many pains, but celibacy has no pleasures.*

JOHNSON

# 5 DOUBLE BIND

A man who cannot tolerate living with his wife or without her. We trace this dilemma to the restrictive, dominating matriarchy of his childhood, to which he reacted with strength as well as conflict.

That sex in humans can break loose as an almost impersonal mechanism, that it can drain all sorts of nonsexual tensions, and that it can be used to serve every kind of purpose other than love, mating, and parenthood is all too evident upon a moment's thought. A man goes to a prostitute for sex without love; she may give herself, not for love or sex, but for money.

In practice I have seen certain men and women who react to any buildup of tension—from studies, from business, from the home, from any source whatever—by an intensification of sexual feelings that they feel compelled to relieve in some way, whether with a partner or by masturbation. Some people experience sex in so detached a fashion that for them love inhibits gratification. They only feel sexually free with a partner who represents simply a body and not a personality. When the personality, the human being, enters, their sexual drive is not enriched, but is dampened or even extinguished.

Emotional disturbances disrupt mating in many other ways. Here is a husband, Art, in whom the sex drive, partially separated from the human relation, was strong enough to begin a marriage that other feelings within him turned into an intolerable battle.

His wife, Amy, sat in my office. She was a rather large blonde, buxom to the point of being slightly plump. She glowed with the freshness of her 24 years despite the strain she was under. This is what she told me:

29

"I am confused. I am deeply in love with my husband, and I am sure he is with me. He courted me for a year and a half. He swept me off my feet. He wined and dined me and tried in every way to seduce me. He could not live without me. I began to give in. Since we were to be married soon, I did give in. [These sexual aspects she tells with great difficulty.] Sex was intense and he was insatiable. Maybe I became so too. But then he began to have doubts about getting married. I did nothing to hold him. I did not want him if he did not want me, even though we were so intimate. Finally I broke it off. But no sooner was this done than the phone began ringing. He couldn't stand it without me. So it was on again. But then he began to feel trapped.

"It was not easy. I was so in love with him. But then I just wanted peace, to be left alone, to have my own life back again. But it was no use. He phoned. He came. He could not stand it without me. It was on and off and on and off. At last I thought it was off for good and left for a vacation from it all. But within the week he had found me and insisted on marriage—marriage immediately, and promises of everything. I knew he could and would keep his promises. He is enormously energetic and smart and generous.

"This time it stayed on, and three weeks later we were married and took off for our honeymoon in New Orleans.

"Even on the train he was not himself. He was subdued. The first morning in New Orleans the weather was perfect. I was eager to go sight-seeing, to explore. But Art had no interest in anything. He wouldn't leave the room. He complained of a stomachache and a terrible headache. He was depressed. He began worrying about money. It was terrible. Have you any idea of what it's like to live with a depressed person? Well, perhaps you do. It is unbearable. After four days of this we returned to Chicago. That was about a year ago.

"Art got back to work and came out of that depression. But for the past few months he has been insisting on a divorce. I am confused, because, although he wants a divorce, he talks and acts as though he cannot live without me. He makes love night and morning. A few days ago he said he could not stand the marriage any more and definitely wanted a divorce. Of course I was upset. I'm still in love with him. Last night I was listening to the radio to take my mind off all this, and he came in and insisted I come to bed with him, because he could not sleep without me. And today he suggested we go up to Wisconsin for a skiing weekend together. Will you see him if I can get him to come?"

I looked at this young woman. Some women are physically attractive but psychologically impossible. Once at a dance I cut in on a gorgeous blonde, but there was something so wrong there that by the end of the dance, even though we had hardly spoken, my interest in her had vanished. Young as I was, it flashed through my mind that something in her make-up must repel other men also and might be tragic for her. But I had no such sense about this girl. She seemed in all ways desirable.

It is difficult enough to evaluate one person, and five times harder to discern the interactions of two in a marriage. I could not but look forward with interest to an interview with this vigorous, smart, able, successful, generous, highly-sexed husband who could awaken in a hotel room in a fascinating city with this charmer in his bed and thereupon get pains in his head and stomach and plunge into a depression. There was a disturbing possibility that this young wife's confusion might stem from her failure to discriminate between sex and love. Perhaps in herself sex and love and romance and responsibility were normally fused, and hence she could not perceive or perhaps even imagine their being split into separate components in her husband.

Her husband came for an interview, not reluctantly but willingly, eagerly in fact. His eagerness sprang in part from a genuine belief that something was wrong in him which he wanted to change. But in part, as soon became apparent, he was also trying to use me to help him get a divorce immediately. This conspiratorial element I totally rejected, but said I would like to hear how it all seemed to him.

He was a rather small, wiry, intense young man, with a shock of somewhat unruly red hair. He was 29 but exuded an air of authority that one might expect in an older man. If his inner tension found expression in sex, one could easily see how he attracted girls and why his sexual activity was above average. The interview went as follows:

Patient: I've been so depressed, so exhausted, that I can hardly work. I have the weight of the world on me.

Analyst: What do you mean by "depressed"? You seem energetic enough now.

P.: That's only since yesterday. Until then I couldn't even think.

A.: Was this improvement after you agreed to come to see me?

P.: Yes—I see—yes. Maybe it's connected. The train trip for the honeymoon was rather delightful, but when we hit New Orleans I couldn't function. I was depressed, wanted an annulment. I almost stood the girl up and didn't marry her. I almost broke the engagement, but I had her on my brain. When I can go to bed with her, that's it. Do you think sex every morning and night for an hour or two is normal or is it a strain? Why does she attract me so? Is it just her body? But I think it is all sex, only sex. We are from different worlds. She reads her way through life. She likes ballet. She goes for doilies, place arrangements at parties, travel, books, interesting guests. I can't stand these things. What I like is food, drink, horses, skiing, the sports page, the comics, comfort, having my feet up. I was born behind the stockyards. I've come up the hard way, had to defend myself in fights with some rough characters, some of the lowest and toughest. I'm lucky enough to be real smart in business. I have a trucking business and it's doing pretty well in spite of the Depression. [The business depression of the 1930's.] But I don't go for culture. I like a woman who doesn't care about musicales, and, if a policeman stops her car, she tells him to go to hell. I've slept with women all the time, all kinds.

A.: What kinds?

P.: Never prostitutes, if that's what you mean. I just go for a girl and she goes for me. We go someplace—her place, my place, a hotel. Sometimes it's great; sometimes I can't even get an erection. I've had all these women since I was 15, but I've never paid a girl.

A.: When did you first have a depression?

P.: I've had some all my life, but not so bad until three or four years ago. Oh, you think it's connected with all these women? It could be, because after being with a woman, many times I'd feel depressed.

A.: Tell a little about the emotional relations in your family during your very earliest childhood.

P.: My mother was in charge of the house. My two older brothers and father were subservient to her. I have a sister eight years younger, but I never had much to do with her. My mother threatened me with Father, told me if I was bad he would beat me. But he never did. She was always criticizing him and blaming him. He always acted guilty, as though he had to make up for something to her. He was only work, work, work. He works in the stockyards—for Armour. He is goodhearted but could never relate to me. We did nothing together. He never brought me anything. He never taught me anything, like playing ball. When I was older and went to a game or a movie or on a date, he never asked if I had a good time, but only why I came home so late. He never stood up to my mother. Neither did my brothers. In fact, my brothers beat on me just the way my mother did, and she let them. My mother babied me. She made special lunches, wouldn't let me eat what the other boys ate or dress the way they did. I guess she wanted me to be something better than they were. I was dependent on her but embarrassed by my dependence. The other boys didn't play with me much, so I kept returning to Mother all the time. She was the boss. I felt a lot of love and a lot of hate toward her. She rode my father too much. My brothers and I were never close. They tried to rule me too. Mother and Father said they could, so they tried, but I resented it. My father couldn't assert himself. Everybody rode him.

A.: What are the very first memories in your whole life?

P.: The first is that the kids would not play with me, and Mother was trying to be reassuring. Another memory was that Father forgot to do something for Mother, and she wouldn't talk to him, and he felt awful. Father was always subservient. He never was like other fathers. He never said, "Come on out and let's hit a ball" or "Come on to a ball game" or come and do anything together.

[Mother seems to be the central theme in these earliest memories. Relationships with other children fail and Mother is the consolation. Father demonstrates that one must please Mother or feel awful. But this implies resentment of Mother for having to do so. Mother is the central figure, as in his life women are. The love and hate for Mother seem to be the clue and key.]

A.: Did you dream last night?

P.: Yes, I dreamed my wife and I were in a train wreck. I tried to save her, get her out, but couldn't. Then a man got me out.

[This dream seems like a frank expression of a wish for his wife to be lost. The man who saves him probably represents his wish toward me, the way he sees me and analytic help.]

P.: You asked when I was first depressed. I was depressed when I was about 17. It was before the stock market crash. All the other kids found jobs, but I couldn't. Mother said I would be president of a giant corporation, and Father said he would get me started. But I went from one job to another. The reason was because I had to direct whatever it was. I had to run the business. I've always had great drive. When I got my own business—trucking—I did well, and it's not an easy business. I've handled every kind of person, some pretty tough ones. I've always had a lot of sex drive too. My mother joked about it. She knew about the girls from an early age, and later I used to tell her, and she'd make jokes and think it was cute.

A.: We are running out of time, and I think I should tell you my impression. The way I understand what we call your dynamics is roughly something like this—and you tell me freely where I am wrong: The main pattern of early childhood seems to be toward your mother and to consist of spoiling, overprotection, and especially domination by her. The brother reinforced the domination, and your father gave no model for standing up to it. This involvement with your mother rather cut you off in your childhood from friendships with other boys and girls. Because friends rejected you, you fell back on your mother. But why did they reject you? Was it *because* of the close involvement with your mother? Correct me if this impression that you have never had any close friends is wrong.

P.: No, I've never had a real close friend.

A.: Your choice of attitude to people is limited pretty much by the ones you had toward your mother. If they are strong, you are threatened with being subservient, as you were with your mother. The escape from that is to *be* the dominating one yourself—you dominate others, become the boss, run the business, handle every kind of person. It is as though, in order not to be the submissive child or father, you must be the directing mother—with everyone. *Identification with the aggressor*, it has been called. At the same time, cut off from playmates, with little relation to your father or brothers, you were thrown back on and close to one single person, your mother—all the love and all the hate you mentioned. Perhaps that is why, without close friends, you seek everything in human relations with women. With women you look for all the love, but also you feel all the resentment, the rebellion, and the need to dominate.

P.: You mean they are all Mother?

A.: And the opposite. You cannot stand being subservient, as you were to your mother. These women are probably both the wish for Mother and the attempt to escape from her.

P.: Then is that why I can't resist my wife sexually? She is absolutely passive sexually. I can do anything I want with her. Other women react much more, are much better in bed—but maybe this is why she excites me. I am completely in charge—can do anything. And is that why I sometimes don't even get an erection with another woman I like better?

A.: Meaning?

P.: Well, I've noticed that I may have a lot more in common with a girl who is more my type, but she doesn't excite me much sexually. With my wife the only thing we have in common is sex. There is nothing else. When that goes there will be nothing. But another girl likes what I like, but I can't care that much about sex with her. That's why I didn't marry earlier and why I couldn't make up my mind about marrying Amy.

A.: And the resentment of mother may make an undercurrent of hostility to all women.

P.: I'm not hostile to my wife. I just can't stand her except for the sex.

[I thought of the dream he described, of his wife's being killed in the train wreck. He could have dreamed that he was divorced, that the marriage was annulled, that he was single and had never been married. It is hard to consider dreaming of his wife's being killed in a wreck as not hostile, but the time was up, and we would wait and see.]

Further dynamics were suggested more or less strongly by the material. The mechanism of *identification with the aggressor* has already been mentioned. Subservience to the mother and brothers was contrary to the child's natural growth toward independence; submissiveness in his father made the mother and brother look down upon him. Probably for other reasons as well, the patient feared and disliked the tendencies in himself to give in to maternal control. It seems that he defended himself against his mother's domination by identifying with her in this; as she was the boss in the home, so he had to be boss with women and in business. Thus he could not hold an ordinary job because he felt compelled to be the director of whatever operation or business he was employed in. He could only function as the boss, not as a subordinate. And, apparently, he was only fully potent with women so utterly yielding that he felt he could do anything he felt impelled to do.

The childhood pattern continued in his having no close friends but in seeking complete emotional satisfaction from women. He lived out toward them the pattern toward his mother: the closeness to his mother, the emotional dependence on her, the being thrown back upon her because of rejection by friends, the hostility to her (which came through to the sorrow of every woman with whom he became close); the guilt for the hostility that got him into situations with women, which he found intolerable and from which he sought escape. As with his mother, he could not live with a given woman or without her. His success in business, when he became the master of his own firm, stood in contrast to his intense but intolerable involvement with women.

This interview alone reveals the depth and power of the motivations that enter into all close human relations, especially so intimate a relationship as marriage. Not always do these motivations appear quickly. Sometimes signs of them are evident in the first hours of the honeymoon; sometimes, as in this case, after a day or two. But often the deeper patterns of reactions only emerge after months or years.

This interview illustrates an aspect of the technique by which the dynamics operating in a personality are discerned. There is a fit between certain factors:

1. The present emotional pattern of a person's life (in this case, toward his business, which he directs well, and toward his wife, with whom intense feelings clash, as they do also in himself).

2. The childhood emotional pattern, which, as here, is continued into adult life.

3. The life history, which reveals this same pattern (perhaps different facets of it at different ages).

4. The first memories.

5. The current dreams. These memories and dreams may reveal, not the entire pattern, but rather one or two essential aspects of it. (In this case, the common pattern of being rejected by friends and thrown back into the relation to mother appears in the earliest memory, but the hostility does not. This hostility, however, is

quite undisguised in the current dream, in which, years later, the pattern toward his mother, and the defense by identification with the aggressor have appeared toward his wife.)

Consistency in these five kinds of data is the most potent clinical tool as yet available for insight into the dynamics, the interplay of emotional forces.

A case such as this, common as it is, cannot fail to impress us with what terrible chaos and cruelty there is sexually and personally in human reactions as compared with the equally powerful, yet clear, calm, well-ordered, so much more considerate and loving reactions between the sexes in many, or perhaps most, animals. Of course this is true not only of relations between human males and females but of all human relations—in which hostility in the form of cruelty, crime and war is intrinsic to the human scene, to human history, to human dreams. And the source is the same as in this example; the source is in childhood, in the first weeks and months of life, from conception through the earliest years— 0 to 6. There and then is determined the adult personality by the way the child is treated. If the child is reared with good human relations, he will mature emotionally into a responsible spouse, parent and citizen; if he is raised with disturbed feelings, his emotional development will be warped to neurosis, psychosis, addictions, self-defeat, cruelty, crime—to all those disorders we find in our mental hospitals, our jails, our divorce courts and our battlefields.

But let us return to the couple under discussion. Art's conflict tossed him back and forth. As he had related, no sooner had he finally won his wife, married and gone on his honeymoon than he panicked. He felt that he might lose his sanity if he did not get a divorce without delay. Since he had so recently expressed to his wife his undying love and devotion in words, sex and marriage, she naturally was reluctant to grant a sudden and ostensibly senseless divorce. Finally realizing his feelings, she agreed. As soon as she agreed, however, he again panicked, and felt he was falling apart. He could not stand the idea of being all alone or of moving into an apartment and eating in restaurants. His wife, becoming upset by all this herself, insisted on going ahead with the separation. His fears of loneliness and lack of a woman to be dependent upon proved justified. No sooner was he living alone and eating out than his anxiety and depression became intolerable. He had managed before marriage by having many affairs. But now he was no freedom-loving bachelor. It looked as though his childhood mixture of feelings toward his mother was now fully aroused and attached to his wife. Feeling desolate, isolated and unable to exist without a home, he began to consider suicide. If only his wife could relent and take him back, he was sure that the pain of this present banishment would burn forever and force him to accept the adjustment to marriage. So he wooed and pressured her—and eventually wore down her resistance until she wavered. He saw that she was about to let him return, and this was enough to fill him again with panic. He could see that his return after the separation was irrevocable—that he could not go back to his wife and then again leave her without incurring her total and irrevocable antagonism and rejection. It was literally true that he could not live with her and could not live without her.

He had no pattern in childhood of playmates, friends or relationships other than the overclose domination-rebellion conflict with a mother whom he could not stand and could not leave. Now the conflict centered exclusively upon his wife, Amy. He could find no surcease in friends, sports or social relations. His stability at work was endangered. Panicked by being married to her and panicked by being separated from her, he began to fear that he would break down mentally or be driven to suicide.

In the end his wife sensed the threat to him that lay in returning to her and felt that she had been through too much to risk reunion. As it turned out, it was she who insisted on the divorce that he had at first in terror sought and then in terror fought.

This was a few months before Pearl Harbor. When America entered the war, Art joined the Marine Corps and, once in the Service, became much more stable, stayed out of trouble, and served well. Art was not the only man that the armed services rescued from an emotional blind alley in private life.

I heard from Art some years after the war and found his later story of great interest. Almost immediately after returning to civilian life he became engaged and also began analytic treatment. It was violently stormy. He could not return to his old free, promiscuous bachelor existence. His new love, Janice, was quite like Amy—a big, buxom blonde—but a little more earthy and doggedly, almost masochistically, attached to Art. Again he oscillated, leaving her and returning. They married. He left again and took up with a woman, Phyllis, for whom he had no respect whatever. His new wife, Janice, had a child. He hated himself for being with his mistress, but he lost all feeling for his wife and had none for his small son; and he could not tear himself away from Phyllis. It was a rough analysis. But surprisingly enough, virtue was rewarded. After about two and a half years, almost suddenly, he returned to his wife and son. He arranged for business in Los Angeles and took off, saying he would bring Janice and the baby as soon as he was settled and had a place for them. She did not know whether she would ever see him again. But he sent for her, and they have been together and reasonably happy since. He located a good analyst in Los Angeles whom he saw from time to time. His first wife remarried at the beginning of the war and settled down and had two children—settled down happily, we hope.

Improvement in treatment depends, as in the rest of medicine, upon the balance of forces:

1. The severity of the disorder, that is, how early in life the disturbed patterns—the psychodynamics—were formed and how powerful, deep-seated, and widespread they are in the personality.

2. The health and strength of the counterforces toward maturity, adaptation and health.

3. The uncontrollable circumstances and happenstances of life.

4. If there is treatment, the skill and personality of the physician.

Art's case also typifies how conflict causes indecision and oscillation, which are seen commonly in many forms. Some men cannot live with or without a girl before marriage; then in matrimony some settle down but others continue the oscillation. Still others find that they cannot tolerate either matrimony or promiscuity and reach a highly satisfactory balance in long affairs (like the elephants?) with women who, because of their own problems, are willing to live with them unfettered by the marriage state. Some escape by alcoholic binges; some only withdraw emotionally; some run to other women, either with sexual desires only or with some feelings for them, only to seek the wife again as the one true love. Women, too, show this disturbed behavior. These are only a few of the variations on the theme portrayed by these notes. For the cause and the possibility of cure, *cherchez la femme* —she is the mother (or father or other) of the earliest years.

Many a husband or wife is so unhappy in a marriage as to

think seriously of divorce, but hesitates at the prospect of the separation being worse than the union. These frequent doubts and fears, and what may be behind them—how much is realistic and rational, and how much from childhood patterns—can usually be seen more clearly when exaggerated, as in the example we have given. The extreme is like seeing the moderate through a magnifying lens. Hence we have presented not a mild, usual bind, but a desperate double bind.

The accustomed behavior of each of us, that is, our usual personality, is the result of a balance of many and strong forces; therefore, it can be tipped in new and surprising directions. Even in a man with such extreme and apparently fixed patterns as Art, I have seen sudden and surprising changes. One such man, in a year of analytic treatment, gained much insight but had not resolved his conflict. His wife then divorced him. He suffered. But only for a month or two. Then he met another woman. She was young and attractive and most loving and considerate. She seemed to fit his needs exactly. He became equally loving, considerate and giving toward her. His conflict vanished. He could love and be loved and could again work freely, effectively and successfully. Whether the analytic help had prepared him to react thus well to what life brought, or whether the fit with the personality of this girl operated alone, the fortunate result was more freedom from conflict and happiness than he had ever known.

How this marriage held up I do not know, but it does recall those men and women of about 30 who come for treatment with the belief that something must be wrong with them, since they have not yet married, although they are burning to do so. The large majority of these are correct; many have internal inhibitions or conflicts that keep them from a final commitment to anyone, even though they can love and be loved and are healthy, attractive and successful, and nothing is wrong with their sexuality. Some have no problems. They simply have not met the right woman or man. One mature young man of 30 said, "Now I have been happily married for a year to a girl I deeply love. I would have waited until I was 40 rather than marry just for the sake of marrying. I was waiting for a girl I could truly love, no matter how long it took to meet her." This marriage was one of the happiest in my experience.

One young woman was 29, and her friends were beginning to

think she was just not the marrying kind. On a rare trip, a conversation started with the man in the seat next to hers. She told her parents, whom she was going to see, about it and added, "I think this is the man I will marry." They were somewhat shocked. But she did, and the marriage has been most satisfactory.

Of course it does not always work out so well—but neither do many other marriages, even though they are off to the most promising starts. We will give examples later of fine girls who soon discover that their choices are very poor husbands, and excellent men who find their wives to be hostile, demanding children. Some of these good people realize that they have "goofed," as one girl put it, lose no time in getting a divorce, and are soon remarried to the right person and go on through happy domestic lives. It is certainly wise, for the sake of the children, to give a marriage two years to settle down before having babies. Other couples do not divorce but muddle through. Some of these couples drive each other to the breakdown, or near it, of mind or body or both, and doom their children to serious emotional disorders. But some reach a reasonable adjustment, which may develop in a few years, or which may not develop for most of a lifetime. One philanderer settled down when his children were grown and he was 50—"I'm not much of a threat any more," he told me—and he and his wife had 20 quite good years together.

*Misery seeks not man, but man misery.*
FRANCES BURNEY

# 6 HOSTILITY AND MASOCHISM IN MARRIAGE

A young woman who cannot stand marriage gives herself as well as her husband a hard life. This pattern of hostility and self-injury was caused by a tyrannical father whom she tried in fear and anger to escape.

Sex is a physiological and psychological mechanism in its own right, but it often serves as a channel, path, or drain for all sorts of impulses and feelings. Rapes and lust-murders express sex cut off from love, mating and parental feelings and used as an outlet for hate, violence and destructiveness. This sexual pleasure in cruelty gets its name, sadism, from its depiction in the writings of the Marquis de Sade. Its converse, sexual arousal through suffering, is termed masochism, from Sacher-Masoch's novel *Venus in Fur,* in which a man achieves sexual satisfaction from being whipped by a woman wearing a fur piece. Originally the word was used narrowly for sexual pleasure in being hurt. It has gradually come to denote any trend toward being one's own enemy. One way among many to assure self-suffering is to marry a person who plays upon this unconscious tendency. One may unconsciously choose a spouse who is overtly or unconsciously cruel; or one may choose a kind and devoted partner but suffer anyway because of inner frustration, hostility and guilt.

Brenda, a petite, blue-eyed blonde of 31, told the following:

Patient: I can't stand my husband—and I don't know why. We went together for two years and now we've only been married two years, yet I can't stand him. But if I'm real nasty to him, then I want to make up. I feel guilty and I'm afraid of his leaving me. I'm hostile to my mother and father too. Since I was a kid, my father has mostly been angry at my mother. When he was angry, which was often, he would lash out at everybody. But the worst

43

part of my childhood was that I had no freedom. Both my parents would say, "Later"—you can do this or that "later." But later never came.

Father was a martinet, and I was always subjugated to his tyranny. He was very strict—a real Prussian. He did give me some affection, though—when I was very young—although he was always a tyrant. My brother was nine years older and hardly ever home. He went away to school pretty young. He didn't play much part in my life. Mother never gave me any real affection, or at least I felt she didn't. She was very negative. I know later on I'll feel guilty for talking this way about my father. He worked hard and was fairly successful.

Analyst: How do you sleep?

P.: Pretty well, and I have dreams every night, but I can't remember them.

A.: Any recent ones at all?

P.: I dreamt that a man I went with died. I'm always afraid of dreaming of someone who died. And I often dream about a girl I know who criticized me when I was only 15 years old, and I am always trying to please her. Why was I so impressed?

A.: What is your very first memory—way back before continuous memory?

P.: Father used to like to play with me in bed. I used to jump up and down on the bed. Once he kissed me on the mouth, and I said something about it and he got mad and told me never to say it again. Also I remember finding a Kotex of my mother's and asking her what it was. She said it was for some trouble she had that made her bleed. I must have been over five years old but those are the earliest I remember.

A.: What about other people in your life, besides your husband?

P.: I have one girl friend and we get along very well. Except for her I'm not very close with anyone.

This is extremely interesting. Some patients talk freely about their present lives but not about the past. This young woman comes with a marital problem and talks freely about her past. This gives us a good initial insight into her pathodynamics, and arouses our interest in how this combination of forces has shaped her life and the inner emotional atmosphere of her mind. What she has told so far fits together about as follows:

The picture in childhood (the "0 to 6" and later) is of difficulties in the only two close relationships of her life. The brief allusion to her brother gives the impression that he escaped from the home as much as possible and played no significant part in her life. Her mother is described as negative and not affectionate, so there is no sign of a warm, easy relationship there, but no overt struggle either. The pattern toward her father is the most vivid. Her relation to him was as to a tyrant, yet also he was apparently her source of affection. This dual relationship appears in her earliest memory, which is highly illuminating. Here her father is a source of play and affection, but the affection has an unmistakable, openly sexual coloring and takes a forbidden form. Her father prohibits her from ever mentioning it. If borne out by further information, it means that she seeks her affection in the form of sex, but that sex is forbidden. Here is one conflict. Further, she only can expect the affection if she is obedient to the father's tyranny. Here is another conflict, because she complains about it and probably represses much hostility toward him because of it. This hostility does not come out toward him overtly, presumably because of her fear of him, and because her need for his love and affection was exaggerated by getting so little satisfaction of her dependent-love needs from her mother.

Her hostility is probably much repressed, for it does not appear in the earliest memories, but its existence is made clear by the current dreams of men dying. The early memory of her mother suggests that her mother may have been more important to her than she at present consciously realizes, if only because of her dependent-love needs, which her father did not adequately satisfy. In this memory her mother is deceiving her or trying to, and the scene is again of a sexual nature. This means that there is some sort of problem about sex, probably of sexual acting out.

The only close relationship in childhood was with her father, and the only close relationship recently has been with a girl her own age. It is likely that this girl friend is in part a mother-substitute and in part provides another person like herself to identify with. The repetitive dream of distress at being criticized by the girl and of trying so hard to please her sounds like trying to please Father —and Mother—and now in adult life, herself. If she were not dissatisfied with herself, she would not be here talking to me.

What then of her chief complaint, her not being able to stand her husband? This is now intelligible, at least at a first guess from this meager but consistent information. With the pattern toward her father, she expects tyranny. She hides her hostility because of her fear, but in her dreams she almost wishes he were dead. She also expects love and affection from her husband as from her father in childhood, but mostly in the form of sex; yet she cannot freely accept love in this form, for by her father's training sex is forbidden. Hence she probably *feels* she is not really getting love and sexual satisfaction, no matter how giving her husband may be. With the pattern toward her brother, she can only expect her husband to go away and leave her; and by her identification with her brother, she would feel impelled to do as he did—escape from her parents in childhood, and from her husband in adult life. We can also suspect, pending further revelations, that if she is hostile and rebellious, openly or covertly, consciously or unconsciously, the defiance and retaliation might take the form of sexual acting out (which means using sex to express other feelings, such as rebellion against parents).

As we have already remarked, we each relate to other persons as objects (for dependence, sexual urges, hostility, love and the like) and by identification, that is, feeling ourselves to be like another person. The child is thus dependent upon its parents as objects, but also in large part identifies with them, taking over into himself much of their feelings, attitudes and behavior. This identification is often less evident than is the feeling toward a person as an object, but is no less powerful. Others often recognize how much the offspring are like their parents.

If Brenda identifies with the figures of her childhood, feels like them, takes over their attitudes and behavior, how will this affect her feelings toward her husband? Being like her mother will make her distant and unaffectionate; being like her father will make her in part affectionate in a sexual way but in part tyrannical. Also her father's anger at her mother was one of the most disturbing features of her childhood. If she is like her father, she will be angry at her mate; and if she is like her mother, she will expect anger and tyranny from her husband and either accept this masochistically or else fight against it, feeling that it exists even if it does not.

She has told very little of good personal relationships so far. Unless she does, the therapeutic problem will be difficult, because lack of a pattern of good feelings in the past means lack of a base for the development of good feelings toward her husband in the present. *A fateful fact about marriage is that each person tends to feel and behave in his marital home the way he did in his parental home.*

Wondering how her dynamics had, as has been said, lived her life for her thus far, I began the second interview by asking her to tell the highlights of her past from childhood on.

P.: I guess the worst part of my childhood was my father's anger at my mother. I couldn't stand it. I didn't know whose side to take. Maybe this has something to do with my being so confused and so indecisive. The other thing I couldn't stand was Father's strictness. He was a tyrant, as I told you last time. I felt shackled and not free—and that is how I feel now in this marriage.

A.: Before telling about the marriage, please tell more about your past. How did you behave in your home?

P.: Well, like my brother, I got away from it as much as I could. In fact, I used to run away from home—I began doing that as far back as I can remember. When I got a little older I would go to the girl friend I told you about. She was the only person I felt at home with. We were close for years. I still see her sometimes. When I got near to teen age I had other friends among girls but no one else really close. Of course Father never allowed me to date, but I was used to slipping away, and so I began to sneak off with older boys. One of them fell in love with me and we had sex. He wanted to marry me but Father forbad it. He was very poor, and Father thought he had no prospects and that I would be stuck with him for life. He married another girl and has remained terribly poor. So Father was right. But at the time I resented his control. I wanted to be free to live my own life. I went with another boy, and after a while he seemed to be in love with me and we began an affair. I've always enjoyed sex, and that wasn't the last affair.

A.: Was this partly in defiance of your father's overly strict control?

P.: I guess it was. And it seemed that only with sex was I close to anyone. I guess you'd say my life then was escaping from home, defying my parents, and finding love or sex or both with an older boy or man. As I got out of my teens I continued this. It was really a series of love affairs. I was satisfied just with the relationship. One day a woman I knew told me I was foolish to make such a point of never accepting anything from a man. If a man cared about me and we had sex together, he would want to take care of me and give me expensive presents. So I tried it, and it was like a series of marriages. Not so many. Sort of a different one every year or so. I saved a good bit of money. All the men were extremely nice to me. They treated me better than any husband I know treats his wife. We always had a lot of respect for each other.

When I met the man I married, Ben, I was really impressed. He was handsome and wealthy, and crazy about me, both sexually and as a person. We went together for a year and a half and then he said he wanted to marry me. He had had plenty of affairs with women, but for him this was love, this was what he wanted. He did seem like a prince in a fairy tale. He had everything—looks, friends, money, success (he is a lawyer), and devotion to me. He said he would give me anything and everything I wanted, and I knew he could do it. This seemed to be the real thing. We began living together, but when it came to actually getting married, I felt nervous about it. I couldn't figure out why. But I should have followed my instincts about it and not let myself be pressured into it. Since we've been married, I just haven't been able to stand him. I feel shackled again. And all the sex that was so great has become nothing. He's lost a lot of his drive and I don't care much about sex myself any more.

A.: What is it you can't stand about your husband?

P.: He is cruel to me.

A.: Cruel? I got the impression from what you just said that he was very kind, considerate and generous.

P.: He is. He is too perfect. He is cruel because he makes me feel guilty. I think he does it on purpose. I lose my temper at him; I'm awful to him, but he is all patience, only wants to please me. If I don't like the cook, he'll get another one. If I don't like the apartment, he'll get another. If I told him I wanted to have an outside affair, he'd probably say yes even to that. He torments me with this. And part of it is that he can never make up his mind—all he wants is what I want. He never puts his foot down, never makes me do what he wants, never makes a decision except to please me.

All this fits the childhood pattern. It sounds as though her husband is in reality a paragon, and that she cannot tolerate a relationship so foreign to what she was accustomed to as a child.

Unlike the hostile, tyrannical father and the distant mother, her husband is all devotion and giving, wanting to please her instead of to dominate her. Surreptitious, prohibited sex outside the parental home had the lure of defiance and closeness, but in marriage it is forbidden, as it was in the parental home. The husband's attitude of only wanting to please his wife tempts her to be the tyrannical one herself ("identification with the aggressor," her father, similar to Art's identification with his mother in the previous chapter). As long as Ben was the forbidden lover, she could enjoy the relationship. But when he became the legitimate husband in a home, then her childhood patterns toward her mother and particularly toward her father were duplicated toward her husband.

Of course I reserved opinion until interviewing the husband. It is hard enough to evaluate the dynamics of one individual; in a marital problem one must discern not only the dynamics of each of the partners but also how these mesh with or grind against each other. If this young woman's description of her husband is correct, it would fit with her inability to tolerate the marriage, but it is safer to get his view of what is going on between them. In many cases I discuss all these dynamics without delay, but this can only be done if they can be put in a way that clarifies what is going on without upsetting the patient. Here I thought it better to wait until I had seen the husband, and meanwhile we needed more information about the patient's feelings toward herself.

A.: Can you tell me how you feel about yourself—apart from this problem with your husband? Have you other problems?

P.: I have no confidence in myself. I'm still hostile to my mother. She tries to control and dominate me now more than my father does—to such an extent that I have no confidence in myself. And I'm hostile too. If I buy something and it's not right, I'm afraid to say anything about it. When we got married and moved into a beautiful apartment, I just remarked to Ben that I didn't care for the color of the walls in one of the rooms. So he said, "Okay, we'll change it." That's how nice he is, and that's how he makes me feel guilty, and the guilt makes me even angrier at him. I don't like housework, but I do it. Of course when I complain he offers to get help, but I'm afraid I wouldn't know how to deal with whomever it would be. And I'm afraid of social obligations. I talk too much and say all the wrong things.

A.: If you don't see people and don't like housework, do you have any interests?

P.: My father is in the building business, and for a while I was interested in houses and even in architecture, but not anymore. I want to be interested in the home, but I can't. I want to get away from it, but I'm afraid to. You'll probably say that I hated being home during my childhood, which I did, and still just don't like it in a home. I feel tied down, hemmed in.

A.: You are right. I would raise the question of whether this traced back to your home in childhood. Have you and your husband any interests in common?

P.: I wish I had interests. I wish I could get out of the apartment and do something—job, volunteer work, anything. I try to make myself, but I just can't. I rarely see people any more, even my girl friend. I've just got to get out of this marriage.

A.: Into what?

P.: Just to live alone, to be free again. Marriage just isn't for me. I just want to have a small place of my own and be free.

A.: What about the interests in common with your husband?

P.: As I said, I guess I don't have any, with him or without him.

A.: And your husband?

P.: Oh, he likes everything. He likes to be on the go. He likes going to political meetings, lectures, movies, all that. And he likes books and what he calls interesting people. And he likes parties. And of course he's absorbed in his law practice and he's always buried in the *Wall Street Journal*, which he always carries around with him.

Arrangements were made for her husband, Ben, to come see me. Very often in marital problems each partner reveals little of self but gives a picture of the other, frequently clear and accurate as far as it goes, but showing the other to be the source of all the difficulty. The wife may complain that the husband is totally absorbed in other interests and has no time or attention for her, while the husband tells of all he does for his wife, who is dissatisfied because she wants too much. But in this case, the husband's story and my impression of him fitted exactly what the wife had told me. He was a big fellow of 39, with thinning blond hair and blue eyes, who could have passed as her big brother. He was all she had said—handsome and charming and, as far as I could perceive, entirely devoted to his wife. He had been around and had had plenty of affairs. Now he wanted to settle down, but very specifically with this girl and no other. If it were impossible for her to stay with him he would survive, he said; he would provide for her as best he could, and in time he would no doubt find another wife. But it was Brenda he wanted. What made this lusty young bear settle on this girl with such constancy after a life of such freedom could only be known from his own dynamics.

It is often said about marital difficulties that "It takes two to tango." I have not found this to be true in all cases. In many marriages the trouble arises entirely from one of the partners. The only generality, it seems to me, is that either husband or wife may contribute anywhere from nothing on up to 100% of the trouble. I do not know if the 20–80's or the 50–50's or the 0–100's are the most frequent. It would be an interesting statistic. A successful, that is, a reasonably, harmonious, happy marriage depends not on the absence of neurosis (i.e., of disordered childhood patterns) so much as on how the childhood patterns of the pair *fit* each other. But probably the more mature the two are and the less disturbed their childhood patterns of human relations, the easier is their adjustment in marriage to each other and to the children and other responsibilities involved.

In this case, as far as could be seen in two interviews with the wife and one with the husband, the problem lay with the wife.

We introduced this young woman to illustrate one way in which masochism works. How many women want to live alone instead of with a handsome, charming, sexy, wealthy, colorful, worldly, devoted husband? Having everything, she is miserable. She feels caged. Her childhood pattern toward her parents repeats itself toward her husband. Down underneath she feels toward him as she felt during all those previous years toward her parents. The old feeling of being trapped and tyrannized over, leading to rage and guilt, continues in the new home. This pattern of feelings, formed in childhood, lives its own life, with little regard for reality.

To clarify the distinction between the child's outmoded feelings for her parents and the present realities of the wife's feelings toward her husband is the first big goal of treatment. Brenda's feelings toward her parents were a natural, normal, inevitable reaction to the treatment she received during her earliest, most formative years. But she is no longer a child and her husband is a

contemporary, not a parent. She has failed to outgrow her childhood feelings toward her parents so as to mature and develop the
feelings of a wife for a husband. The conspicuous lack of any
mention of children in the two interviews is a manifestation of
this failure as are the repeated references to the specific parental
warning against tying herself down for life. If her masochism wins
out, she will leave love and marriage to be isolated from people,
devoid of interests, and to face a bleak, financially insecure, lonely
middle age. This is the challenge to the analyst.

The extent of this challenge becomes even more apparent if we
review the box score for each partner on the seven components of
marriage. Enough has been said about Brenda and Ben for the
reader to evaluate them on these points.

1. Love—defined as closeness, identification, and selfless interest
in the spouse.

2. Sexual attractiveness, desire and healthy functioning with the
partner.

3. Sense of romance.

4. Parental drive and functioning.

5. Responsibility, personal and other, such as for home and in
breadwinning.

6. Maturity.

7. Fit of the two personalities.

People who knew all that went on in this marriage in later years
would not, unless they enjoyed more than average insight, have
considered the analytic treatment a success. But knowing the
depth of the problem and seeing it from the inside, I would consider the outcome a therapeutic triumph. When the girl came,
she was headed for an emotional breakdown, and this was not only
avoided at the time, but, with considerable security, prevented for
the future, chiefly by working through her hostility and guilt and
their sources. The second threat was that her masochism would
cause her to abandon the love of a devoted husband and a superior
person, that she would scuttle her security by withdrawing from
him and her few other human contacts, and that she would be
left with no adequate way of supporting herself as she entered
middle age. Her sexual activities, as came out soon after treatment
began, had the meaning of secretly defying her father and hence
piled up guilt, which increased her tendency to punish herself. The
marriage itself, although it looked hopeless, managed to survive.

It fell not in the one-third that ends in divorce, but in the upper part of the second third: those marriages that endure, but with difficulties.

Immediately after the interview with her husband, Brenda's major dynamics as described above were discussed with her. Her insight was keen and realistic, but it alone could not remake childhood patterns of reaction to her parents, which began so early in life and which were in no way diluted by other relationships. There was no sibling, aunt, grandparent or near neighbor with whom she could have a free, easy, good friendship, feeling that they understood her and were on her side. She did not escape to some other family from the stresses of her own, as so many children do. She ran away, but to nothing—later to loose relations with pre-teenagers, and to one girl friend. It was a struggle for her to try to free her adult attitudes and feelings, as a wife to her husband, from her almost all-encompassing patterns of reaction as a child to her parents. While slowly improving, she acted out many of these patterns, including the running away from home, and even the gestures toward surreptitious love affairs, which never materialized or were consummated, but remained gestures.

What took place while her husband was away in the service I do not know, but five years after the war, while in the Philadelphia area, they stopped in to see me before returning to Chicago. The marriage had held together. They had one child, a daughter, now 2 years old. Brenda was obviously a little easier in her acceptance of the marriage, which was still slowly improving.

There were two impressive features: One was Brenda's perseverance in treatment despite her almost irresistible impulses of anger and escape toward her husband. The other was the steadfast patience and fidelity of her husband, compounded no doubt of both mature and infantile patterns, in the face of his wife's hostile, provocative feelings and behavior. He knew that she had a problem but was getting analytic help, and he waited it out. Thank goodness his faith was rewarded. On our box score, it was perhaps mostly the fit of the two personalities that maintained sufficient equilibrium, however unstable, for them to continue together through all the storms.

Hostility has a place in the emotional life somewhat similar to that of heat in the physical world. Just as all physical friction produces heat, so all psychic friction generates hostility. Any threat, frustration, or irritation makes us angry. This is, I think, because a fundamental mechanism of adaptation is, as we have already mentioned, to meet every danger by destroying it or by escaping from it—by fight or by flight. When what distresses us arises from within, from inner conflicts, from an internal sense of inferiority, from self-made frustration, then we cannot destroy it or escape from it. Often in such circumstances we project our hostility onto others, attribute our troubles to them, blame someone or something outside ourselves. Hostility threatens family and society; no one enjoys being the object of another person's hostility. Hence children generally, and properly, are trained to control their hostilities. Therefore hostility, checked by the parents, may be directed against the self ("I could kick myself") and causes the superego (or conscience) to react with guilt and shame. Unfortunately it does not cause enough guilt or shame in many people to prevent crime and war. Aggressive war is only a larger form of crime. We have to fight the aggressors to survive, just as we have to have a police force to combat crime. But in good, decent people hostilities cause guilt and are often self-directed, and hence people very often behave unconsciously in self-injurious, masochistic ways and are their own worst enemies. As Churchill said, it is very hard for anyone to know his own best interest.

Marriage, we have noted, provides an ideal arena for the acting out of hostility to others and, masochistically, to oneself. In any close relationship the old emotional patterns of child to parents and to others tend to emerge. Sometimes they come out almost as soon as the marriage ceremony is over; sometimes they take years, even decades, to reveal themselves openly.

Masochism or self-injury arises from guilt and self-directed hostility, whatever the source. In some cases self-injury in any of a thousand forms is no more than a threat. In other cases the threat is realized because the self-injury is to some extent acted out.

Examples are probably at hand in everyone's experience. I will describe another couple very briefly without going into detail. The wife was a most attractive girl, married to an equally attractive man, and was the mother of two boys. We might call this couple Cliff and Candy.

Candy had a deprived background; her parents and older brother and sister were in the home but showed very little interest in her. She had a childhood with no really good relationships within her family. Therefore there was no emotional pattern for good feelings within a family in adult life. As we must stress, people tend to behave in their marital homes as they did as children in their parental homes, however different the realities of the marital home may be. Cliff had a certain amount of deprivation from his parents also, and this drew him and Candy together. This was the deeper emotional element they had in common, that made them understand each other, that made them *simpático*. But Cliff had developed more effective defenses than Candy against his sense of deprivation and rejection. He also had the advantage of being a man, and having work he could wrap himself up in. Work itself can be a great escape, defense and compensation. Through work many men and some women can drive for the recognition, appreciation, rewards and love that they lacked in childhood from their parents and of which they continue to feel deprived, or for the love they had and strive in their work to hold. That is why there is a compulsive element in the unremitting drive of some men to work.

Candy felt, with some justification, that her husband was too devoted to his work (engineering) and not enough to her. She complained, and he responded with a real effort to be home earlier, have cocktails before dinner, take her out to dinner and to the theater, and in general to do all he could to satisfy her needs. But her needs were too neurotic, that is, too much an expression of the deprivations of childhood rather than of the realities of a mature, adult married life. Her complaints continued despite his every effort. It got so that he lived in the stream of her hostility and criticism. Nothing he did was right. She acted out her parents' rejection of her in childhood by rejecting her husband now in marriage. Of course the children suffered. She saw an analyst but made little progress in changing the situation. In her mind all her frustration was caused by her husband, not herself. She failed to discriminate between her justified complaints in childhood and the realities of adjustment as wife and mother.

Then it happened. Cliff met a girl who sincerely felt that he was the greatest thing that walked the earth. His wife continued to feel that he was totally inadequate. At last Cliff was offered what his soul craved, and he and the girl fell madly in love. He became determined to have a divorce. Now Candy woke up—but too late. She had pushed him beyond the point of no return and masochistically precipitated herself into a divorce. Freud called it the "repetition compulsion"; she had acted out the childhood pattern of deprivation, hostility, guilt and self-punishment and had re-created for herself in marriage the rejection by her husband that she had suffered as a child from her parents. The divorce went through, with great anguish for all involved. Cliff's new marriage was of course not idyllic but was vastly happier. Everything was bitter for poor Candy who was, in her ego, the innocent victim of her own unconscious, undone through her pattern of rejection by her parents asserting itself in her marriage. Lacking a childhood pattern of good relations with parents, she failed to make good relations with other men after the divorce. Too late she realized what she had lost—a husband to whom other men she met did not measure up and whom another woman appreciated. She became depressed and, when I last heard, was again seeing a psychiatrist, this time not to save a marriage but to prevent serious depression and potential suicide.

It seems terrifying that what parents do or omit doing during those early formative weeks, months and years of their child's life can so fatefully influence that child's destiny. Terrifying and grossly unfair. But the world of adults is only the world of these children a few quick years later. The destiny of humanity is determined by how its young are reared. If we do not face this reality squarely, we will continue, by unenlightened child rearing, to bring up generation after generation of hostile, suffering adults—neurotics and psychotics, and criminals and aggressive war-makers, who will bring about destruction and agonies compared with which the unhappinesses of divorce, bad health and poverty seem only minor inconveniences. For not only in their marriages and private lives do individuals act out their frustrations through hostility and masochism, but, acting with others similarly affected, they may account for the hostility and self-destructiveness of whole nations.

*No one has ever loved anyone the way everyone wants to be
loved.*

MIGNON MCLAUGHLIN

*Those who want much are always much in need.*

HORACE

*The hand that gives, gathers.*

RAY

# 7 GIVE AND GET IN MARRIAGE

A very common marriage conflict—the good husband who gives to his business the devotion his wife craves for herself—and how such an interplay develops, and the problems of ameliorating it.

There is a kind of marital problem so common that, if my practice has provided a representative sample, it can properly be rated a sociological phenomenon, at least among certain strata of our society. This might be called a simple "give-get" conflict, and it would be helpful if everyone contemplating matrimony were well acquainted with it. But then it seems self-evident that the fundamentals of the human emotional life—that is, our attitudes, feelings and behavior toward ourselves and toward others—should be taught in school from the lower grades on up through college. Marriage is only a special case of human relations, and the essentials of marriage should be taught as soon as young people are concerned with it in its earliest form, dating.

It would be more proper to say that the essentials of marriage should be taught as soon as these instincts and feelings begin to exert their power in the adolescents and pre-adolescents. Actually, a background of knowledge of the human emotional life should be laid in advance, long before this period. Certainly such instruction should be made available not later than high school, for these forces are so powerful that every adolescent is to some extent confused by them, and needs all the clarification, insight and help available.

These forces can make a person's greatest happiness or his most extreme misery.

John and Jane are an average middle-income American family with three children, all now in school, the youngest in kindergarten. The husband was a loved child. His father was too occupied with his business to have been much in evidence. His mother was pretty well adapted to her husband's absence and to getting her chief satisfaction from home and children. She pinned great hopes upon John and perhaps he was somewhat favored by her over his sister, perhaps not. Probably his mother felt that he would be a greater source of pride to her than her husband was. At any rate, she gave John the best of care and possibly a little too much devotion. Certainly she was always there during his grade school years; she served him breakfast, saw him off to school and was waiting there with milk and cookies when he returned. She was a good, orderly housekeeper, and she was pretty much the boss of the home. As John grew up, his picture of marriage, formed from that of his parents, was of a good, kindly father coming in from his affairs to a well-run home in which his mother was at the helm. His father acceded to her wishes and did so gladly, for it saved him the trouble of making decisions and it kept the peace. He worked and earned, and Mother was satisfied with home and children. John was a miniature of his father. He went to school instead of work. He earned high marks instead of money. He behaved well in the home, and his mother was delighted with him. He went on to college and then to business school.

The sex urge drove him, and he had some adventures and affairs. The mating instinct asserted itself and he married. Jane was very attractive and very bright. Their three children came in fairly rapid succession and by the time the third child was two or three years old, John and Jane had been married nearly ten years. John was just passing his middle thirties. Sex with his wife was no longer the novelty and thrill and irresistible passion that it was. As John's interest in his wife diminished, his absorption in his business increased.

The old pattern was emerging. As his father went out as breadwinner, now so does he. Now he must make top grades in his particular occupational field as he used to in school. Then his wife will, like his mother, be proud of him, his income and his other successes, and like his mother will have a well-run home and well-behaved children always awaiting him for dinner with open arms. He is satisfied with himself as a sincere, conscientious husband and father who is doing good work in his chosen occupation. His mother and father were pleased with him because of his behavior in childhood, and now he takes over their acceptance of him into his own self-image, his picture of himself. And it is confirmed by his friends and co-workers.

How could his wife see him any other way? Astonishingly though, at least to him, she does see him very differently. This is less surprising if one learns that despite their having chosen each other, her early emotional background was rather different from John's. In childhood Jane lacked warm, understanding, giving love. And this meant that she lived in a different emotional climate in her own mind and had other outlooks and attitudes toward herself and toward life.

John called me and made an appointment. He was a small, slender, fair, outgoing man, a man on his way up in a large company. He told the following:

Patient: Over the last few years, our marriage, now ten years old, has been getting worse. At this rate it will soon reach a crisis. Jane and I are getting to be at swords' points. Sex has become infrequent. Is it possible that these things could be my fault, that I am doing something wrong or not doing something I should without realizing it? Can our marriage be salvaged? I still want to save it, but it is meaning less and less to me. Marriage no longer means much, but the children do—they and their future. Jane is not stable and is a poor housekeeper. If we got a divorce, she would not raise the children well. I think the trouble is really all hers, but I hope there is something in me that can be changed to help matters. Jane is impractical, a poor organizer, can't run the house. Dinner is not cooked or is not on time. A water pipe leaks and she doesn't call the plumber. The furniture is not well arranged. The refrigerator is not stocked. The house seems empty, dark, depressing. Jane has no interest in my work and never asks about it. She is never satisfied sexually and complains so much about not enough love-making that I've given up trying to satisfy her. But Jane says that the only way to improve the marriage, or maybe even save it, is for me to get analyzed for my sexual inadequacy and for my lack of affection. She blames me for the whole trouble, because she says I never give enough affection and never want to have sex. She seems to be threatening me, telling me I'd better see a psychiatrist and be a good lover, or she will leave. Even when I try to be demonstrative, she still accuses me, and the more she accuses me and attacks me and neglects the house, the more I withdraw.

Analyst: Please tell me a little about your home life when you were young.

P.: My parents did not have a very good marriage. They were not terribly fond of each other, but they were good-hearted. Mother was especially so. She was always very good and very warm, and she babied me and catered to me. The only children were me and my sister, three years younger. Father was almost always working and I didn't see much of him. He tried to do what was right, but there was no closeness between us and we never talked about things that mattered.

A.: Has your sister problems?

P.: She seems to have an all-right marriage and to be reasonably happy.

A.: What is the very first thing you remember, way back before continuous memory?

P. Let's see. The first thing I can remember is Mother taking me to kindergarten.

The very earliest memories are astonishingly revealing of central major trends in the personality. The major trends seem to cause one to select for remembrance just those little scenes which best express them. Here we see the prominence of the mother and care by her and the outside interest, the school.

This is as far as we got in the first interview. In the second he went on:

P.: This problem with Jane is the only thing really wrong in my life. I've gradually been gaining confidence in myself. I have gradually made good friends. I like my job and am doing well in it. I get on well with the children. My relation to Jane is practically the only bad one I have in life. She has blotted out her childhood. She makes friends but often loses them. She can be good with the children but then fails to make arrangements for something, say a party, and disappoints them.

The mutual respect, admiration, affection, and interests Jane and I had when we were first married have been lost. Jane likes to discuss artistic and intellectual things, but I don't feel like it when the house is in such a mess. When I come home, I can't find anything, dinner often isn't ready, or she'll tell me to take her and the children out to dinner, although I have work to do that evening. If I want a snack there is nothing in the refrigerator. I've given up expecting breakfast at home.

A.: What do your complaints come down to?

P.: Well, I guess you could call it domestic inefficiency that I object to—things misplaced, beds unmade, servicemen not called, all that. And social inefficiency as well—she's careless about letters of congratulation, gifts, entertaining.

A.: What else bothers you?

P.: I want my wife's interest. But no, maybe I don't. Maybe I rebuff her. I don't want her suggestions about what I should do.

A.: Do you think a vicious circle is building up between the two of you? And if so, what does it reduce itself to?

P.: As we have been talking, things have become clearer in my mind. My chief complaint is *inadequate house management;* her chief complaint is *inadequate love life.* And this is what makes the vicious circle you spoke of. If I phone to say I'm delayed at the office, Jane's tone makes it clear that she thinks I arranged it on purpose.

A.: You mean she is very easily frustrated?

P.: Exactly. When I come home at night I must be on guard, because if she has had any problem or disappointment she will be annoyed and hostile. What I want is for her to be *more responsible* and *less hostile.*

As usual the one spouse tells more of the pathology and dynamics of the other one than of his own. In this case John has shown Jane to be a deprived person underneath, which makes her constantly frustrated, demanding and hostile. He has depicted her ego (the conscious, official part of her personality, with all her higher powers) as childish and irresponsible. Often the description of one spouse by the other is correct or partially so, but I have learned that one cannot count on this. The other partner must be seen.

To emphasize this point it is worth a brief digression to mention another case. Gus, a handsome and apparently healthy and wholesome man, complained that his wife, Gail, was infantile, that she was extremely neglectful of the house and of their young children, that her person and house were filthy, and that she was so hostile that she attacked him. The picture was of a rapidly deteriorating schizophrenic. But I got no clear idea of his own dynamics. When I saw the wife, she presented a very different picture. The husband, she said, from his own background held a belief in male supremacy and was so extreme and hostile in this that she simply could not tolerate it and was on a full scale sit-down strike. We tested this by a brief separation in which she and the children visited her parents. Overnight she became her old self. This couple moved away because the husband was transferred, but I heard later that the wife had obtained a divorce despite the husband's resistance, had married, and was her former happy self.

There are two morals to the tale. The first is the necessity of hearing *both* the husband and wife. The second is the powerful effect people have on each other, especially when bound together in the intimacy of married life. With this husband, Gus, the girl, Gail, was behaving indeed like a schizophrenic. What would this have led to if the marriage had continued? I once saw a mature, stable man who was so depressed that he could barely function. This turned out to be a reaction, unrecognized by himself, to his wife's internally generated hostility. It was possible to get her into treatment, which was, happily, successful. Her hostility to her husband lessened in a few months and his depression disappeared.

I had to meet Jane and see the picture through her eyes. I hoped that all was not so dark as it looked and that the drift to divorce might somehow be reversed.

Speaking with Jane for only a few minutes quickly and sharply brought out the contrast between her personality and John's. Both came through strongly, both were highly intelligent, but John, although outgoing, was deliberate and steady, while Jane, with bright blue eyes and a ready smile, would attract attention in any group by her quick mind and varied interests, as well as by her femininity. If the two complemented each other, they would, other things being equal, have a good and interesting marriage. In a way each provided qualities the other needed. How Jane saw the problem will appear from the following abbreviated notes:

Patient: The problem is whether it is possible to make a go of the marriage.

Analyst: What is the central difficulty?

P.: It is John's lack of interest in me, generally and sexually. He apparently can go indefinitely without wanting me or even hardly touching me. I am the opposite. I respond strongly to people and to everything—art, literature, music—and there is always an erotic coloring to the enjoyment for me. John doesn't understand this at all, and his not understanding it makes me so angry. I feel so frustrated and blocked and angry that I cannot do anything— not even get a divorce or take a lover.

A.: Tell a little about the emotional relations in your earliest childhood.

P.: My father was mostly busy and I saw very little of him. He traveled a lot, but when he was home he was always preoccupied with business. Mother meant well but we were never very close. My sister, three years younger, wasn't close to her either. Mother was always active in the community, always had something to keep her out of the house a lot.

A.: Did you resent this?

P.: Yes. I got used to it, but I think I always missed her and was very angry at her underneath for it.

A.: What are your very earliest memories?

P.: The first is of my father saying that I was spoiled. The second is having fun at a neighbor's whom I used to visit. I liked it better at my neighbor's house than in my own home. Then I remember, when I first went to school, being told that I was no good at the little paintings we did, and how devastated I was by this.

[We note the criticism by father—overspoiling—the fun at the neighbor's in preference to her own home, and again the criticism at school for her performance, which may appear today in criticism from her husband.]

But the question is, how can I live with nothing from my husband and with no sex? I didn't want to come to see you because John thinks everything is my fault, and if I spoke to you, he would take it as proof that I was neurotic. He tells me all the things he wants done and I do them. He lacks any human feeling; he had it once but hasn't shown it for years.

A.: You said you do all the things your husband wants done, but you know he complains of the opposite—that you don't run the house very well or handle entertaining well, or anything really.

P.: That's only because I'm in such a rage at him. He gives me nothing and doesn't seem to have the slightest idea of my needs. I don't know if it's because of his talking with you, but he seems to be waking up a little to what is going on in his own home now and to be concerned about the children. Anyway, it's nothing at all for me to run a home efficiently, take care of the children and their activities, and do plenty of entertaining. I haven't done any of these things because of simple revenge. I told you I felt blocked. Divorce would harm the children. Somehow I haven't felt right about taking a lover. I've just taken revenge by letting the house go.

[Here is a most encouraging sign. If her neglect is the result of conscious hostility, it is of course much more easily reversible than if it were an internal sit-down strike.]

A.: Do you think that your revenge may have the opposite effect from what you want—that it may be causing a vicious circle by making John react with more anger to you and therefore with even more rejection and neglect of you? Sometimes in adult life we defeat ourselves if we demand too directly. Sometimes we get only by giving.

This comment began a discussion that launched treatment, although the goals and the form of analysis were not yet evident. Jane quickly made clear that she wanted her husband to see me regularly for his part in their difficulties, but that she would not even consider going to a psychiatrist in a systematic way herself.

Since we were still in an exploratory, diagnostic stage, this was not unsatisfactory. A pattern of deprivation and hostility formed in her childhood seemed a central key to *her* side of the tussle with John. I discussed this pattern with her almost immediately, in as unthreatening a way as possible, without attributing to her any blame or neuroticism (neurosis being disturbed childhood patterns tnat cause difficulties in later life). At the same time it is important that only the truth be told. I said that, as she well knew, the extent, form, and nature of one's wants and the way in which one handles his frustrations are largely conditioned by one's experiences during childhood. Therefore she and her husband had differences in their needs, in what and how much they expected from life and from others, and in their reactions to frustration. But no matter what one's early childhood, every marriage involves *getting* somewhat less and *giving* somewhat more than each of us dreams of and anticipates. If she did the efficient job her husband desired, maybe the vicious circle of their marriage would be interrupted.

When John came in again, what he said confirmed my impression of his dynamics and I was able to discuss these impressions with him very openly. The essence of his dynamics was his continuing toward his wife the pattern toward his mother, taking her for granted and not fully appreciating her needs, which might, I agreed, be intensified by his wife's early deprivation. But every wife has some limitations; no wife is the ideal mother of our childhood wishes. For him, as for her, it was a matter of getting a little less and giving a little more in a real-life marriage than he had dreamed of since childhood.

The idea of giving and getting was the main theme of the therapy for both of them. The immediate goal was the clarification of how their present attitudes, formed in childhood, impaired their achievement of harmony. The object was to make the most of the present reality, since each had so much to offer, instead of pining hopelessly and angrily for some dreamed-of potentiality.

It was not clear at this point how much trouble would come from Jane's underlying residue of deprivation from childhood. She would certainly have to come to terms with her past. All the same, the trend in John's personality that contributed to the tug-of-war between them, although quieter and less obvious, was no less of a contributing factor to their difficulties. As we have previously remarked, sometimes the difficulties come almost entirely from the husband or the wife. Not infrequently the problem stems almost entirely from the wife's persisting pattern of childhood deprivation, which makes her excessively demanding and chronically hostile. But in this case the husband's naiveté about his wife's normal needs certainly increased Jane's sense of frustration. This was all to the good therapeutically, because it increased the chances that insight alone without a long analysis would help John change appreciably, just as it promised to enable Jane to relinquish her tactic of revenge by passive aggression through her sitdown strike.

When I brought up with John his wife's feminine needs, he said, "At eleven o'clock I'm tired and want to go to sleep and not have intercourse first." I replied, "Sex is not just the physiology of intercourse. Your wife needs all the kinds of attention a man can give to a woman. If there is to be intercourse, the woman wants to be wooed and gotten into the mood. Her needs for physical sex are only part of what she wants more broadly: masculine attention, appreciation, affection and love. She wants to be told that she looks pretty, that she made a fine dinner, that she handled a difficult problem well, that she did a good job with the children, that she was attractive when you were out together, and that she handled the entertaining at home well. She wants your interest in things that interest her. She will be less demanding of physical sex, which you rather resent, if you better satisfy her broader feminine needs, and she will be much more apt to handle her responsibilities well, which is what you want, if she gets plenty of appreciation for doing them."

Does it seem strange that it could be necessary to discuss these elementary matters with a man who is successful in life and who has a wife and three children? We traced back his attitudes toward his wife to their sources, in his relation to his mother. We also spoke of his wife's needs and reactions in relation to *her* childhood pattern.

The interactions of both and the sources in their childhood patterns were then discussed with Jane. Each one saw what was central to the struggle between them and what each must do to build reasonable harmony and happiness in its place. The positive attributes of each were also defined—all Jane's excellent qualities and all that John actually provided for her. For Jane to get a divorce and face life seeking a better mate, with or without her three children, seemed a poor risk compared with trying to make her relationship to John work. And how could John know whether a second wife would not have hidden troubles worse than Jane's?

The first goal of this therapy was to clarify the conflict and bring it into perspective. It was to show what each was feeling and doing, and why, and to visualize the alternatives. This was done through insight and discussion. Its purpose was to achieve a reorientation of attitudes which would make both of them realize what they would lose by breaking up, and gain by true reconciliation. This was not full personal analysis, designed to change by therapy the childhood pattern of each. Instead it was what is called "ego reorientation" to help them see what they would do to themselves and to each other and to their children if they did not change and build a good relationship between them. The hope was that the threat on the one hand and the promise on the other would be pressure enough. Working in this way through insight, I hoped to force them into steady improvement in their feelings and behavior toward each other. The desire to find pleasure and avoid pain works with the drive to maturity; and nature's powers of healing are what help us to change, to free ourselves from the entrapments of the childhood patterns.

This worked substantially almost immediately. John showed appreciation and attention; Jane easily ran everything efficiently, as she said she could. This improvement led to the resumption of sexual relations, although John's drive did not match Jane's need. The children became happy again.

The first principle of therapy is, as we have said, *primum non nocere*—to do no harm. A second principle is the same as in sports: *Never change a winning game, always change a losing game.*

With such a good start, I thought it best to continue as we were doing and not to bring in another psychiatrist for John or Jane. This does not mean that there were not ups and downs and backslidings, nor that I ignored the potential for trouble from the pathodynamic childhood patterns of each. But the trend was toward improvement and the difficulties were manageable as they arose. For example, John would feel at times that Jane was backsliding in her responsibilities and he would flare up in anger in spite of his efforts. This I agreed was bound to happen and, I reminded him, making a satisfying marriage was never quick or easy for *anyone*. Jane objected that, although John's treatment of her had improved greatly, his behavior had an artificial quality. "Naturally," I said, "everything we learn is artificial and self-conscious in its first stages. This is a good sign, not a bad sign; it means that he is trying and that he is moving toward change." Or Jane would at periods of anger become bitter about what she had missed over the last years and invoke her "rights as a woman." The important thing, I reminded her, was to keep this a winning game—the relationship was better, the job was to keep it improving—and not to pine over the past. As to rights, this had only an abstract meaning. The only substance was the reality of what we knew of her and of John and how to get the most satisfaction out of what each could offer. And this was the point: marriage, like the rest of life, offers less and demands more than *any* of us wants. *Make the most of the reality; don't frustrate yourself over the potentiality.*

Of course the differences between John and Jane were clear.

Different people use different physiological systems in varied proportions to gain satisfaction. Some especially enjoy eating, using the gastrointestinal system; others get great pleasure from athletics, using the muscular system. John got his satisfactions chiefly through intellectual and man-to-man social activity in his business. Sex was not the chief system for his gratification. Sex can be a great drain for any kind of feeling (hostility, dependence, love, togetherness, and so on), and for most people it is a great diversion, consolation and refreshment. Sex was all of these things to Jane; it was the chief channel for almost all of her feelings. This important incompatibility was apparently so deep-seated in their makeups that the chances of analysis changing either one appreciably in these outlets, intellectual and sexual, were slight, if indeed such an attempt were advisable.

Of course there were the deep-seated childhood patterns underlying the marital conflict. Could ego orientation and insight help? Would analytic treatment for one or both be indicated later? Were there strong hostile and masochistic trends that would cause one or both to injure the other and himself? Or was the balance of forces in each personality and between them such that this ego reorientation had halted the vicious circle and started them on a permanent path to ever-increasing mutual satisfaction? The unconscious is complex and powerful, its effects always unpredictable. Meanwhile we were playing a winning game and, since both John and Jane had so much to lose by breaking up, so much to gain by getting on better, we continued on this basis.

The outcome was fortunate. Improvement continued over the years. Typically, it was easier for John than for Jane. There were two reasons for this: John had had more security and love from his mother than Jane had had, and he had the pattern of taking the home for granted while he made a success in school. So now, with a well-run home and success in the company, his pattern was pretty well satisfied. But Jane, with her inner dependent-love needs strengthened and sensitized by early frustration, was, as a woman responsible for home and children, largely cut off from outside contacts and gratifications. As she saw and worked through all this, she made steady progress in managing her needs and frustrations, and her husband was won over to accepting and even approving outside interests for his wife, although this ran contrary to his mother's narrow, undiverted concentration on the home.

Jane, always interested in politics and community problems, became active, well known and popular. This helped to satisfy her needs as she worked analytically to control these needs and her inner sense of frustration.

Five years after the war they were doing well. They had come or were coming through the next shoals and rapids of marriage—the matrimonial passage in which the husband is at the peak of his career. It is a time when the husband is even more absorbed in his job and his increasing power in the business. He is more self-sufficient. He has gained recognition from his associates, and his success compensates for his passing youth in attracting certain kinds of women. He is more easily tempted into infidelity because, now in his mid-forties, he sees the shadow of age five or ten years ahead.

Jane had reconciled herself to the futility of expecting and demanding from John what it was not in his makeup to give; and she had learned how much of her frustration derived from her own inner pattern. So she ran the home and pursued her own outside interests, was exposed to her own temptations, and made a life for herself as best she could, restraining her envy, feeling of deprivation and resentment toward John. In striving for an equilibrium they had grown further and further apart, and here lay the danger. The children were grown and one after another leaving for college. The maturity in John and Jane showed them in retrospect the life they had shared and the deep satisfactions, despite the battles, in marriage, home and children. They saw that the only choice was to make the most of what they had together and that nothing—neither success nor pride nor interests nor romantic adventures—was worth the sacrifice of the good that they provided each other. (But maturity does not always prevail, as the next chapter will show.)

John and Jane's situation illustrates another point: in order to understand a person one must usually maintain two opposing attitudes. We must be entirely open-minded and free of preconceptions, always ready for the unexpected, but at the same time we must be ready to draw on all our previous experience and knowledge.

Almost always, in my experience, there is some deep-seated emotional similarity in childhood patterns that draws two people together into marriage. In John and Jane's case the similarity was not clear. Perhaps it lay in their attachments to their mothers. John tried to gain his wife's love in the same way he had successfully gained love from his mother. But, unlike John, Jane had no established pattern to assure her of her husband's approving love.

In some cases the wife or husband has an intensified longing for maternal love because of being a little spoiled and overindulged as a child; in others (and this is more common) there was some deprivation. Perhaps the father, like most, was so preoccupied with the competitive struggle for existence, security and status that he was not much in evidence. If the family was in a low income bracket, the mother may have been fatigued emotionally and physically with the labors of home and children and not have had enough to offer in feelings, patience, time and understanding. If the family was in a relatively high income bracket, the mother may have been too busy pursuing her club and community activities. In either case the child feels insufficiently loved. And this feeling—a true, inevitable, realistic reaction during the earliest, formative years—continues for life. This creates an inner emotional atmosphere that leads to several consequences.

It creates an *internal* sense of being deprived, unsatisfied and insufficiently loved. This comprises two feelings: an increased need to *be* loved over *giving* love, and a sense that one is not loved enough, a built-in feeling of frustration. These two feelings may in the days of courtship enhance a girl's attractiveness. Many such girls are especially alluring. They are so girlishly eager to be loved and this eagerness shows through so clearly that most men find it an irresistible appeal to their masculinity. Perhaps this is particularly true for a man who has been in the position of the child craving his mother's love—for now he finds *himself* in the stronger, adult position, as the one to whom the girl appeals for *his* love. Thus he is "out from under" the childhood position to his mother.* He may also be attracted, by identification, to someone who craves even more strongly than he what he himself yearns for, that is, maternal love. (And one who was deprived may be attracted to one who was gratified in childhood.) The girl, on her part, usually seeks maternal love through the channel of sex and romance; she turns her dependent-love needs from mother to men or to one single man. The most direct path for her to express her need is through sex in a setting of love, which becomes especially prominent in her relationship with a man.

* Saul, L. J.: *Emotional Maturity*, 2nd Edition, Philadelphia, Lippincott, 1960.

In the case we are discussing, Jane, deprived in childhood, especially craves love and has particularly strong sexual needs and sex appeal. Since she is so attractive, we can see why John married her. However, wanting the reassurance and demonstration of love through urgent demands for attention and sex may well lead after the honeymoon to a vicious circle. With this couple the requirements of home and children took more and more energy out of Jane and thereby increased her already strong inner needs for replenishment. Meanwhile John's powers were being directed more and more toward his job. If Jane were strong and were firmly identified with her husband's orientation, she would tolerate the frustrations of being a wife with a hard-working husband, who is wrapped up in his work but who is well-meaning and at heart devoted to hearth and home. Thus when I asked one wife how she liked having a husband with two jobs, she unthinkingly replied, "Great!" and then the conversation made clear that she was referring to her husband's enjoyment and enthusiasm for the two jobs he was then carrying. Another wife, somewhat younger and who had three small children, found it difficult to have her husband in a job that required many nights out; but she knew how important it was for them all, and was so proud of her husband and what he was accomplishing that she did her best to accept the deprivation.

Jane was much younger but not that strong. Strength is largely a matter of how much one can give and how little one requires. Jane felt increasingly deprived and became more insistent on what seemed to her to be her rights; and of course, with the frustration came resentment. Not all wives identify with their husbands' successes. Jane felt that John was getting recognition and esteem at work while she got nothing and only did what a housekeeper and nurse could do. She was a little envious of what John got out of work, a little competitive with him. John sensed Jane's increasing need of him, her sense of deprivation, her resentment. He never liked his mother to be displeased with him, and he did not like his wife to be. He tried to give her more attention, time and affection but he disliked her demands for these. Though he tried, he became somewhat cooler and more distant. Sex had lost its irresistible urgency. He was happier following his interests at work than doing what was becoming a chore in his home—the job of being husband and father. Jane felt this and noted an artificial quality in his feelings toward her. She felt more deprived, more demanding, more resentful. But John wanted a home like the home of his childhood, so that he could be free for his successes, then at school, now at work. His reactions to Jane's mounting frustration increased further. The vicious circle between them was in full spin, spiraling downward.

The children, of course, are also affected by these increasing tensions. If they are involved long enough, strongly enough, from early enough in life, there will be effects upon them that will last all their lives. Today many parents know this or at least suspect it. Sometimes it is because of the children that they come for help. All the more reason for the efforts of the dynamic psychiatrist to arrest and reverse the downward spiral.

# 8 PASSIVITY AND REGRESSION: THE PERENNIAL CHILD

A reaction that is related to "give-get" and the psychological sitdown strike, as exemplified by husbands who give up under the responsibilities of wife and children and job. This reaction we traced back to the kind of wing-clipping in childhood that can cause an exaggeration of what everyone feels occasionally.

The baby and small child are completely dependent on the mother (and father or substitutes) for satisfaction of their needs, that is, for their survival. The feeling that goes with this dependence is love. Being loved brings the assurance of the food, shelter and care that are necessary to survival. Thus we can conveniently speak of the dependent-love needs. Conversely the parent, originally the mother, who carries, bears and nurtures the child from her own body, is responsible for meeting the child's needs; and the feeling that assures this, is love for the child. The child must *be* loved and have responsibility taken for it by the adult—the parent *gives* the love and all that the responsibility entails. This is the "instinctual response system" between child receiving and parent giving.

On the long road from the helpless, love-needing dependence of childhood to the relative independence and responsibility of the adult, certain feelings and attitudes may, if the child is not properly treated, be left behind, may fail to mature. Some parts of the emotional development proceed; others are inhibited or warped and persist with little change in the adult. It is like the children once raised by traveling circus troupes in big vases of varying shapes,

73

which let parts of their bodies grow normally but molded other parts grotesquely; or, a less grisly analogy, like a young tree growing in a dense forest, striving to mature fully and in perfect balance, aiming to catch the sunlight but becoming bent, stunted or twisted by darkness, crowding and climbing vines. Thus, because of the early influences upon them, many children mature well in certain parts of their personalities, while failing to do so in other parts; certain of the childish needs for love and dependence may persist and not be outgrown in favor of giving and responsibility. These may be in relation to wife, children, career, breadwinning, or in any other area. A person may be quite mature in some areas and painfully infantile in others, depending on his early experiences.

A simple example came to my attention when a young mother of three came to see me about her husband. We will call them Eleanor and Ed. Eleanor said that Ed was a fine husband and father, devoted to her and the children, a good lover, and of a uniformly good humor. He had only one failing and it was about this that she wished to consult me. His devotion was confined to his home; he had none for his work. A college graduate, he had had a series of rather lowly and poorly paying jobs—low level work in business, door-to-door selling and other employment suitable for college students during the summer but of no interest in themselves, and not adequate for supporting a family of five, or for potential for the future. Her parents would finance treatment for him, if I felt it held promise. I explained to her that my schedule was filled at the time but that I saved time each week for consultations and referrals of people to other analysts. Although some disagree, my own experience has demonstrated beyond doubt that the selection of the analyst is of the greatest importance: his personality as well as his interests and abilities should fit as well as possible the particular needs of the individual patient.

Ed came for an interview, which I will not recount in detail. What Eleanor said was completely confirmed by him. There had been very little model for responsibility in his mother, and his father had been away most of the time. His own efforts at any responsibility, such as helping to clear the table or running errands, were rebuffed and discouraged. Apparently these were rejected as nuisances. He was most loved when he was inactive, passive. Then his mother was devoted. She was also overanxious about his playing and associating with other boys. Thus his childhood pattern, his 0 to 6, was a loving family life as an only child, as long as he stayed home and was "good" (meaning quiet). His passivity was rewarded, his initiative blocked. Thus he became a homebody, at home in the bosom of his family but not so out in the world. His wings were clipped.

The outlook for therapy was poor because no nucleus of independence and responsibility was discernible in his whole life to build on. Yet normal maturation includes a drive to use one's power. He accepted referral to an excellent analyst for his problem. The treatment did not go well.

Passivity, whether for breadwinning, as in this case, or in any other area, usually has four main sources: a fixation to the childish enjoyment of inactivity, hostility, inhibition of normal drives and regression. Each of these sources may be present in a given individual in different strengths and proportions.

The simple enjoyment of inactivity is similar to the baby's and very small child's enjoyment of lying back and being taken care of, his every want fulfilled by others. However, even in infants this passivity is only a small part of otherwise ceaseless activity. Of course rest from responsibility is normal and healthy. We all withdraw into complete passivity for sleep, and only a balanced life is wholesome—a balancing off of responsible giving and effort by rest and replenishment. But passivity can also be a continuation of childish needs to such an extent as to be pathological, a neurotic problem, as in the man just mentioned. This kind of passivity is a fixation to a childish (perhaps we should say "babyish") attitude.

But this man also revealed another source for his deficiency as a provider for his family. His mother's restriction of his natural exuberant activity, her oh-so-gentle molding of him into the good little home boy, was of course a warping of his emotional maturation. We all are impelled biologically to live out our lives, to fulfill our life cycles, to mature and then to senesce and die. Impairment to the process of maturation is frustrating and threatening. Failure to mature makes us inadequately equipped to cope with the world, inferior to others, and insecure. We react with the fight-flight response: attack and destroy the danger, or flee from it. But if the danger is internal, it cannot be grappled with, destroyed or escaped; instead it generates an impotent rage. Ed managed to hide his rage at his mother from her and even from himself. She would not have tolerated it; he would not have been loved, if he had showed it.

Married, Ed repeats toward his wife the old pattern toward his mother. He is the good devoted boy in the home. But besides being unaccustomed to making his way in the world and not wishing to, he uses this passive withdrawal as a weapon of hostility: "All right, Mother, you hold me back from growing up in the world, then I'll do what you say—but to such an extent that we'll just see how you like it!" This is passivity used to express hostility, the so-called "passive aggression." It is the sit-down strike that Jane, described previously in "Give and Get in Marriage," used consciously in neglecting the house as revenge on her husband.

Interestingly, treatment is more promising if the passivity expresses hostility than if it is a simple fixation, simple childish pleasure in inaction. For hostility is mostly uncomfortable and for this and other reasons is reducible.* But simple passivity gives satisfaction, and what gives pleasure is relinquished only with great difficulty. If a drive to responsible activity is there but is blocked by hostility, the task is only to unblock it; but if the passivity has never been outgrown in favor of this drive to responsible activity, then a long process is required for growth out of something that is clung to as pleasurable. Hence alcoholism, sexual perversions and misbehavior, and generally all symptoms that give pleasure are difficult to change. It is almost like working with something that is not there. People only change if they feel strongly that the change will relieve suffering and increase pleasure.

If the passivity is the result of normal drives to activity and responsibility being blocked while they still exist strongly in the person, then therapeutically the most favorable situation exists. It is the third source: passivity as blocked (inhibited) mature drive. For example, a father insists too much that his son be a great success. The son has drive and wants to succeed but is on a sit-down strike against the excessive parental pressure. Another son is always criticized for what he does; his activity becomes blocked for fear of criticism. Another is so intensely competitive that success means to him defeating or killing off every rival. Striving

* As Coleridge wrote in "Christabel":
  *"And to be wroth with one we love*
  *Doth work like madness in the brain."*

is therefore so fraught with effort and anxiety as to become inhibited.

Sometimes the child is in such conflict with his parents or others, or as an adult is so burdened by internal pressures or by situations in life that exceed his capacities, that he gives up, breaks down, collapses, and is unable to continue his responsibilities. This is passivity as regression from adult life, back to the dependence and helplessness of childhood. Such regression may affect only certain parts of the personality, or it may be comprehensive enough to necessitate hospitalization. Such passivity as regression from external situations beyond a person's tolerance are of course clearly seen in the neuroses of war. It is a matter of external pressures impinging too strongly on a person's "specific emotional vulnerability." Thus one man would break as soon as he was drafted. Another would tolerate combat better than the next, but then when relieved would break when he heard that his wife had been unfaithful to him. Others would tolerate just about everything except the authoritarian discipline—and so on. The strongest men break and regress if the pressure hits them in their most vulnerable emotional spots.

Ed's problem turned out to be a good illustration of passivity as fixation. Of course these four categories (fixation, hostility, blocked normal drive, and psychological escape into regression) are not hard and fast, are not mutually exclusive; all are usually present, but in varying proportions. In some persons one reaction predominates strongly over the others, as hostility did in Jane and, as it turned out, fixation in Ed.

All this sounds, I fear, rather didactic, but it is of the greatest practical importance. Each person should understand the nature and strength of the passivity versus the responsible drives in himself—and in his prospective mate.

It is tragic when a good man finds himself wedded to a woman who turns out to be infantile in her lack of interest or capacity for responsibilities for home, husband, and children. And what of the girl who, aglow with love, entrusts her security and that of her children to the breadwinning capacity of her husband? Certainly she should know that a man's relation to his work is no set, stable thing. It is subject, like everything else in the personality, to a whole range of variation. It is influenced by intelligence and energy and, of course, by the emotional relationships in the man's childhood.

The capacity for responsibility is, as we have seen, an attribute of maturity, and conversely responsibility builds maturity. A man's capacity for interest and accomplishment in his work is a vital part of his personality for himself and for his family. He may be so compulsive in his application to his work that his wife bitterly objects, somewhat as Jane did. But before a wife objects, however legitimately, to her husband's excessive application to his occupation, let her consider the other extreme: the men like Ed, who, however charming in every other respect, are emotionally infantile as providers.

It is difficult for most men to find a happy medium. Even if a man's own emotional balance and maturity make him desire a happy medium, external pressures of the world, in our society, bear down heavily upon him. When a man is young he must make his way to a certain level of income and security, and this is no easy task. When older, he has responsibilities that he is usually unable to shed. He is caught in a more or less all-or-nothing position. Usually it is not possible, in certain strata at least, to do half a job or three-quarters of a job. The competition is strong. At any age and stage he may wish to let up and have more time for his family and for leisure, but life rarely lets him achieve this well-balanced life.

Thus the balance between interests (work, family, society) and the balance between responsible effort and recreation are both difficult to attain because of the external demands of life and the internal balance of forces within the personality. Perhaps this is part of the reason why it is said that it is the very rich and the very poor who take the worst beatings from life.

Perhaps too it is because of the unremitting daily demands of life that so many people long for surcease from work—for passivity—and are apt to forget that the exercise of one's mature adult powers, if not excessive, is one of the greatest of all blessings. Put conversely, one of the worst punishments for a man—and for a woman too—is to force him to be idle, to prevent him from using his abilities. For in this the personality is like the body. If vision is not used, it dims, as animals long in caves lose their sight. Muscles, even if in peak condition, weaken in a few weeks if they are not used. So too do the reflexes for sports and arts, from golf or skiing to piano playing or singing. The proper use of one's body, mind, and feelings for mature, responsible, giving, constructive purposes is indispensible to the maintenance of health and strength. To let one's natural endowments atrophy bespeaks an emotional problem.

Looked at another way, the progressive thrust of maturation is opposed by a counterforce of fixation and regression back to the childhood patterns. These patterns affect different motivations. Some persons carry the weightiest responsibilities without flinching—Winston Churchill, for example (but he said he would not want to live through it all again). Others carry on, but the inner protest, the regression which is not given in to, contributes to ulcers, high blood pressure, or to other symptoms. Others under their first adult responsibilities do regress, even to the point of breaking down. And still others never get started at all.

Ed started, but barely. His wife suspected nothing while they were students together. Not until six years and three children later did she realize that he had a problem, and even then she did not perceive its severity. He accepted treatment, which was to be financed by his mother and his mother-in-law. The analyst knew that this arrangement played on the problem, but reasoned that if a start were made and any progress at all achieved, Ed might then gradually become willing as well as able to contribute financially. It was the only way an attempt could be made.

It was evident in a few weeks that the attempt would fail. There was no sign in his history, dreams, memories, or present behavior of any motivation toward this or any other financial responsibility. His unconscious motto was: Anything is better than work. There was no therapeutic urge and hence no progress. The analyst cannot hypnotize or anesthetize the patient and actively *do* something, as the surgeon can; of course such methods have long been tried —hypnosis, Pentothal, shock, and the like. Improvement on a sound, permanent basis is the result of alterations in the balance of basic forces in the personality.

In Ed's case, the progressive forces toward work were overwhelmed by the childhood fixation. It seemed clear that there was not enough for the analyst to work with, but he tried valiantly and far reduced his fee to bring it to something that Ed could afford himself. But Ed was more inclined to enjoy treatment at the expense of his mother than to use it for any real change in his attitudes and functioning. Despite all the analyst's resources, the treatment never took hold. Some persons from their first contact with analytic therapy feel that it was developed just for them. Some begin with a powerful resistance, usually from things within them that they fear to face or reveal or experience; but it is usually favorable for improvement to have this defensiveness appear early so that it can be dealt with immediately. The balance of forces in others is such that analytic intervention cannot influence them appreciably and start them toward health and maturity. Ed was a legitimate failure (in contrast to the illegitimate ones resulting from faults in treatment).

His analyst arranged to maintain contact with Ed by occasional visits and phone calls. This kept the relationship going and enabled the analyst to watch for anything that he might be able to do by way of prevention or help.

Ed dragged along earning less than his family could subsist on. He would keep an inadequately paying job for a time because he enjoyed it. One that required much work he soon relinquished. The parental families contributed in order to keep the family going, but their financial resources were limited and they could not continue this support indefinitely. Their attitude gradually shifted from wanting to help Ed get up the first rungs of the ladder to impatience and dismay at the character deficiency they were being forced to acknowledge.

Faced with the withdrawal of their help, Eleanor, the wife, felt that she had no choice but to find remunerative work herself, in addition to the already weighty job of caring for home, husband, and three children on a subsistence income. She found work that enabled her to pay for help in the home and still come out ahead financially. Fortunately she was sturdy physically, but the strain soon told. The chief effect was to make her irritable. She tolerated this irritability in herself toward her husband because it was his fecklessness that overburdened her. Even so, she was not entirely easy about her shortening temper with him because he was a warm, interested husband and father, and what with his shortcomings, could not but appeal to the maternal in her. She inevitably responded to this appeal, which derived so directly from his childhood pattern toward his mother. But her blowing up at the children filled her with guilt and self-reproach, and she became somewhat anxious and depressed.

Sex, as we have said, is the great diversion and consolation; it channels and drains every kind of tension and feeling. Eleanor, feeling more and more deprived and increasingly resentful toward Ed, her give-get balance tilted far over by little get and excessive give, began to think of a love affair. This might provide masculine consolation, a needed outlet, diversion and change from the home, and drain some of her hostility, her wish for revenge against her husband. She was not conscious of all this. All she was aware of fully was the build-up of this urge and these fantasies. Her background and training were such that her reaction to this impulse was guilt—and, when inevitably she met a man who might make such an adventure a reality, she panicked. She feared that yielding to such desires might involve her in feelings and situations destructive to herself as well as to her family.

To save herself, she called her husband's analyst. That is how, in the position of consultant, I heard the story, told to me at her own request. The analyst referred her to another, not wanting in any way to jeopardize any possibility, however slight, of helping Ed by seeing his wife also.

She was right to be afraid of such entanglement. It would mean too much to her. It had too hostile a meaning, which, intended for her husband, might cause suffering to the children; and she was already so filled with guilt that she could not trust herself to use such an affair for release and happiness without too large a component of self-punishment. But the temptation was so strong that she sought help in fighting it and allaying it.

We will return later to the matter of marital infidelity; here we may note that the impulse to indulge in extramarital sex is very commonly stimulated by anger at the spouse. But some personalities are such that they do not react with infidelity no matter how angry they are—they respond, but by other mechanisms and in other ways.

While his wife was thus struggling with the pressures from her external circumstances and from her own emotional responses to these, Ed increasingly felt the strain. He was reproached, sometimes openly, sometimes silently, by his wife and their parents. Inevitably the children began to show signs of upset. He felt shame, which is a reaction to weakness and makes one feel undeserving of love; and he felt guilt, which is caused by injury to another and makes one feel deserving of punishment. He too found his outer and inner worlds less and less happy, more and more uncomfortable and burdensome. His fixated passivity kept him from the one simple solution: earning a reasonable income by doing a proper job somewhere near the level of his abilities. His make-up, as we have seen, was deficient in fighting spirit, so important in life and for analytic treatment.

I wondered what his unconscious would decide. His solution was just as pat as one might have anticipated. He could not relieve his wife's burdens and make his home happy, so he began to think of a change. He began to talk of divorce. Eleanor was now even harder pressed. She wished she could feel "good riddance," but now Ed's virtues were a handicap; apart from poor providing, he was, as she had always known, a good husband and father. She loved him. Difficult as life was with him, what would it be without him —no husband for her, no father for the children, and even less income from him or none? And if she stood the rejection emotionally and could in her heart accept another husband, what were the chances of finding one when all her energies were going into working to support herself and the children, while still running the home?

As for Ed, it gradually became apparent that his pattern from 0 to 6 was turning his wishes toward another home more nearly like his parental one; he was thinking of divorce and then a second marriage, this time to a wife who would be rich enough to be a good provider for him. And since his pattern was of warmth and charm toward women, especially older ones, he felt that this would work out.

Eleanor first endured the disillusionment of her husband's neurotic improvidence; then she sustained the burden of working in addition to running the home; now came the psychic pain of rejection and the prospect of a bleak future. Her strength was exceeded. The potential deterioration that began with the temptations to infidelity now progressed like a malignant disease. Her irritability increased. Instead of smoking a cigarette or two after lunch and dinner, she now reached for one at every minor demand, frustration or tension. She became an addict. Of course I know the argument that smoking is a habit and not an addiction, but the distinction is, in my opinion, a sophistry. For smoking, instead of merely being a pleasure, comes to meet an emotional need and becomes more and more compulsive—the person is forced by inner compulsion to smoke, just as he may be addicted to overeating or to alcohol or to women. Eleanor's smoking increased to half a pack a day, then a pack a day, and soon she was chain-smoking at least three packs a day. She tried to cut down and could not; tried to stop completely and could not; and finally gave in.

This giving in was the first real crack in her ego, her defenses, her character. Not able to resist smoking, she began drinking martinis before dinner every evening. She began to have trouble sleeping and tried to help this by drinking at bedtime. She overate and began losing her figure. Life was too much for her. She fought, but a losing fight, always giving more ground.

The marital vicious circle was in full whirl. And the children, as always, were caught with the parents in the downward vortex. They became irritable, had nightmares, behaved badly, did poorly at school, and more and more became problem children. So the home was transformed more and more into a place into which Ed's pattern fitted less and less. It is said that divorce brings out the worst in people. No doubt it is often the best solution and the only solution. Couples who are destroying each other sometimes do divorce and make good second marriages. And in many an instance it is clear that no marriage is far better than a bad marriage; for a bad marriage can breed hatred and can destroy both body and soul. But the process of separation is apt to be nasty. At any rate, for better or worse for him and his wife and children, Ed finally insisted and won out. The divorce became a reality.

Eleanor and the children moved in with her parents, forced by the divorce to return to all the tensions she had had with them as a child. I have used as a slogan: G.D.M., meaning "generations don't mix." Eleanor and her parents were no exception. Through all this Eleanor had the indispensable help of a psychiatrist in a clinic and, for part of the time, of a social worker in an agency.

Needless to say there can never possibly be enough therapists to help the millions who need it. The only practicable solution is prevention. This has many aspects. The basic one is of course the proper rearing of children so that they mature adequately and do not have childhood patterns that disrupt their own lives as well as the lives of those to whom they are important.

Before our eyes the neurotics, dropouts, and juvenile delinquents of the rising generation are manufactured where all of these are made—in the home. The only sound basis for control of children comes not from cold discipline, but from a good relationship with the parents, from loving and being loved, and from good parental examples of mature behavior.

When I last heard, Ed had indeed remarried, to a woman with a small but definite private income. Perhaps it was because of this support and freedom from the responsibilities of parenthood that he was now able to carry satisfactorily a simple clerking job, and he was interested enough to take some courses in a business school. Eleanor reached a frustrated stability, living near her parents, being helped by them, and working half time while the children were in school.

Here is a similar case: Jack was attractive, strong, energetic, and the son of financially comfortable parents. He seemed a fine catch for any girl. When Josie married him, their friends rejoiced for them both. It took a few years for Josie to realize that Jack was not capable of sustained work; he was like Ed. This marriage, however, did not run as tragic a course as Eleanor's and Ed's. Josie, an outstanding person, managed a job as well as home and children, without breakdown or deterioration. Very few women in my experience have been capable of this. Jack's parents helped out to some extent, and the marriage survived. Jack's problem, and the tensions with Josie that it created, could not but have ill effects on their sons; but Josie was superior in her handling of the difficulties, and Jack, however childish in the workaday world, was a loving father; so the children had a reasonably good life. But it is still sad to think of as superior and talented a girl as Josie, dissipating so much of her warmth and happiness in the internal heat and friction of a marriage with a husband with such pathology in his make-up.

It is quite different when such pathology (pathological dynamics or pathodynamics) shows up earlier. It would be a boon to the girls (and in the reverse situation, to the men) if these passive trends, and other disorders as well, could be spotted while the young men and women were still students. Sometimes they show up in the senior year of high school or college as anxiety or other symptoms. In interviews these are often found to result from the fear of graduating from the protection of school, which is all the student has ever known, out into the unknown milling and mixing of life with responsible tasks and inexorable demands and all the problems of understanding and dealing with people.

For example, a young woman, an excellent student, was courted in college by an ardent young man. In the beginning of their senior year they made plans to marry about six months after graduation. Let us call them Kay and Ken. As the year progressed it was evident that Ken was not doing well in his studies. Actually, he had never been an outstanding student. It was not clear whether he had unrealized capacities, but it seemed to be generally accepted that he was extremely able but not working up to his potential. It is interesting how often one encounters this estimate of a student without any solid factual basis for it. In this case, it seemed to be deduced from Ken's many talents. He sang, he built hi-fi sets, he could draw, and he was a superior dancer. He was very good at tennis and other sports. The deduction was that if he applied himself to his work he would easily be successful in whatever field he chose. This assumption reflected his opinion of himself and his parents' opinion. He did poorly in his senior year but graduated. He obtained a position, but then did only marginal work. This caused second thoughts in Kay, and a closer look. She came to talk with me about it. Perhaps in the not too distant future, when psychodynamics is more advanced scientifically and psychiatrists more skilled in its application, young couples contemplating marriage will profit in many ways from psychiatric interviews. Kay was highly perceptive as well as intelligent. She had done what all girls and all young men should do before letting themselves become seriously involved. She had pieced together from Ken and his parents enough about his 0 to 6, his early childhood, and his later life as well to have a pretty reliable picture of his underlying pattern. It was this:

Ken was an only child. He was a loved child. This gave him the warmth to which Kay responded. But he was loved too well and not wisely enough. He was too much doted on. Everything he did filled his parents with pride, and they thought no child was ever so cute, so bright, or so accomplished in every activity he tried. Ken quite naturally took over his parents' extravagant opinion of himself. He grew up with this self-image. Never was there a child who could do so many things so well. But as he became older, vague, disturbing fears crept in. On closer examination his performances in science, music, sports, and the social graces did not quite measure up to the standards achieved by other boys his age. Meanwhile, his whole orientation was toward winning the praises of his fond parents; but he was accustomed to winning praise by showing off skills and not by solid, responsible accomplishment. When he did not do well, even in school, his parents had excuses: he had great potential but had not yet found himself. Thus he was warm and affectionate but striving for praise, rather than geared to sustained responsible work, even in studying and getting good grades. All that he did was more a subdued showing-off than an expression of any genuine interest.

This became very evident toward Kay herself. When she suggested postponing the marriage, Ken replied that this was not his idea of love—if she really loved him she would love him for himself alone and not be concerned whether he did well in his work or not.

This of course was the key. This revealed his immaturity. All his life he had been loved unconditionally by his father and mother. Now he wanted to marry but failed to see the difference between the love of a child by doting parents and the mature love between husband and wife. He failed totally to see the responsibilities toward wife and toward children that were involved in marriage. When Kay explored his finances, she found that he was planning to marry with enough money for a two-week honeymoon and no other resources, except an insecure job with minimal pay and uncertain prospects.

It became clear that Ken thought marriage meant getting from a wife all the love he knew from his parents, only now with sex included. His own responsibilities hardly occurred to him; he had always been provided for. That he himself would be in the parent role as an adult, now called upon to provide financially for his own marital family, had not quite reached him. It was evident that, having been too strongly on the receiving end from his parents, he was deficient in appreciating the needs of a wife and children. Indeed, the closer look revealed no evidence that he was capable of supporting himself if he were alone in the world, let alone being capable of all the interest, energy output, and giving of self involved in meeting the emotional and financial demands of a wife and children. In his psychology he had not made the transition from child receiving to parent giving. Despite his looks and strengths and talents, he was still much too much a child himself for any girl to count on him for her security and happiness.

He did not even see the problem until Kay made it an issue. At first he blamed it all on Kay, on circumstances, on his parents, on his stars. Only after some weeks was he forced to face the fact that there was a real problem within himself. And this realization opened up new hope for his maturing. Not to see this means, in some young men, mounting inferiority feelings, frustrations and impotent rage. In some cases the tension rises as the youth becomes a man in years, but the discrepancy increases between the maturity he needs for living, but cannot achieve, and the infantile orientation, which he cannot rid himself of because he cannot define it.

The engagement was broken, but Kay said she would see if Ken changed. This unhappy experience brought him for analytic help and may have saved him, his wife and his children from the suffering of a marital failure. Perhaps no one is more than 70 per cent mature, but a certain minimum is essential for making one's way through life—at least 51 per cent, let us say, and preferably over 60 per cent.

The war intervened and I do not know the end of the story. There was enough to work with in this young man, however, that with good analytic help and his experience in the armed services, he may well have gone on to mature sufficiently to work and support a wife and children and have a reasonably good life.

Whether coming into money solves many or any of the marital problems arising from the husband's limitations as the breadwinner, I do not know. Perhaps if this is his only major deficiency as a husband, if the other six of the seven components of marriage are adequate (Chapter 3), if this is a circumscribed area of pathology, then maybe money could keep the ship of marriage on an even keel.

In a way the ability to earn a living is a purely male problem; for despite permanent argument and endless variations in our culture, breadwinning is the basic responsibility of the man, as running the home is for the woman. Therefore failure in the wife of responsibility for the home is the equivalent of the husband's failure in providing the necessities for it. And one certainly sees in an office practice numerous examples.

Fred was about as adequate a husband, father, provider, friend, citizen, and all-round good man as one meets in a lifetime. Frances, his wife, was his equal except in one area. And this only came to light gradually, just as a husband's inhibitions in earning often emerge only after some years of marriage.

Frances was unusually intelligent, attractive, and capable, but it began to become evident that she had no interest in any responsibilities having to do with the home. She could spend endless energy on community affairs but never had time to call the plumber. She was praised by all who knew her as the finest secretary the bridge club ever had, but she moaned like a martyr when she did any accounts for the home. She was indefatigable at tennis, but the mere prospect of replacing a burned-out light bulb in the home made her feel overburdened, and this item was placed on a list of things she would do when she had time (and anyway, she reasoned, it was a man's job). When someone phoned about any sort of problem she gave sage, balanced, disinterested counsel, speaking for hours on the phone, but brief phone calls to the butcher or baker or laundry wore her out. I need not go on.

In her personal relations with the children, two daughters and a son, she was a fine mother, judicious and sound and full of humor. But her failure to provide a well-run home introduced tensions between herself and her husband that inevitably embroiled the children and damaged their emotional development. Frances in the home was the counterpart of Ed, in our earlier example, at work. In anything that was not an obligation, that meant to her *play*, she was superb. But in anything that involved domestic responsibility she was either entirely derelict or else did what was required, but so grudgingly and with such a martyred air that Fred and the children were enraged and hated to accept whatever she did do. They came to hate any dependence on her, and she treated the normal, even the minimal obligations of wife and mother as inexcusable demands and impositions.

Her parental home had been an unhappy place; her only pleasure had been playing with some friends, other little girls, at a neighbor's. She developed in her marital home the same pattern, as we all do in some form—the same pattern or some reaction formation against it. As long as she could play and be praised, she was a happy child, throughout her life. When she had to carry responsibilities for the home, she became martyred, irritable, hateful and withdrawn.

By the time this pattern came out clearly, the first child had arrived and the second was on her way. Fred recognized this childishness in his wife and feared for her welfare if he sought a divorce. Fred was sociable and his business required some entertaining. Frances liked being entertained but hated being the hostess herself. Fewer and fewer friends came to their house. Fred located a small cabin in an idyllic setting near enough to town for weekends. Frances raged against the idea of owning it, because she feared she might somehow be expected to have some responsibility for it. They grew further and further apart as the decades slipped by. Fred made a life of his own while living in his own home with a wife who was so distant as to be almost a stranger. He would not desert her or the children. But he learned bitterly that no marriage at all is better than a bad marriage. He also learned to make the best of his wife's good qualities and to appreciate the children for whom Frances had, in some respects, been a really good mother. He learned to enjoy what he had, and he tried his best to enjoy life without the love of a wife.

In childhood he had been accustomed to much affection and closeness. Now, although he tried to accept it, the deprivation and hostility he endured from Frances—the all give and no get—and the isolation in his own home, resulted in mounting strain. Yet he was not of the make-up to find in another woman what his wife did not provide: the normal, honest loving and being loved between a man and woman. He did not break down. He only developed common psychosomatic symptoms, the warning signs of the stress, signs that his life was being shortened by many years. He was being killed slowly by the passive aggression of his wife, by her emotional pattern, which she did not will, which she did not put there, but which was her inevitable reaction as a small child to the influences upon her by her own parents. Her personal relations with Fred had been good enough for them to fall in love, court and marry, but these good feelings had been corrupted by the narrow pattern of her inner childish rejection of domestic responsibility.

# III    Sex Outside Marriage: Extramarital Sexual Regression and Other Types of Infidelity

*To a man the disappointment of love may occasion some bitter pangs . . . but he is an active being—he may dissipate his thoughts in the whirl of varied occupation. But woman's is comparatively a fixed, a secluded, and meditative life. She is more the companion of her own thoughts and feelings. Her lot is to be wooed and won; and if unhappy in her love, her heart is like some fortress that has been captured, and sacked, and abandoned, and left desolate.*

IRVING

*You lie and hate it and it destroys you. . . .*

HEMINGWAY

*There is only one kind of love, but there are a thousand imitations. (Il n'y a que d'une sorte d'amour, mais il y en a mille différentes copies.)*

LA ROCHEFOUCAULD

We are now acquainted with some common varieties of marital difficulty, the emotional forces that underlie them, and with what we find when we follow these forces back to early childhood. The difficulties have been intramarital, between husband and wife. There are marital problems, however, that involve a third person. We will first consider one particular form of infidelity which, because it is primarily a return to behavior characteristic of adolescence or earlier, we will call extramarital sexual regression. We will illustrate some of its dynamics for people at different ages, and mention only briefly some of the other forms that unfaithfulness takes.

# 9 IN THE TWENTIES

How rejection of responsibility can involve wife and child instead of, or in addition to, breadwinning.

Some time ago, impressed by the return to teenage behavior of a series of male patients who were past fifty, I contemplated a paper on this subject with the working title "Late Life Regressions." But then I realized that this adolescent acting out was just as common in the forties, in the thirties, and even earlier. Here is a sample:

An apparently wholesome, clean-cut American couple, whom we will call Hank and Helen, court in college and marry a year after graduating. Hank is then well established on a stipend in graduate school, on his way to becoming a clinical psychologist. They are very happy and have a daughter. When she is six months old, Hank begins to have some doubts about his choice of a career. These doubts increase. After a few months he decides that he should take a year off and "think about it."

This decision is typical and interesting but usually a bad sign. Doubts about career? "Take a year to think about it." Embroiled in an extramarital affair and don't know what to do? "Think about it." Sometimes to this is added: "talk about it," endlessly, compulsively. As though certain basic orientations, motivations and feelings can be resolved by meditation; as though one must stop living while thinking. Why didn't Hank go ahead with his training, which would always be useful in any field, *while* he sought a more satisfying pursuit? I have often found that the person who must do nothing while he tries to find himself professionally has an inner block against doing anything. He resists any prolonged, responsible training and work, and is acting out an unconscious wish to do just what he is doing: nothing. He is thinking of what to do, but living out what he more deeply wants—the passive-dependence of the small child, who is active kinetically, always on the go, but incapable of channeling this diffuse energy into any serious sustained responsibility. For this reason such persons often take aptitude tests but do not follow through.

Hank took his year off and on their small capital they lived inexpensively at a sort of camp. Something came out of his thinking, but it was not certainty and drive in his career; it was the extension of his doubts to encompass his marriage. Now he was not only unsure of his choice of profession; he began to doubt his choice of a wife. It is not uncommon for these regressions to occur about the time a child is born, sometimes because it strikes some specific emotional vulnerability (such as the arrival of a preferred brother or sister in the person's childhood), but most often, I think, it is because of retreat in the face of added responsibility. A child really seals a marriage, binds one so irrevocably, and imposes such lifelong weighty responsibilities.

Now Hank thinks about his marriage also and, typically, he believes that to do so he must withdraw from Helen in the meantime. He cannot send his baby daughter back while he thinks about her too, although doubtless he would like to. But he does pull away from his wife and sleeps in a different room—and they are in their early twenties, when the sexual drive is at its peak. This is a rather bad sign. Sex is so powerful a drive that the regression must be alarmingly powerful to stop it.

His wife came to see me. One cannot be sure of such things in a few interviews, but from all I could learn and discern, she was as emotionally healthy a girl as one meets. This was apparent in her descriptions of her parents and her feelings for them, in her present relationships, in the course of her life, in her outlook, earliest memories, and dreams—all the criteria we mentioned before. I wished I could give her a more hopeful picture of her husband's future. But here she was, married only a few years, with a baby of six months and a husband who had gone into a severe regression away from her and the child, as well as his career. His withdrawal of interest and responsibility in both areas was unprovoked by any perceptible external pressures; apparently it was a symptom of a deep inner weakness. He was one of those who regress at the very threshold of getting started in life—in career and in marriage. Some of these young men regress all the way to breakdown. Even then, however, they may with the resilience of youth and over a period of years gradually come back to some level of workable maturity and adjustment in society.

Underlying Hank's passivity was an extremely infantile dependence. He had been much babied and overprotected by his mother. She hovered over him and helped him with everything. He was kept living in a symbiotic relation with her. His healthy maturational forces of growth drove him enough toward independence to work and marry. But his pattern toward his mother of passive-dependence led him to seek the same sort of envelopment by other people—by institutions such as school and church and, after marriage, by his wife. He often dreamed of his wife with a baby, and he associated the idea of a baby with himself in relation to his mother. Thus part of him—too large a part—continued to feel like a baby toward his wife, as he had toward his mother. Then when his child was born he had dreams of being pushed out, of actual rivalry with his own child for his wife's devoted attentions.

Fortunately Hank's drives to maturity were fairly strong and the insight and support he received from his analyst succeeded in less than a year in tilting the balance in the direction of responsible, productive activity. He began to move out of PRD (passive-receptive-dependence) toward RPI (responsible-productive-independence). He began to realize what was going on despite his inner revolt against it. He stopped sitting and "thinking"; he found a satisfactory job, and he reestablished the feelings of a husband and a father toward his wife and child. He was turned from the way in to the way out.

Hank regressed from both occupation and marriage. Sometimes only one is affected centrally, the other secondarily, as in the man who is so dedicated to his job that he neglects his family. Sometimes the family is the only butt of the regression.

A young man in his mid-twenties has finished his training and is on the first rung up the ladder. An accountant, he has an excellent job with a large firm and is doing outstandingly well. He has a good-looking, steady wife, and three fine children. We will call him Richard and his wife Ruth. Off to so good a start in career and marriage, strong, good-looking, popular, young and healthy, he has much for others to envy and much for himself to be thankful for.

But so treacherous are the latent emotional patterns of early childhood that, rather than counting his blessings, Richard starts an affair with another woman, and before he knows it he feels himself to be half "in love" with her—he is attracted to her sexually. But if one penetrates to what is behind attractions with such destructive consequences, one almost always finds that an early childhood pattern is being acted out, a pattern in which hostility is generally the central force, truly unconscious but no less implacable hostility, usually toward the mother. Fall in love with an emotionally mature, stable and superior girl, marry her, have three healthy, happy children, and then all but murder their spirits by allowing oneself to become involved emotionally and physically with another woman. I think this only happens when the triangle fits a pre-existing childhood pattern. Thus Richard continues his work while his withdrawal of love and his unexpressed unconscious hostility wreck the wife whom he has accepted and the children he has helped produce, the human beings for whom he has the greatest, most personal biological responsibility.

A married woman, a patient, once rejected something I was saying as "just typically masculine thinking." Whatever limitation this implied, men have formulated a certain wisdom among themselves. For the married man it may be terribly hard to learn to "look but not touch," but it is essential for his own selfish welfare.

A traveling man with ample opportunities to be unfaithful once told me that he sometimes took advantage of these opportunities, but only if they were sure to be transient and purely physical relationships. (Of course sex is a component of mating and reproduction, so it cannot be purely physical.) He said that as soon as he saw in himself any flicker of emotional involvement, of serious personal interest, then he immediately broke the relationship—definitely, finally, and completely—for, although he enjoyed his fun, his sex as play, he was most positively not going to do anything that would disturb or threaten to disturb his marriage.

A young wife, true to her husband, who had been away for two years in the Service, met a man who attracted her irresistibly. He was married and was also in the Service. She decided to yield to their mutual desires because he would soon be gone. But that very day she received a letter from her husband overseas. He was so completely trusting of her that she could not betray his confidence. She broke the date. She and her husband both went through the war faithful to each other because, powerfully as they were tempted to indulge in sexual affairs, highly as they valued them, they valued far more their marriage, their home, and their children. And on being reunited each wanted to greet the other, to look deep into the eyes of the other, with a sense of complete honesty and openness, which could only rest on a mutual faithfulness. I sometimes wonder, as the ethological studies of birds and animals in nature indicate, if faithfulness is not more common among those species who mate for life than among human beings, so many of whom are neurotic, that is, warped in their relationships by how they were treated by their parents, especially from 0 to 6.

Another illustration of this is provided by Len and Liz. They too were in their early twenties when he was transferred by his company to San Francisco, a transfer that came just when their first child arrived. The company would have delayed the transfer, but Len was ambitious, this was a promotion, and he was eager to go. He left when the baby was ten days old. His wife was to join him in a month. He had known San Francisco in his childhood, was somewhat acquainted with the city, and was able to find suitable living accommodations for his wife and small son. At the end of a month they arrived. His wife felt he had changed somehow. In a week she was sure of it and said so. He confessed that a week after his arrival there he met a girl with whom he was madly in love. His affection was soon completely withdrawn from Liz. They shared a double bed, but by the end of another week he slept half out of his side because he could not stand touching her. Then he moved into another room. Liz, as seen in interviews, as described by Len, as seen by all who knew her, was a healthy, wholesome, normal, feminine girl. She had a perfect figure, was very pretty and totally tempting. Yet there they were, two years after marriage, with both of them at the peak of their sexual desires; they had courted and loved for three years and had had a child. Yet suddenly Len is so repelled by her that he cannot stand to touch her. Now, precipitously, when he is a father, he desires a different girl. How the mating process can be deranged by the force of disturbed personal relations!

Len had enough conflict over his feelings and behavior to seek analytic help. In a few months he was back in an improving relationship with his wife. If only all such situations could be so easily reversed. Not that the end of this story is as yet known—the unconscious is treacherous, and I have not learned what the next decade brought to Len and Liz.

Len's main dynamics were a simple, garden variety of self-preservative rebellion. His father, to whom he was very close, had subtly and directly engineered his entire life. His father chose each school for him, each subject, and even his career, holding up a vision of future success and renown. Throughout, Len showed no signs of open resistance or rebellion. His mother was soft and weak and went along with his father. However, she too rebelled underneath and even tried a partial escape by interest in another man—which may or may not have had an effect on Len's pattern of escape from marriage. Len grew up successful and popular. Readily accepted by girls, he would go with one intensively for some months but drop her at her first hint of marriage. However, one girl was so attractive, so looked up to him, so praised him, was so compatible sexually, and was so liked by his father and his mother that, despite his own doubts, he married her. No sooner were they married, however, than he felt trapped—the same feeling he had had for so long toward his father, whom he had never dared even attempt to escape. In his mind, as revealed by his associations, he grouped his father and his wife together and felt himself to be under the yoke of both. His trip to San Francisco was for him an experience of escape. The girl he met there seemed to him to be entirely selfless, making no demands whatever, leaving him totally free. Thus he felt he could find escape from home and yet have this girl too. A secondary theme was the fact that as a child he had been in San Francisco for a visit, and while there he had had a young nurse who was not circumspect about being unclothed before him. He had been greatly stimulated and had never forgotten the experience. Moreover the new girl was blonde, unlike his father and Liz, who were dark haired.

When he returned home he found Liz repugnant, but the more he pushed her away, the more she clung, which was in contrast to the girl in San Francisco, and which he found intolerable. His father aggravated his feelings by saying, "You have to go back to your wife!" This was just the pressure he was trying to get away from. And his child as well as his wife represented the trap.

Yet he was in conflict and tried to work it out. He saw an analyst and learned these dynamics. He saw how much his normal, mature mating instincts were warped and deflected by his rebellion against his overcontrolling father. It developed that Liz had had some re-bellion against her own father, and this (in the usual way) had been an element in their mutual attraction—only to become divisive later. She too saw an analyst. The happy result was that they again came to identify with each other instead of rebelling against each other. The only reason for my caution about this excellent outcome stems from my experience with these childhood patterns, which sometimes insidiously reassert themselves years later. But in this case the response to insight alone was so prompt and effective that we would expect the release from the trap of childhood to grow into permanence.

# 10 IN THE THIRTIES

Whether a person is unfaithful or not is largely a matter of his or her individual makeup.

We have stressed the basic finding that different wives —and husbands—react differently in accordance with their own individual dynamics, formed by the emotional influences upon them during early childhood. One girl of high caliber, Polly, had been married to Peter for about ten years (they were in their early thirties) when he began going out with other women. Polly, a girl of integrity and spirit, saw only one solution: Sauce for the gander was sauce for the goose. If he had affairs, then she was free to try them herself. There were three children, and she would not break up the home. So she had her affairs—very few, each long-lasting, each with a very superior, carefully chosen man, with whom there was the highest mutual regard and indeed love, and always with a man who was single or a widower or divorced, so that Polly was sure that she was in no way whatever injuring a home. On this basis she saved her own home and kept relatively good relations with Peter. The children thereby were raised in a reasonably harmonious, stable marriage. How much heartache and psychic pain underlay her solution, I do not know.

Some women are totally incapable of such a solution. In their dynamics they are strictly monogamous, one-man women. The thought of sex with a man other than their husband is not only not inviting, it is repulsive to them. Sometimes, however, if the terrible emotional strain and pain of the husband's unfaithfulness lasts long enough, even such an utterly devoted, loyal, one-man woman may turn to another man herself, turn in the way that Polly did, with no hostility to another home, seeking an unattached man who offers love, emotional as well as physical, some healing and balm to the open wound inflicted on her heart by the husband who for so many years was her only thought.

Another girl, Rosemary, had a sound marriage, and two children. Her husband, Rex, was perfectly open about extramarital sex, and could be because in their particular psychology, it was "only physical," it was always strictly within the bounds of the physical, and devoid of emotional involvement. At least this was their conscious attitude. When he visited a foreign country in the course of his business, he wrote amusing letters about sex with girls of other races, climates, and customs. Rosemary freely spoke of her amusement at these transient, physical adventures of Rex's. She in turn was always touched by lonely men, and occasionally consoled them by providing the best of consolations. Rex did not mind until, in one case, there was a flicker of emotional interest on the part of Rosemary, and then in jealous anger he put his foot down.

Another outcome is quasi-bigamous. Shortly after beginning my practice, Susan, an attractive woman, consulted me about her husband, Sam. He had no interest in treatment for himself but came for one visit. It was possible to be of some help to his wife in the following situation:

Sam, a successful businessman, had been devoted to his wife and to their five children for over fifteen years. He had always had an eye for other women and an exaggerated sexual interest in them, but had not let this affect his behavior, home life or career. Suddenly a full-blown affair erupted with a woman, Shirley, who had a husband and four children. He found Shirley irresistible, and she found Sam the same.

As is typical in these cases, rationalization played its part in self-justification. Susan had freely admitted her part in the squabbles from which probably no marriage is free. But Sam gradually built this up to such distortion that it appeared in his mind that there never was love or good times or children or a home. With the passage of time his rationalization grew. He seemed to deceive himself with the conviction that he was a long suffering husband driven by an inexorable, unrelieved shrew into the companionship of another woman.

Shirley eventually divorced her husband and got an apartment for herself and her children, and Sam shared it with her. Susan, torn to the quick, continued to keep her home together for the sake of the children and because she knew nothing else to do. So Sam lived with her and remained a good husband and father in this, his own home, but also divided his time with Shirley. In short, he now lived in two families.

Susan survived this kind of life; and for the sake of the proper development of the children, she maintained in their minds as best she could a good image and relationship to their father.

Perhaps all such compulsive infatuations as that between Sam and Shirley are the product of two disordered childhood patterns meshing in some way, a *folie à deux,* a joint neurosis, which causes prolonged pain to the respective spouses and to the children still in the formative stages of their development and certain to be damaged for life.

Five years after the war there was no change in the situation, except the growing up of the children and their departures from the two homes.

# 11 IN THE FORTIES

A brief theoretical statement; and a husband who, in this "dangerous age," remains effective in his work, but acts out a childhood pattern that spells desertion of wife and five children in favor of a young girl and a lower caliber of associates, although he saw that there was a problem and sought psychiatric help.

The turning of a man away from his own wife and children to another woman is seen at all ages. Sometimes, as with Len, it strikes like lightning. With others it is slow, creeping, insidious, an almost imperceptible slipping into an emotional quicksand. This analogy is apt, for many husbands resist this slow sinking; often they fight against it, and once engulfed they feel not happiness but torment, not release from the bonds of marriage and convention, but an entrapment from which they cannot escape, from which they cannot any longer *will* to free themselves.

It is in this disintegration of will that one of the ultimate tragedies of the mind resides. We have used a concept of the mind with three groups of forces:

1. The id: the biological urges, such as for food, shelter, love, sex, mating, and survival.

2. The superego: the results of training and identifications in forming ideals, standards, morals, ethics, and conscience.

3. The ego: the powers of (a) perception (of outer world and our own impulses and reactions), (b) integration of these (through memory, reason, intellect), and (c) the executive powers of directing our behavior, that is, control and will.

(The experiences of early childhood shape the patterns of reacting to others and to ourselves; they also make the ego what it is.)

These three parts of the mind of course are part mature, part childish. If a child is reared with love, security, and respect and has models of harmonious, mature relations in his parents, then all available evidence shows that this child will become an adult with predominantly mature motivations toward responsible, constructive love for others in his id, superego and ego. We all also have residual childish, egocentric, hostile patterns of impulses within us. These impulses appear in our dreams, even in our waking fantasies— images of selfish, grasping behavior, of the most abandoned profligacy, of every kind of sexual act, of unrestrained hostile, destructive deeds. But this does not mean that they need be acted out in real life, and they are not, except as crime.

Should education not make clear to the young, as forcefully and consistently and repeatedly as possible, this distinction, as it exists in our own minds and in drama and story, as contrasted with real life? We all have these hostile impulses and therefore the fantasies they create. We live in a world of such fantasies: on television and radio, in the theater, in stories, and throughout our schooling in literature. Yet every extravagance of sex, promiscuity, perversion, licentiousness, brutality, sadism, and criminal action must remain entirely internal, entirely in the fairyland of fantasy, while we live as responsible, productive, loving family members, friends and citizens. (Those who act out any of these impulses are criminals and have no place in society or must be controlled by society.) In the mature adult these impulses, the results of lingering childhood dangers and frustrations, must be very weak, relative to the mature motivations of the id, superego and ego. They must be weak relative to the strengths of the moral, ethical standards of the superego and relative to the judgment, control and will power of the ego. The more mature the id impulses, the more the drives to responsible, loving productivity and good will, the less the strain on the conscience and will power.

This abstract formulation is meant to remind us of the simple "structure" of the personality, which is useful in giving a model or picture of the interplay and balance of forces that make each person what he is, in impulses, wishes, thoughts, fantasies and behavior. And it is meant to emphasize the fact that we all have all sorts of urges and temptations, but we do not all act on them. Any man would like to wake up with some other beautiful blonde or brunette in his bed; but what is a fleeting or not-so-fleeting fantasy in one husband becomes rank and brutal desertion of young wife and child in another. Yet in view of the other forces in the personality, if a man like Len ("In the Twenties") has mature impulses in his id, such as love and responsibility, if he has mature standards of behavior and a conscience, if he has maturity of judgment and self-control, then his behavior will cause him sharp pangs, conflicts and torments. And in the end these may help him to become a more fully mature person who provides much greater enjoyment and satisfaction for others and for himself.

This I had learned before Mel came to see me at the request of his distraught wife, Madeline. As she pictured it, he was having a fine time extramaritally with another woman, May. Mel came—a man of 46, stocky, broad-shouldered, attractive in looks and personality, and at first glance direct and straightforward. A second look revealed that aura of inner suffering that one sees so often in men around 45, an aura that seems to appeal to certain women. His expression reflected anything but happiness, peace or freedom. He was hollow-eyed and tragic in his seriousness, and although he could smile and had a sense of humor, the impression he gave was one of anxiety, conflict and depression. His wife seemed like a perfect mate for him. She was about 5'4" and had frank blue eyes and a trim, perfect figure, although she was 40 and had five children. Her suffering was undisguised.

May was 21 and just out of college. Mel had been slipping into the involvement with her slowly and inevitably, bit by bit, over the past four years.

Mel's marriage had not been ideal prior to May's insinuation into the scene. The hostilities between his parents had made him insecure personally and had split his identifications. He could not very well side with one parent without feeling disloyal to the other. His wife, Madeline, was distinctly deprived in childhood, but well enough treated to develop a strong ego and strong moral standards (part of her superego), with the ability to keep repressed her feelings of being too little loved. She was one of those small, vivacious girls, capable at anything she attempted. Mel was very dependent on her and afraid of losing her. She was not always easy to get on with, because of her readiness to feel unloved and her resentment because of this. But the marriage worked: the sexual aspect was entirely satisfactory; the children were handsome, and they were well brought up, except for the squalls between their parents.

Mel was in the sales division of a large company and was away frequently on business. He met May. Mel and Madeline lived in a suburb; May had an apartment in town. She encouraged him. We can understand how, unhappy within himself because of his own inner patterns of feelings, he was responsive to the accepting smiles of a fresh young college girl. His need exceeded his judgment and his will. His marriage, satisfactory though it was, had its storms and tensions, had the demands and resentments of a wife who felt insufficiently loved, was anxious, and was drained of energy by five children. Here was May offering herself, the great diversion, the great refreshment. It took between one and two years for the affair between Mel and May to become full-blown, for all reserve to be dissipated.

With this, as is usual, a general deterioration was evident in Mel. He began to see less of his friends and more of people who drank heavily, were more promiscuous, cut corners in their business dealings, and were generally less honest and responsible toward their families and fellow men. Some were living together out of wedlock. Most were less conscientious in business and less well-off or secure financially. Briefly, they were people with less integrity, stability and responsibility. They condoned, even accepted, more readily the living out of this kind of hostility against wife and children—and also accepted what went with it: the lies and behavior that a man uses more and more in his efforts to deceive a true and faithful, if human, wife who is doing her best to preserve the home and do what is best for the children. The "other woman" often becomes an addiction. The husband may try to break off, but as with alcohol or tobacco, when they fill a neurotic need, he is not able to; he lacks the "ego strength." He cannot break off, and he cannot stop the lies and deceits that are exactly like those of a drug addict who stops at nothing to indulge a craving that he himself has come to despise. The superego (standards, ideals, conscience) and ego (judgment, control, will) yielded partially to the pressures of the childhood pattern. Mel vowed that he did not want this involvement with May, that his wife and children were his only loves. There was a compulsive element in his seeing May—and generally behind compulsions of all sorts is hostility. This is another form of oscillation:

he loves his wife and children and home, and wants to live with them in love, but is unable to give up the girl, who exerts every wile to hold him.

For brevity I will only give a few salient features of what I learned of Mel's dynamics. He had always had a problem about women, had to have their love, but felt insecure and lacked confidence in his personality and in his potency. Even though he was past 45, with a wife and five children, he was trying to prove something to himself with May—in a way using her to prove that he could have a relation, an affair, and be successful, uninhibited and sexually potent with a girl who, in his mind, fitted a certain category of women.

The disturbed elements in his childhood pattern were: considerable neglect by his mother, for whom, like Madeline's mother, children were a burden; and contention and hostility between his parents. As a result he clung too much to his mother while repressing his resentment to her, and was resentful of his father for treating his mother harshly. He could not identify wholeheartedly with either father or mother as adults upon which to model himself.

Now in his marriage he had (as we so fatefully and inexorably and unconsciously do) re-created the outline of the childhood emotional interplay. Instead of two parents he now had two women. He craved the love of each one and clung to each like a child, but at the same time he was living out his hostility unconsciously by causing them both suffering—and of course causing his children not only present suffering but damage for life. The result was a torment of guilt, so that from the situation came not happiness but anguish.

Wife and paramour corresponded to mother and father, but not in a strict, narrow way. Mel showed the "split mother image" commonly seen in these cases. Madeline, his wife, meant to him in part the mother whose love he must have, but whom he resented because of her lack of giving. He spited her, unconsciously, by going to May. But also, Madeline and the children represented demands and responsibilities, and he fled from them to May, who was mother in the sense of escape from the burdens of family obligations, a person who consoled him like a mother. But she was also a playmate with whom he could identify, someone who meant rebellion and escape. I suppose all men would like such a dream girl, one free and loving and always available but without any expectations, demands or ob-

ligations, just sex and play and an inexhaustible fountain of love
and affection. But the Mays have their needs and childhood patterns too, and sooner or later they must end the idyl. The day
comes, this year or next, when she will demand the marriage she
has hoped for but never suggested. Then come the tears, the rages,
the threats, the gestures of suicide. And the man is guilty and
weak and now afraid and confused, his capacity for decision paralyzed. But are there also girls so hostile and so masochistic, so
lacking in the mating and reproductive drives that they are satisfied forever to be "the other woman," smashing a marriage while
getting no marriage for themselves? There is no end to the variety
of ways in which childhood patterns shape the designs of adult
behavior.

Analysis was relatively new in Chicago in the 1930's. Mel had
been to see an analyst of the type that believes that if he mostly
listens passively to the patient, who lies on the couch for five meetings a week, and that if this goes on for enough years, all will come
out well. The analyst refused to see Madeline. He said he was not
concerned with the marriage or other externals; his patient was
anxious and his task was simply to make the unconscious conscious.
We know today that this is one of those half-truths: the analyst
cannot step in and direct lives or live them for his patients. On the
other hand he must have a down to earth, realistic, practical
knowledge and grasp of what is going on. Otherwise the patient,
free-associating on his back on the couch for five or even three days
a week, goes off into a demi-world, a confusion of fantasy with
reality, of past with present. What his conscious ego gains through
some insights it more than loses through failure of enough reality-
sense to use the insights effectively. As a result he regresses more
and more, lives more and more in fantasy, becomes more and more
childish and dependent upon the analyst. He often takes the silence
of such an analyst as sanction for whatever he is doing. But the
most malignant consequence is the feeling that what he does in
reality is not particularly important, it is just something to free-
associate about.

Mel told me that he was doing what he was doing because of this
and that incident in childhood, which amounted to "his father and
his mother and his brothers and his sisters and his aunts." As he
talked it was clear that analysis was for him an intellectual exercise, a play of fantasies and memories, which was of no realistic,

practical use to him in clarifying and dealing with his problems and those of all concerned. In fact it had the opposite result: as he sank into this never-never land, he thought the analyst was sanctioning whatever he was doing, and that this meant they were somehow getting "deeper" analytically. This encouraged his retreat from reality into a childishness and confusion. He was all but killing his wife by his behavior, he was involving the girl, he was doing irreparable damage to his children, he was lying, cheating, deceiving, he was abandoning his friends for more or less disturbed, immature personalities, slipping from his mature functioning, risking his job and career—but he was free-associating. As he sank deeper into the so-called analysis he sank deeper into his problem, into regression and confusion.

This twilight state is a sinking back or regression into the attitudes and feelings of early childhood. These feelings develop and are transferred to the analyst (transference). Unless they are recognized and properly handled, the patient becomes more and more toward the analyst like the dependent child he once was toward his mother and father. For this to occur on a limited basis is an aid to insight. The patient sees in his feelings toward the analyst the emotional forces he has been struggling with unconsciously, and through this he is helped to help himself in reducing, resolving and controlling them. But if he is not helped in this way, then the regression is useless therapeutically and may do more harm than good.

Usually, following the old infantile pattern, the patient represses his hostility toward the analyst and is not aware of it; but it still produces guilt toward the analyst, as it did toward the parents. There is as little chance of the patient's seeing all this, even if pointed out to him, if the analyst has not dealt with it properly from the beginning, and as little chance of extricating himself from the analysis, as there would have been of separating him as a child from his mother. Typically he believes that he is just on the verge of a great insight—as though he would gain such insight if he has not done so after two or three or more years, and as though an insight alone would solve such situations. Often the hostility in the transference to the analyst is displaced to a wife or to others in life, thus compounding the problem rather than relieving it.

This is no criticism of analysis itself. It is only to point out some relevant misconceptions and misunderstandings of thirty and more

years ago which, with progress in the field, are avoidable today.
But of course one must be as careful in choosing his analyst as he
would be in choosing his surgeon, his lawyer or his automobile
mechanic, or anyone having much responsibility for his well-being
and happiness.

Madeline, a sincere, honest, fine person, was in such anguish
over this situation as no human being (or any animal, for that
matter) should have to suffer. Mel's behavior struck directly at her
own specific emotional vulnerability. Her pathodynamics were, in
brief: lack of love and interest from her parents, making her cling
excessively, but in a controlled and hidden way, and making her
resentful and hostile through deprivation, while loading her with
guilt for her hostility. For, if she showed her hostility, she would
lose what parental interest and love she had. Besides, it was against
the strict moral code of her family, which dictated that a child have
only feelings of love for his parents and siblings. In addition to
these reactions, she took over her parents' attitudes toward herself,
seeing herself as relatively unlovable and unwanted. In reality she
was charming, cuddly, and appealing and sort of heartbreaking.
Also, fortunately, she was of the small, spunky breed.

"I am terrified," she said, "that Mel will leave me, but I'm afraid
I may deserve it. I have demanded too much and lost my temper at
him too often. And now that I'm terrified, I'm afraid he will want
to get away so much more. We get on well when we are away alone
together. I couldn't sleep at all last night. I couldn't change the subject in my mind. I have a feeling of doom. If he should leave me,
I couldn't exist."

[This does not convey the tensing, blanching, tears, clasping of
hands—the effects of inner writhing with psychic pain.]

Analyst: Have you other close relationships to people?

Patient: Except for the children, no. I have good friends but all
my feelings that really matter are attached to Mel. He is the only
one. Do other marriages have such happenings as this and survive?
I'm afraid I demand more of Mel than he can give. I am not close
to people because if I were, they would get to know how I really am
and would not like me. I feel awful at times when I find myself
wanting to treat the children the way my mother and father treated
me; I want to be just the opposite. When I found out about May I
was so furious I could have killed Mel. Of course I don't mean that.
I mean that I said the most awful things. I screamed at him. It was

the first time I was openly mad at him. He said he was sorry about this girl and did not want to hurt me, but that he was glad it was out in the open. Yet he insists that he loves only me and the children. He is very good with the children.

This inadequate sample is meant only to give a little of the flavor of our conversations. There is no need to describe Madeline's dynamics further. Only one major point should be re-emphasized; namely, the high, strict moral and ethical standards of her parental family. Largely because of these, as well as her guilt and self-depreciation, she searched her soul to find whether it was chiefly her own doing that had driven her husband to his infidelity. She did, I think, contribute to it, but this was because of the deprivations that they both endured in childhood, the deprivation, resentment, and guilt that drew them together in the first place, the deep-seated underlying feelings that they shared and that made them understand each other. If her husband had not had his particular dynamics, including the weakness of his ego's controls and judgment and his superego's principles, he would not have taken up with May; his tensions would have come out in some form other than infidelity. We will mention a few brief examples of this later. In this marriage we see a one-man wife devoted to a no longer one-woman husband—actually, it appeared, to a two-woman man.

If Madeline in truth had contributed to Mel's extramarital involvement, then one would think the course of common sense would have indicated that his analyst, instead of refusing to see her, would have called her in (she would have come willingly, in fact she requested to come), made clear to her where her behavior was pushing her husband, and advised her to get some help in modifying the patterns in herself that were threatening her home; in which case Mel would have had the realistic expectation that his wife would change and become more like both she and he wanted her to be.

At any rate Madeline saw the dilemma she was in. If she reacted with hostility to Mel's behavior, then she feared that she would drive him into May's arms. But if she tried to ignore it, then why should Mel not go ahead and enjoy May, since his wife raised no objections? The same conflict existed in regard to sexual relations. If Madeline assented, and their sexual relations were always mutually gratifying, then was this not condoning May? But if, tormented by the thought of lying in arms still warm from embracing

May, she refused, then would not cutting herself off as Mel's sexual outlet drive him all the more to May? If she accepted his behavior, did she not sanction it and relieve his guilt for it? But if she opposed it, did she not increase his guilt, making him feel so guilty toward his family that he would try to escape it by leaving? Incidentally, the idea that if a marriage is good sexually it must be good in all other ways does not hold up in my experience, as this example shows. Nor does the reverse hold true.

Madeline felt that she should divorce Mel, which she had ample grounds to do. But he was the only person she deeply loved with the constancy of the craving she had had for her parents. Then too she would be left alone with the care of five children, for whom no father was worse probably than a faithless one. At times she felt the situation to be intolerable, felt that she was not the kind of woman who could or would share a man like this and live with this kind of hostility directed toward her.

Madeline was stuck on dead center. All she could do was try to stand it and wait out May—knowing, though, that this might mean waiting years or forever, or that the vagaries of her husband, now embroiled in treatment with an analyst who would not or could not tell anything to anyone, might lead to his wanting to marry May. Where his unconscious hostility and guilt would lead him was unpredictable. Standing it also meant seeing friends, who gradually had deserted Mel (for such behavior cannot long remain secret). It meant going against all her own standards by snooping in spite of herself—looking for lipstick on shirts, stains on underwear, odor of perfume on jackets, wondering about every trip, watching the mileage on the car. Because of Mel's deterioration she was always doubting, always suspicious as to whether he was deceiving her or being honest, telling truths or lies, worrying about his every absence. It meant the decay of all trust in him. And then she feared that her very dissolution of confidence in him, inevitable as it was, would itself jeopardize re-establishment of the marriage. And with her own high standards and tendency to self-depreciation, she despised herself for her behavior, or even the impulses to it, although they were only those of a wife trying to defend herself and her brood against the inroads of a woman who was a stranger, a ruthless or thoughtless neurotic or criminoid home wrecker, heartlessly robbing her of husband and father.

What this all comes down to is how the individual's personality will react in the given circumstances: stay on despite suffering, keep the home harmonious for the sake of the children in spite of everything, turn the children against their father, as revenge on him although damaging to them, expose the other woman and attack her legally if a lawyer can be found to do this, or divorce; suicide and murder are often thought of but rarely committed. In the absence of any practicable solution for a given person, the triangle is apt to continue until something gives, someone breaks, or fate intervenes. Distorted childhood patterns, caused by faulty upbringing trap a person and lead him unconsciously to create his own suffering and that of those closest to him.

In this case fate took the form of an international criminal regression, against which background whether or not a mate was loyal seemed suddenly of less consequence; a regression in which groups sought their own egocentric gratification and power; a regression in which all the sadistic fantasies of tens of thousands of disordered, frustrated, hostile childhoods were wreaked in reality upon helpless victims; a regression in which powerful groups of men and women brought about death and agony for the most selfish satisfactions and goals, when cooperation could have made a more secure and happy life for all humanity. This hostile egocentric regression resulted in World War II. Although marital fidelity paled in significance against this background, it was one of the very values, one of the manifestations of emotional health and maturity for the individual and, through the children, for the race, which we fought to preserve.

Two years after the war I received a letter, of which the following sentences are excerpts.

"I have a lot to thank the Navy for. It took Mel away from May and away from his analyst, and maybe it was good for him to get away from me. Maybe it's only because I'm a woman that I never believed that the 'Army Builds Men,' but the Navy did something for Mel. Maybe it only pulled him back to reality. It did bring him back to something more like the man I married. Maybe I was unfair to Dr. ———— [his analyst]. I've heard that the real results in psychoanalysis sometimes come only in the years after it is over. Maybe Dr. ———— did a good job after all, but I can't help the feeling that he drove Mel into a mixture of utter confusion and utter egotism. However it was, Mel came back less egotistical and more realistic. He looked up Dr. ——— but found that he had moved to Los Angeles.

"He started with another analyst and this has been very different. He keeps Mel's back off the couch and his shoulders to the wheel. The floozy [May] used every trick to hang on to Mel—offering her all, playing on his guilt, tears, threats of suicide—but in the end she married someone else. And *they* moved to Los Angeles. Mel was getting so upset before the war that I was sure he would lose his job. Now he is working well again. The company is humming and Mel is overworking, often at night. Once I might have objected, but now I'm so thankful it is not another woman that I wouldn't say a word. I don't dare uncross my fingers, but the children have a father and I have a husband again. Could he have proven to himself in the Navy whatever he was trying to prove with May? Because now he doesn't seem so—well, so restless and compulsive."

Madeline had gotten help with her own problem, and with May gone Madeline and Mel had had a fresh start, with something learned, we hope, of life and of themselves; they had gained a wholesome respect for the unconscious forces that motivated their lives, and were grateful for having saved their home for the children, with all it meant for their future lives.

The outcome is not always so fortunate, and one reason among many is that there is a point of no return, beyond which the marriage is only rarely reconstituted. This is the point at which one or the other partner "goes cold." The husband, even against his wishes, may lose all feeling for his wife; he may even go to the extremes of defenses against her by a sense of repugnance (like the young man who could no longer bear contact with his beautiful young wife). This coldness may develop in reaction to his wife's hostilities to him; it may develop from his inner problems, which have transferred his attachment to the other woman, leaving for his wife, to whom he was once devoted, only the rejection and hostility of his whole emotional pattern. So, too, the wife may exhaust her tolerance for her husband's disloyalty with another woman, or may turn cold because of other behavior of his, or from a pattern in her own makeup of which the husband is an innocent victim (for example, Ben and Brenda, discussed in Chapter 6).

# 12 IN THE FIFTIES

A man in whom a mere tendency to philander comes into the open with the beginning of a general regression of the personality; and how a strong wife finds a design for living with this.

When "extramarital sexual regression" occurs in the fifties, the external situation is apt to be different from what it is in the forties or thirties or twenties, although the underlying dynamics of the individuals still give it its particular form. In the fifties the children are usually grown up and some or all have left the nest, are away at school or out in the world, and perhaps married and beginning to be settled. They say there is no fool like an old fool. Certainly childishness is more striking at fifty than at twenty.

Norman, of medium, rather stocky build, with serious dark eyes, was in his early fifties and was at the peak of his career. In fact he had his business run so well by an excellent manager that it was no longer taxing and demanding. He could take it fairly easy.

Although he had been faithful to his wife, Nel, except for a possible brief slip or two along the way, he had always liked to flirt with women. All men do; his flirting was just somewhat more evident than the average—more conspicuous, less controlled. Like so many men of any age who have been too strongly dependent upon their mothers (whether from overindulgence or overprotection or deprivation or whatever), Norman always had an eye not only for women in general, but a particular woman in any given situation. On a train or boat or plane, at a party or a meeting, at the theater or any entertainment or sport, he would always select one particular woman to fix upon. In age she might be anywhere from barely

past childhood to fifty or more, although the younger ones were preferred. If she had feminine charm, figure, face and manner, Norman would be "in love" with her for that place and time. This is
probably not unusual among men. Some carry it to philandering.
Some become Don Juans and may never marry. Others are well
aware of this perennial series of light, sexy loves, but whatever
their fantasies they do nothing to jeopardize their marriages. Very
literally, they look but do not touch. The wise wife will not try to
hold the reins too tightly, if she and the children have the husband's
basic love and know he will never let anything disturb their home.
But Norman now touched as well as looked.

In his early fifties, he finds himself in love with Nancy, a sophis-
ticated woman of the world about 12 years his junior. He tells his
wife, Nel, that he is in love with Nancy, but is not ready yet to
talk about it. He explains that she is no common woman but a very
superior person, and then wonders why his wife is angry at this.
Nel, a small, wiry, dark, determined woman, will not stand for it,
but will not rush into divorce after nearly 30 years of marriage
and four children. She suffers as much as any wife in such circumstances, but she has a strong ego (i.e., sense of reality, judgment,
control and character). She watchfully waits and finds an excellent
job that she likes. Norman sees that she is withdrawing from him
and really will divorce him.

Strength consists in part in who is more dependent on whom. An
affair is a great culminating experience, or should be; but to have
one at the expense of open hostility and rejection from the wife
who is your anchor gives one pause. Of course we are speaking
only of a man's own egocentric feelings and not of the suffering and
damage to his wife and children.

There follow months of Norman's claiming he has broken off
permanently with Nancy, only to have it turn out, as is so routinely
the case, that these are lies. The usual series of deceits and deceptions and the deterioration of ego and standards follows, until he
is no more to be trusted in anything. Then Nancy sees clearly what
the situation is and rejects Norman.

Now he has to struggle to re-establish a relationship with his
wife. He has now regressed to behavior like that of a naughty,
guilty child. He was "not ready to talk about it," but now he can
think and talk of nothing else. He is so childish, so threatened, so
preoccupied that he cannot be trusted with the simplest responsibilities. The business continues, thanks to the efficient manager.

He struggles to get back on his feet psychologically as well as to reconstitute his marriage, for his wife finds him too much of a strain to be around. She turns out to be the stronger; he is more dependent on her than she on him. He finally sees an analyst, who finds the task of analyzing him a difficult one. There are some persons (Len for example) in whom the progressive and regressive forces are in about equal balance; and some of these people react to awareness of these forces, that is, of what is causing their feelings and behavior, with a burst of insight that is almost like a religious conversion, and which signals a shift in the direction of maturing. But Norman's ego was weak and was corrupted by lying and deceiving his wife, which also warped his judgment and his grasp of reality. His control and will were not strong. He had so far retreated into passive dependence on Nancy, as well as on his wife, that there was no potent force of masculine pride and independence to spring into play at the spark of insight. Instead he was one of those who react to understanding of themselves with a "so what?"

Such a man presents a special problem in analytic technique. A completely passive procedure can do more harm than good, as we have illustrated with Dr. ———— in the case of Mel and Madeline. With his passive-dependent-submissive wishes already so strong toward his wife and his mistress and dominating his whole feeling and behavior, Norman could easily sink into this childish attachment to the analyst, too. He might tend to use the analyst's sympathy as sanction for his regression and release from guilt, and the whole situation as a comfortable retreat into fantasy, letting the analyst do everything and hoping somehow, sometime, to emerge cleansed, purified and mature. On the other hand, if the analyst accurately interprets and correctly points out reality, Norman may feel that he is not getting support for his regression, and leave. If so, he probably will have been saved much time and money and his wife will have been spared the protraction of vain hopes. But with a real will to solve his problem, and with an analyst who sees the psychological realities clearly enough, Norman's retreat may be halted and he may start on the long, slow road back from childishness to relative independence, effort, productivity and responsibility. Fortunately he was prevented from sinking deeper into childishness in life and in the analysis.

Norman had the virtue of honesty. With his full consent, all aspects of the situation were freely discussed with his wife, Nel, who was by now bitter enough, but still very understanding and still loving. Despite her disillusionment and disgust with him, she would not abandon him so long as there was any chance of his getting back on his feet.

Fortunately, Norman and Nel's children were grown and away from home; it is a bad thing for children at any age to be disillusioned in one parent or in the stability of the relationship between parents, but at least when they are no longer small twigs, bending them will not cause such serious warping and damage to their personalities and lives as it does in the earliest years.

Nancy meanwhile saw that there would be little satisfaction in her future with Norman. He was too weak, too dependent on her, too unreliable, too untrustworthy with women, finances and alcohol; he was an insecure bet as a provider, even if divorced, with an ex-wife to support. The excellent manager kept the business going, thus assuring some stability of income. It sometimes seems that if there were nothing, if the wolf were at the door, the husband would be compelled to make a mature, responsible effort. Necessity is a hard master but under him we become potent, as Freud said. But by no means is this always so.

Norman continued working but his effectiveness, which should have been at its prime, dwindled. This is seen in men who may relinquish important positions and become involved with another woman, or other women, and with or without alcohol sink into companionship with questionable characters (see Chapter 8, "Passivity and Regression"). Some, like Ed, have never gotten started, but here we speak of those who have worked, often successfully; then, at what should be the peak, they decline. It is a great emotional strain to be around an extremely dependent, attention-demanding, passive person, however outwardly charming he may be. It can be utterly exhausting. A man may be wealthy and shower his wife with gifts, but the underlying childish demands, the hanging on her emotionally, may drive her to divorce him to save her sanity. Or she may announce that there will never be a divorce. In this case, Nel did not divorce Norman, but she did build her own life.

Nel had the emotional and physical strength and the intellectual ability and knowledge of people to finally locate a position in industry that suited her talents. She became the breadwinner. Emotionally she achieved a workable independence of her husband. She grew to enjoy her job, her independence and her income. Norman came to terms with this. Less was required of him but he had to accept an apartment in which his wife was not always there to greet him. As Norman accepted this, Nel came to like the arrangement and even to be grateful to Norman for her freedom, which she now cherished, and which he, whether willingly or perforce, now acceded to.

She no longer cared too much whether he saw another woman or not. She felt free now to do just as she pleased. In this case she did nothing so far as men were concerned, but she relished fully the knowledge that she was free to have affairs. Thus the marriage was saved by working out a new kind of "fit" between them. When I heard from them a few years after the war they were healthy, rather youthful grandparents who, in spite of spells of turbulence, had pretty much come to terms with the relationship as it now was.

Again we caution that all endings in such cases are not this fortunate. The regression, as we have seen hitherto, is not always limited to a retreat from wife and children; it can involve the job instead of the family, or it can encompass both. And, especially when it includes both the domestic and occupational fronts, it is occasionally part of a general regression of the personality, with or without alcohol. In the extreme, the person is so childish as to be unable to make a go of life and must spend some time in a mental hospital or its equivalent.

Norman's case causes one to wonder how it is possible psychologically that a man, who for most of a lifetime has held a responsible position in his work and who has been relatively stable as a husband and a parent, can in his fifties regress so far that he cannot function in any of these capacities. If he drinks, there is a tendency to blame it on the alcohol. No doubt the dynamics differ greatly from person to person; in one such instance, they were as follows:

The man was much more dependent upon his wife than he realized. His flirtations, which rarely went far, had been on the pattern of escaping dependence upon his wife (in childhood, upon his mother) by playing the strong man to weak women.

In his fifties, however, one of these women drew him into an all-out affair. The usual deceptions and lies to his wife ensued. As is so frequent, his wife's suspicion was aroused and was readily confirmed. After initial attempts to win back and hold him from "the other woman," her hurt and dismay and subjection to lies and deceit more and more caused her to withdraw emotionally. This was in part jealousy and simple self-protection against rejection. The result for the husband was a diminution in her previous stalwart, unwavering strength and support. His dependence had lost its sustaining rock. His whole personality structure was shaken. He lost interest in the other woman, and also in his work. He began to drink. His regression became more apparent. The other woman lost interest in him. A vicious circle was generated with his wife. The less reliable and the more childish he became, the more his wife was forced, for her own security and that of their children, to stand on her own. The more she did this, the more she withdrew, the more childishly helpless and irresponsible and alcoholic her husband became.

There is another force besides dependence that can be a cause of regression. That force is the self-punishment or masochism we have previously discussed (Chapter 6). In fact, there seem to be two great poles around which most major motives and reactions cluster. The child is little and weak and therefore dependent on his parents and needful of their love as a guarantee of security; he is, in reality, inferior to the parents physically, mentally and emotionally. He fights for their love, and thereby becomes rivalrous. He seeks to compensate for his inferiority to those older than himself by building his self-esteem.

The other main cluster of forces is around the fight-flight reaction, but especially around the fight, the hostility. Hostile, aggressive transgressions normally cause guilt, which in turn makes the tendency to self-punishment, and self-punitiveness, or masochism, is cumulative. In the man we have been discussing, Norman, the past flirtations may have been contrary to his early training, but his guilt did not damage him seriously until he had a flagrant affair which injured his wife and children. This, and his wife's disapproval, increased, and released the latent tendency to self-injury.

Even if the wife understands all this and forgives and forgets and welcomes back the husband, with or without the other woman, the regression may have gone too far for the husband to reconstitute the marriage. If he can relate to his wife only as a helpless, dependent, guilty child, the outlook is poor. And whether or not he

can be helped by analytic psychiatry depends, as usual, primarily
on the balance of forces in his makeup.

Sometimes the man has regressed so far that he becomes a hostile, masochistic person. His passive aggression, that is, his helpless
irresponsibility, may have put him unalterably on the road to destroying himself and dragging down his wife and any others involved. If he is in the grip of forces that cannot be influenced, even
by therapy, then his wife may have no choice but to rescue herself
and the children as best she can.

*There is no worse evil than a bad woman; and nothing has ever been produced better than a good one.*

EURIPIDES

*No better lot has Providence assigned*
*Than a fair woman with a virtuous mind.*

HESIOD

# 13 WIFE TOWARD HUSBAND

Although we want wives to be angels, they, like husbands, can be tempted into extramarital sexual regressions.

Nearly every kind of problem is seen in women as well as men. When one deals with the basic needs of small children, the sexual difference between the parents is negligible, or at any rate secondary. If one needs food, shelter, care and affection to survive, it is relatively inconsequential whether this is provided by the mother or father. Once the pattern is formed, other emotional forces, other early experiences, determine how transferrable this pattern is from the parent to others. Therefore a girl who has had a certain kind of experience with her mother can transfer this pattern to her husband, just as a man transfers it to his wife. Within certain limits and modifications (for example, male aggressiveness fuses more easily with hostility, and femininity with receptivity), husband and wife are interchangeable. One might say that if each had had the childhood of the other, then in the marriage each would have had in his dynamics the make-up of the other. But externally the husband bears the burden of the responsibilities for breadwinning and the wife the relative loneliness and isolation within the home and the exhausting, unremitting demands of small children for care and attention. And in wars, which are still with us, the two roles differ.

Thea had a model husband a few years her senior. Since she had married at 20, her three children were grown and had left home to start out in the world. Tom, her husband, at 45 was small, vivacious, youthful-looking, self-assured, athletic, kind, personable, popular and devoted. He was interested in his business and extremely successful at it. His easygoing nature and success in business gave Thea freedom for her own pursuits in the home and in the community, with ample time for golf and bridge. She had always been a good mother. How could she at 43 risk all this for the sake of a clandestine affair with a neurotic man (call him Bud) a few years older who had a wife and not yet fully-grown children? It is hard to believe that this behavior does not contain a large component of masochism, that is, tendency to self-injury. She feared it and therefore came for help in understanding it and dealing with it.

The marriage had not been ideal, but how many are? Her husband, attractive as he was, had ample opportunities and was tempted to have an affair here and there; but he simply was not the type. Thea with all her freedom also had been tempted and for all I know may have yielded, but if so, it was in so quiet, brief a fashion as to arouse no attention. If it occurred it was not deep, and it was transient. But this present involvement with a rather petulant, demanding man threatened the whole structure of her life: husband, children and financial security, with all the freedom and privileges that it provided.

Our point is only the obvious one that wives can be as unfaithful, surreptitiously or otherwise, as husbands. It is worth mentioning an example of the variability of the forms masochism can take: A woman soon found that her husband was cruel and tyrannical. She could not defy him to his face, but avenged herself secretly by starting an all-out love affair. Some women—and men—damage themselves by being caught. But this affair was kept hidden for 20 years. However, this woman was reared with a strong conscience. She developed enough guilt to generate severe anxiety and some psychosomatic symptoms.

Thea had been raised in a home with the highest standards and had been well loved. Her childhood background was excellent except, as nearly as I could tell, for three features: she was a little too much adored, there was a little too much emphasis on being the best (narcissism, "bestism"), and she was pressured and molded a little too strongly and consistently in this direction by her proud and doting parents. She must be the best in grades, in athletics, in extracurricular activities; she must marry a wonderful young man —and her parents were thrilled when they first met Tom, because he was the living ideal that they had held for her. Throughout her married life he was perfect in her parents' eyes. If she had seen him with those eyes alone the marriage would have been idyllic. Her parents had also imparted to Thea good, mature standards of social behavior, and had taught her, for example, that one to whom so much had been given in health and intelligence owed something to society, to her fellow man. Unfortunately there was just enough unspoken overpushing for Thea to rebel. But the rebellion was repressed because she received so much real love that she loved her parents in return and identified with them and accepted their standards, which moreover her judgment told her were mature.

Now, at 43, with her children grown and out of the home, living with a husband who was often away, with all this freedom, Thea felt in her own mind the old pressures and the old rebellion and wish to toss them off and be free at last, to be free before the final imprisonment of age. She wanted freedom from living up to the standard of contributing socially; she revolted against being, in her own eyes and those of all who knew her, such a mature, superior person. The good and mature had been vitiated by the internalized parental pressure toward it, pressure by the most loving, well-meaning parents, who could not quite wait for her own maturation but had to force the growth a little.

As might have been expected, the neurotic Bud, who attracted her, represented in his own dynamics a similar underlying rebellion. But Thea's parents had been loving and she loved them; she could not thus throw over all their standards without feeling hostile to them, and such hostility in the face of love could only generate deep guilt. Hence her conscience, her superego, would make her choose a form of rebellion that must somehow assure its own punishment; her freedom, if she declared it, must be in a form that punished her, made her suffer. And indeed if her affair with Bud materialized and became known, she would be ruined. This sort of rebellion is common enough in adolescence, but, as we have seen, may not emerge until the period of freedom that comes when the children are grown and have left home.

Other dynamics were also present. The give-get problem we discussed in an earlier chapter appeared, as was to be anticipated, when her love needs turned from parents (especially her mother) to her husband. As is usual, or rather inevitable, her husband could not give her all that she as a young child desired from her parents. Her husband was another striving contemporary like herself, with his own dependent-receptive love needs turned toward *her* for satisfaction. Frustrated by Tom's being only a husband and not meeting the residual childhood longings for the overly strong adulation of her parents, Thea generated mounting resentment against him.

Also Tom fitted her pattern of jealousy toward her three younger brothers, who were three, eight and ten years younger. Thea was pushed out of her position as the only child by her brother, Tim, who was three years younger. When her parents raved about his wonderful qualities, Thea fumed and her resentment burned slowly but constantly against him. Now she transferred to Tom, her husband, this early hostility and competitiveness generated in childhood toward her brother, Tim. She had to rise above Tim then, and above Tom now—depreciate him, emphasize his every deficiency —although her reason saw clearly his superior qualities. But the pattern dictated that she must win out over him, be the only favored child. In childhood she yearned to be favored over her brother in the hearts of her parents; now she craved this favor over her husband in the eyes of the world and in the eyes of another man. She was filled with guilt and self-reproach for these hostile, selfish, ungrateful feelings of which she was herself not really aware. She felt the hostility but did not, until treatment, recognize the source.

Of course many people have younger sisters and brothers without this degree of hostility to husband or wife. There are many reasons why such a pattern develops and why it is transferred to one's spouse. One reason is that the intensity of the sibling rivalry is largely determined by the parents. If they so adore the first child and then switch their adulation to the second or third, the first will react strongly. Certainly the pattern of sibling rivalry causing marital problems is extremely common.

Sometimes the hostile, depreciatory competitiveness is intensified by some special qualities of the second sibling or by unavoidable circumstances. One girl's sister suffered for some years during infancy from a chronic illness which focused almost all the parents' anxiety and attention upon her, removing it from the girl who for three years had been the adored only child. Ever after, the girl strove ambitiously, had to be superior, had to win every boy, and after marriage soon developed these hostile competitive feelings toward her husband, whom she tried so hard to love and be a good wife to. Another girl, Vicky, had a twin brother who was preferred by her parents. She hated him for being a boy, to which she attributed his being favored over her. She must, simply *must,* share everything with him, do every little thing he did, have everything he had, be with him constantly. When she married, she did the same with her husband, and at first both she and her husband mistook this for love. But soon she could not even permit him to have his work to himself. She must share it too. Togetherness masked old hostility to the brother, the favored male, and became pathologically exaggerated. The husband was ruggedly stable, but eventually she herself went into a severe depression.

Thus there were at least three sources in the emotional patterns of childhood for the slow buildup of Thea's hostility to her husband —irrational, unrealistic sources, not caused by his actual feelings or behavior: rebellion against pressure for too high standards, excessive expectations, and resentment for displacement by a sibling.

The husband as breadwinner, being financially independent and having an occupation to hold his interest and take his mind off these mating problems, is in quite a different position from the wife who is financially dependent upon him and psychologically has no other great area of her life to occupy her. Despite divorce laws, the husband as wage earner has a great advantage psychologically over the wife, who relies on him for support. He is burdened with the breadwinning, but he has the great benefit of this whole area of interest and human relations in addition to the financial income his work provides. Perhaps the hold of a hostile wife on the husband is through the children whom he loves and whom he knows need a good mother. The hold of the husband is partly financial.

At any rate Thea's present dynamics, as just sketched, demonstrate the tendency toward potentially self-injuring regression. At 43 she was struggling with emerging conflicts of her childhood with her parents, which had been for the most part covered over all these years.

She obtained analytic help but treatment was difficult. She was so greatly tempted to enjoy the outside affair that she did not wish very strongly to be helped to forego it or no longer to desire it (which would be most unlikely) ; but she did see the damage to her husband and her children and the cost to herself. Typically her dreams were not of happiness with her lover, but were of being ill or apprehended for a crime or of some other form of suffering or retribution. In these dreams, as well as in the realities of her life, she could not fail to perceive the punishment she would inflict on herself for a neurotic freedom sought by hostile rebellion, rather than a real freedom from the inner pressure of the old conditioning. She came to see that the gesture of rebellion would bring punishment, not freedom; that the real freedom lay only in deconditioning the childhood pattern, in diminishing the residual feelings in her own mind that drove her to impossibly competitive behavior directed toward unattainable goals. If these were not resolved she would never be free. It was within herself that the conflict lay and must be resolved. Testing in life might well be important but need not be masochistic.

The goal of treatment was for her to achieve the freedom she wanted through the necessary shifts in her own attitudes, so that she could live rationally and more by her ego, her own sense of reality, her own judgment, and less by feeling that even her mature behavior meant, irrationally, compliance with parental pressure. If every good thing meant to her subservience to her parents, she would continue to rebel endlessly and to punish herself and yet never resolve her conflict. Treatment got her on the road to this goal. It moved her toward reducing her strong masochistic trend toward punishing herself by destroying her marriage and with it her whole security and position in life. It is dangerously easy for an established, respected, secure wife and mother to transform herself almost overnight into a lonely outsider looking in.

Getting on the way out, on the way to the goal, is about what we settle for in such a case as this at the present stage of analytic knowledge. If a person is well on the way out of the childhood fixation, regression or conflict, then we cannot complain too much about the rate of the progress. That, given the correct personality and skill of the analyst for the given patient, is a matter of the balance of emotional forces in the patient. The earliness of the injurious treatment (trauma), its consistency, the amount of balancing off by good relations, and other considerations determine how deep-seated and fixed the problem is, how amenable to analytic treatment. Thea was well on the way out before the war came. She did not manipulate herself into the status of an ostracized, impecunious divorcée, and she consolidated her progress, as letters after the war informed me.

*I have been faithful to thee, Cynara! in my fashion.*
DOWSON

# 14 FAITHLESS BUT FAITHFUL

## Personality can be fixed but surprising.

George was raised by a depressive mother who died young. He later married a girl, Gertrude, who was nice but quite colorless. It was only a matter of months before George began having outside affairs. These usually involved the wives of friends but were not limited to them. George suffered from unbearable anxiety when he was alone. He tried for a time to relieve it by drinking but this only made it worse. Hence, on any trip or under any circumstances he would have to have somebody sleep in the room with him. The person usually was, of course, whatever woman he could find. If he could not get a woman, he would ask a male friend or relative to spend the night with him.

The strain on Gertrude's fidelity became too great. The more I observe these things, the more it seems to me that extramarital affairs are frequently triggered by hostility. Usually the person, without knowing it, builds up a great pressure of resentment against the wife or husband and under this pressure goes out and has a sexual affair with someone else. It is a form of revenge, a drain for the hostility, an escape, and probably a channel for many other impulses as well.

So George and Gertrude drifted into one of those settings in which wives and husbands are freely traded about. It is one of the sad ironies of life that such freedom, instead of bringing all the fun and joy that it presumably should, more commonly has an opposite effect. Perhaps all the freedom and gratification cannot assuage the inner unhappiness. It may be that the underlying neuroses (childhood patterns) are such that genuine satisfaction cannot be obtained. It may be that such behavior goes so against the cultural standards and early training that it generates too much guilt. It may be that the basic biologic relationship is between one man and one woman for the rearing of the young. It may be

131

that it conflicts with maturity of personality and mating. Whatever the reason, instead of some joy and deep satisfaction, the opposite is commonly seen, and such was the case with this couple.

George, despite all his sexual freedom, despite the fact that Gertrude was a reasonably good mother to their two children, finally decided that he would terminate the marriage (they were now both in their early forties). While he was watching for an opportune time to broach the matter, his wife became ill. The doctor gave her six months to live. George was informed of this but Gertrude was not. George now did a complete about-face. He became a model and devoted husband. Nothing was too much trouble, nothing was too good for his wife. He spent much time with her, since she was at home during most of this period with occasional visits to the hospital. He gave her gifts and bestowed all the little attentions that are so dear to every woman. She wanted a certain car. He put in extra work, purchased it for her as though she would shortly be well and enjoying it, and drove her about in it at such times as she was out of the hospital. The end came with merciful suddenness, after she had only been back in the hospital a few days and while she was making plans for the future without the slightest idea that she would not recover. She died with her now completely devoted husband at her side after the happiest six months of her life. Perhaps underneath it all she knew the truth, but if so her defenses were unshakably successful, for this is all that showed on the surface.

The rest of George's story proves, however, that a leopard rarely if ever changes its spots. When the doctor told George that his wife's end was near, he wrote a letter to Martha, a lifelong friend of Gertrude's, who lived in Los Angeles. It was a fine letter, showing consideration and goodness. He said that he did not want to disturb her or trouble her, that he felt that she would want to know of Gertrude's condition, that no obligation whatever was implied that she come visit Gertrude, and that no one in the world except himself knew of the letter. It was only that he felt she might reproach him if he did not inform her of the condition of her lifelong friend.

The letter arrived just as Martha was getting ready for a week's vacation. Forthwith she obtained a plane ticket for Chicago and spent her vacation with Gertrude—the last week of Gertrude's life.

The evening after the funeral George took Martha to dinner and for two or three hours poured out to her his feelings and his troubles—the chief one being which of his many women to choose for remarriage. After he was well talked out Martha, who was divorced, asked why she was not in the running. She was leaving the next morning for Washington and suggested that George come along. They decided that he would arrange to get a month off, and that they would live together to find out whether they were congenial. If so, they would return and marry.

They *did* marry and then returned to Chicago. But his pattern immediately reasserted itself in a new series of affairs. Martha could not tolerate this and they were divorced in less than a year. Not only did Martha divorce him but he was ostracised by his friends and the local community and finally, because of his upset, lost his job. He did not seek analytic help despite the urging of friends. I wondered what would happen. He seemed at an impasse. In animals, "emotional death" is a recognized phenomenon, occurring when their mechanisms of adaptation are overstrained and cannot function. At this point, although still in the prime of life, George, isolated and seeing no way out, suddenly died of a heart attack.

# 15 MORE ABOUT TRIANGLES: SILVER LININGS AND DANGERS

**Sometimes even a triangle can have good effects, and breaking it can have dangers.**

Even in a triangle the primary interest may be in the welfare of the other persons, in other words, may be predominantly true, mature love, so that this interest acts as a counterforce against hurt and damage to others. For example, Dave fell in love with a woman, Dorothy, after he was already married and had children and while Dorothy was in the process of being divorced. He loved her in the sexual and romantic sense and wished that he were free to marry her. On the other hand he would not hurt his wife or children by leaving them. In his love the component of interest in Dorothy's welfare outweighed the selfish components of getting what pleasure he could from her, to such an extent that he did what he could to help her find a suitable husband after her divorce came through. Their love continued, but on the plane of true friendship, of real feeling for the welfare of each other, the sexual elements being suppressed. And so they lived, each in love with his own mate, each happy with his own children, each secure in the community, loving each other from a distance and expressing it only in friendship. The gains in richness of personal relations overweighed the frustration of the sexual elements.

When one observes the cruelty acted out by a husband or wife against a devoted partner and innocent children, it is natural to deplore this cruelty and difficult to refrain from judgment, and perhaps we should not refrain. But it is important to note that such judgments usually, perhaps always, must be directed only to the ego—the forces of mature reason, judgment and control.

135

For example, when I was an inexperienced resident in psychiatry, I was called one night to see an attractive man of 40 who had been brought to the hospital because of an almost successful attempt at suicide. We will call him Leonard. We pumped his stomach and he recovered. Next day he was in mental agony all right, and was full of rage and possibly guilt. Maybe it was these that caused his suffering. He was in an agitated depression, and was angrily resistant to talking and to accepting any help.

His wife, Louise, gave the history, the point of which was this: She was a few years his junior. They had been married fifteen years and had three children. Six years before this incident, Leonard had fallen in love with another woman, Tina, but he still loved his wife and children. Tina used all her wiles to persuade Leonard to get a divorce and marry her. In the end, however, Louise won; Tina tired and married another man. Leonard at first was enormously relieved; but then plunged into a despair that culminated in the attempted suicide. His wife, Louise, had seen it coming and had called several psychiatrists, but Leonard refused all help. His ego was so strong that through all this he discharged his very responsible duties as an accountant in an important position. But beneath his mature ego was a serious disturbance, which had pushed him into the triangle with Tina, the turmoil of which was more tolerable to his dynamics than was monogamy, although he had no real complaints about his wife. His childhood pattern had so dominated his mature mating and paternal instincts that when he tried to live maturely with love and responsibility toward wife and children, his dynamic equilibrium of forces became unbalanced, and the infantile motivations catapulted him into a suicidal depression. He had unconsciously acted out his hostility against Tina and against his wife and children during the years of the triangle. When the triangle dissolved, his hostility turned against himself. Poor Louise and the children; would they prefer the anguish of the other woman or mature, moral behavior that spelled psychosis and incapacitation or self-inflicted death? I never found out what eventuated after his discharge from the hospital. His intention was to go to a private psychiatrist, whom he was willing to see with the challenge of demonstrating in a few visits whether anything could be done to help him adjust.

*The dog is promiscuous. . . . But the wolf is monogamous. He mates for life, is intractably faithful, and if widowered will probably not re-mate but will remain a bachelor to the end of his days.*

ARDREY

# 16 THE FAITHFUL REGARDLESS

**Persons who are not provoked to infidelity even by extreme frustrations and pressures in their marriages.**

From the samples of marriages we have sketched, it must be evident that whether a husband or a wife is faithful emotionally and sexually is predominantly a personality characteristic. It is, as we have stated, a matter of their main dynamics in the marriage relationship.

Thus some husbands carry on outside affairs with no provocation from their wives whatever, whereas others under the most extreme provocation never stray from the marriage vows, never become involved with another woman. This is not a matter of sexual potency or desire. The same holds of course for wives who are faithful in feelings and body to their husbands. Some, even under provocation and temptation, do not wish an outside affair; some are even repelled at the thought, in spite of or because of being accustomed to full gratification with mutual orgasm in the marriage. Others feel deprived and unloved at home and strongly desire from another what they feel the spouse does not provide, but their dynamics are such that they do not know how to take such a step or are unable to do in real life what they dream of in secret. And there are many other variations. It is a matter of the personality make-up or, more narrowly, of the individual's particular dynamics toward wife or husband.

Life is complicated—it involves finding one's way externally and dealing with all the conflicting internal mechanisms that motivate us. Therefore we all seek guiding principles. A man or a woman in a difficult marriage usually asks, "What do other people in my situation do?" This question was asked, for example, by a

137

wife in her late thirties whose husband was involved with another woman.

He had used the usual lies and deceptions so that his wife no longer knew if he was telling the truth or not and had lost all confidence in his integrity. She feared that she would be thought a sissy and a coward if she did not righteously divorce him. But then, she pondered, what of the children, what of their financial security; would there be remarriage or only a broken home? Such questions raised doubts. She asked what other women facing such a situation did. Of course I had to answer that it was a purely individual matter, for there was a wide spread of reactions to such a husband. At one extreme would be the woman who, knowing of her husband's mistress, loaded him with affection and gifts in her efforts to hold him. Then there are those who struggle to save their marriages until their feelings pass all endurance and drive them to separation for self-preservation. At the other end of the scale is the wife who instantly sues for divorce.

These differences are not in the wives alone, but also in the husbands, and in the relationships in each marriage. One husband is strong, independent—and inconsiderate. He goes his way regardless and lets his wife and children take it or leave it. But in another man, initiating a serious extramarital liaison turns out to be the first step in a deterioration of his whole personality, a slide into neglect of family and job, sometimes into alcoholism and often association with less reliable, less mature companions; and sometimes the slide is all the way into a mental hospital. The range of individual differences is great. Therefore, while making full use of experience, we must study and deal with each problem specifically; for the situations (age, children, occupation, social and economic level, housing, conditions of living, relatives and similar factors) and the histories and the personalities of the wife, husband and children, as well as the interactions between them all, are unique in each case.

Economic status may also be an important factor. The poor seek extramarital sex as compensation for the frustrations and deprivations of poverty, the difficulties in living and their hurt pride and envy, while the wealthy have the means to indulge every whim of their own or of their paramour. But many of the poor are strictly monogamous, just as many of the rich are.

One man, Vic, as wealthy as he was attractive, married and then had any girl he could persuade. He was divorced and repeated the performance. If it took a Cadillac or a trip around the world to seduce a girl into yielding to him, he was quite willing and able to provide these inducements. Each of his wives was loyal and devoted and deeply in love with him. His philandering grew out of his own dynamics—really pathodynamics, for they were pathological. It was not the money that dictated his behavior nor his moral upbringing, which was extremely strict and reinforced by the weight of his church. The critical factor, the really determining cause, lay in severe neglect by his mother, which exaggerated his needs for the love of women and also created a deep-seated hostility to them. As an adult he transferred to women the original hunger for his mother's love and also his hatred toward her. This gave him an intensity that most women did not in the least understand, but which, covered over as it was by much gallantry, consideration and generosity, they found irresistible. They did not recognize that soon they would be not the recipients but the givers—and the butts of hostility as well—until it was too late and they began to realize that they were not beneficiaries of love, but victims of demands and hate.

Another man, Ted, also very wealthy, had a wife who was unlike Vic's in that she was not a well-balanced, mature, easy-going woman. Vic's wives gave no cause whatever for extramarital affairs; both were nice as could be; both were one-man women. Ted's wife was full of problems and complaints and criticisms of him. He traveled much, he had money, and he had all possible opportunities. Yet he remained constant. He had other reactions to the tensions she created, but extramarital sex was not his particular channel of expressing his needs, conflicts and tensions.

Cultural standards and customs are undoubtedly important. But in seeing husbands and wives from different parts of the globe, I am struck not by differences, but by similarities. Whatever the custom of the country, however much freedom is socially approved, I have yet to see the sanction outweigh the power of jealousy. Jealousy is biological. I see it clearly in our dogs. Just pat Angy, and Shep jumps up to push her out of the way and have the attention and affection for himself. Be demonstrative to a child your dog does not know, and his jealousy may even endanger the child. Perhaps women accept polygamy in countries where it is the custom, but I cannot conceive of a woman—or a man—not suffering violent jealousy when asked or forced to share a mate.

The very small statistical sample an analyst sees in his office practice, however, shows that the critical, that is, the weightiest, basic determining factor is the individual's dynamics. These dynamics will of course be influenced to a degree by the culture in which the child is reared. But the basic biological needs, drives and reactions are the same in all cultures. We have sketched vignettes of a series of men and one woman who engaged in outside affairs, and seen that, in these particular cases, this behavior was not rational, but was a hostile, sexual, extramarital regression.

A few vignettes will demonstrate the other extreme—persons who never disregard and break their marriage vows and the unenforceable secular laws, despite long provocation by their spouses. I do not mean that external provocations, pressures or temptations never play a part in illicit sexual affairs, whether with or without love. A good man may be tempted beyond his resistance by a seductive woman, and vice versa. I have seen a husband or wife impelled into an affair that they never would have entered if they had not been in a rage at their spouse at just that time. How we behave is always a matter of external temptations, frustrations and pressures causing us to react in accordance with our specific emotional patterns. We all have our Achilles' heels, our specific emotional vulnerabilities. And though we may judge others, we do not know how we ourselves will react in a powerfully emotional situation unless we have been through it.

Certainly it takes considerable maturity to ride the tempestuous horses of the sexual urges, mixed as they are with the mating instincts and all sorts of other feelings. No wonder our sexual desires often seize the bit and run wild. But I do not think that a man or woman carries on an outside affair that pains his spouse and children, damages them, in some part destroys them, unless there is a powerful undercurrent of hostility against them, however conscious or unconscious this may be. In my experience such destructiveness to one's own chosen mate and to the children one has created is not a purely incidental result of weakness or even selfishness alone. It is not merely an unfortunate by-product; it is a direct expression of latent resentment, hate, cruelty—in a word, of hostility—whether the person is aware of it or not.

My heart sank when Bill told me about his wife Bertha. Bill was an altogether excellent, sincere young man of conscientiousness and integrity, small in size but broad in humor and good will. When he told me about his wife, he remarked in all innocence that she hated her father. "Why?" I asked. "Because," he said, "her mother hated him, really drove him out of the house and turned Bertha against him." "How early in Bertha's life was this?" I asked, and he replied, "Always. Since her childhood, since before she can remember."

It was early in my career, but I knew by then the truth of the adage that as the twig is bent, so the tree is inclined. Bertha, small but full-formed, was fated by this conditioning, unless there were powerful counterforces (and my questions elicited none), to continue for life this pattern of identification with her mother and hatred and rejection of her father, a pattern in which no harmony existed between the parents, but in which, rather, the mother drove the father out of the house, while never divorcing him. The danger lay in the near certainty that Bertha would unconsciously act out toward her husband her pattern toward her father. The only hope I could see was that Bertha might transfer to Bill the pattern toward her mother, feel close to him and identify with him, and turn toward someone else the hostility she had for her father. There must have been some warning that this would not be the case in the courtship, but the steps to marriage proceeded against the naive Bill's own intentions.

Bill's Achilles' heel was too strong dependent-love needs toward his mother, a reaction to a little too much indulgence, overprotection and anxiety on her part toward him since his birth. One cannot but be sympathetic with this, for it was well intended and was a natural response of a young mother to her second child after the death in infancy of her first. Bill's being an only child further fixed him in this pattern of feelings toward his adoring parents. He could not stand anyone's being unloved, whether himself or others. He was attracted to Bertha because she had this trend in common with him—overly strong closeness to mother. His own dependent-love needs were masked by his athletic prowess, his kidding with the boys, and his hearty good fellowship.

They dated. Bertha was insecure and unhappy. She was grateful to Bill for his attentions and this led to their being "pinned." She was very pretty and was appealing because of her loneliness. Bill's parents felt for her, sympathized with her. Against his judgment, Bill yielded to her tears and wishes, and the pinning became an engagement. Still he wanted to escape, but Bertha's needs and the pity and sympathy Bill's parents felt for her eased him into marrying her, as a shoe horn guides a foot into a waiting shoe.

It did not take long for Bertha's pattern toward her father to begin to emerge toward Bill. She became critical. This and that were not right. He was just starting his career with a small but growing business, but Bertha complained about the house, the furniture, the appliances. She wanted more and better right now. Nothing Bill did was quite right in her eyes. Nothing satisfied her— his hours of departure or return, his attention to his job, his athletic recreations. She liked social climbing. He preferred friendship, fun, and the outdoors. Once in a terrible rainstorm the basement flooded. He went down at two in the morning and stayed until four moving their trunks, groceries and equipment and plugging and pumping as best he could, while Bertha slept. In the morning as he was leaving for the day's work, Bertha complained that he had done a clumsy job.

The key to Bill's personality was mother-love, mostly in the form of appreciation. He had been on the baseball and swimming teams at college, and his parents traveled long distances to see him compete. Probably Bertha could have twisted him around her little finger and had him eating out of her hand if she had given him simple *appreciation*. But she did not know this, and perhaps was as incapable of giving it as she was of giving warmth or love or affection to any man; for she was trained by her mother to hate the only man in her childhood, her father.

This hostility was reflected in coldness, and this encompassed her sexuality. Bertha was frigid. Frigidity need not interfere with a marriage in any consequential way. We have noted an excellent marriage with five children in which the wife never experienced an orgasm. But she liked sex anyway and her easy-going husband was satisfied. They got on excellently and were the best of parents. Bertha's frigidity, however, was not confined to failure to achieve orgasm. It was expressed in a total rejection of sexual relations. She was too tired, or had some vaginal spasm, or had or thought she had a discharge. A few times a year she gave in. She never became pregnant.

Thus she was a burden in every area of his life—work, home, financial, recreational, social, affectional, sexual. Bill got nothing. He gave everything, and all that he gave netted only rejection, criticism and hostility. Need I say more? If ever a man was justified in turning to another woman for some satisfaction of his simplest, most normal masculine needs for femininity, one would think it would be Bill. And he had charm and health and a lot more to offer. Yet under this frustration he stayed within the bounds of the marriage vows. His own dynamics, including the close affectionate, loving harmony between his parents, precluded extramarital sexual activity as a solution. It simply was not in his dynamics of the conjugal relationship. If it had been, it might have led to other difficulties, but it might have alleviated the inevitable vicious circle that developed between them. I have not meant to be unsympathetic to Bertha in this vignette. She was the innocent victim of her own pathological dynamics, formed in reaction to her well-meaning mother's influence. Her life was doomed to be blighted by this mother-attachment with hatred of father, no matter whom she married. I have only meant to show that Bill, also the victim of her pathodynamics, reacted to them, but not with sexual acting out.

As time went on, the vicious circle intensified. Hatred piled up between them. In some ways Bertha was better after Bill had begun to be enraged at her. Now her own guilt was appreciably relieved. The more hostile Bill became, the more justified Bertha felt in her own hostility to him. She could feel it as a realistic, natural reaction that any wife would have to such an angry man. This couple was not in treatment—Bertha never would consider it for a minute. Her pattern of hostility to her father and hence to men must have made her fear the transference of these feelings to an analyst. I thought she might consider going to a woman, following the pattern of closeness to her mother, but she would not. This was in the early part of their marriage, after only a year or so. At any rate Bertha defended herself against seeing her own makeup and its contribution to the discord by projecting everything onto her husband—it was all his fault, he alone must change. He did see a good analyst for a time and derived considerable help in withstanding the demands, frustrations and direct hostility of Bertha.

They came east occasionally for some fifteen years after the war and always stopped to see me. It was tragic to see these young people caught in such dynamics, gradually becoming hard, bitter, hostile, frustrated, and aging prematurely under the strain, and yet remaining true to each other. It is such prolonged tension and stress that usually cause some kind of serious physical illness. Marriage can cause illness and death as well as life.

Apart from the exceptions mentioned, the wives of the husbands with the extramarital sexual regressions did not themselves show any inclination toward other men as an emotional release, and some even felt repelled by the idea. I could add many cases of men who, like Bill, did not stray, even under severe provocation. But I think Bill adequately demonstrates the point without going into the details and dynamics of other couples. However, one husband put it in a rather poignant way, worth quoting. Of his wife I will only say that her insecurity, caused by the crushing dominance of a martinet of a mother, made her suffer in her own mind; it kept her chronically depressed and indecisive. Her husband bore it all quietly for years, a pillar of strength to his wife and children, and never took advantage of his opportunities for liaison with a younger, happier woman. Once when he was nearing 50, he talked to me about this. "I am grateful that I am white, gentile, educated, and financially comfortable, that my wife and children and I have good physical health, that I live in the United States, that we are settled and rooted in Chicago, in some ways the greatest city in the country. If my wife has difficulties I only feel that, blessed as I am in all other ways, she is like a bird with a broken wing that has been entrusted to my care and protection."

His dynamics, the result of his 0 to 6, permitted him to think and feel and behave in this fashion, and this strength far over-balanced the egocentric, the infantile. Perhaps in the future authors of plays and stories will have to tell more than hitherto of the history and genesis of the dynamics of the personalities they portray; not only *how* their characters think and feel and behave, but *why* they do so; not only what the underlying patterns of motivation and reaction are, but their genesis, how they came to be that way, how they were formed by the emotional influences of early childhood. For nothing in nature is comprehensible except in light of its history.

Infidelity is often a neurotic and sometimes psychotic pursuit of exactly the man or woman one imagines one needs for satisfaction in life, a satisfaction always sought but never found. I have often seen young men, so healthy, vigorous, attractive and successful with women that one wonders what more they want from life at their age. Yet, ironically, many are restless and unsatisfied; with the most delectable girls they find only the most transient gratification, hardly worth the tension and turmoil. Often they are as unsettled in career as they are with women. So many of the men I have seen, of all ages, who are the most successful in seducing women are also the unhappiest in their relations with them. They dream of an ideal that is an unrealistic fantasy and that remains forever unattainable.

# IV  Repetition in Marriage of Childhood Patterns

*Whether we consider the rocky layer enveloping the Earth, the arrangement of the forms of life that inhabit it, the variety of civilisations to which it has given birth, or the structure of languages spoken upon it, we are forced to the same conclusion: that everything is the sum of the past and that nothing is comprehensible except through its history.*

TEILHARD DE CHARDIN

Emotional patterns in the parental home tend to emerge in the marital home, but how much this occurs varies.

Throughout our lives we all continue to be in part the child we once were. In other words we are all fixated in some degree in the attitudes, expectations, feelings and reactions of our early days, weeks, months and years as these developed toward those who reared us, in response to their treatment of us. But these responses are many and complex. How many and how fixed are the responses that can disturb a marriage? There is wide variation: some disordered childhood patterns seem not to be transferred to the marriage at all; others only partially; and others almost exactly. We will illustrate each of these three kinds of outcome.

The emergence of a childhood pattern occurs in other personal relationships as well as marriage. The word "tendency" to repeat these patterns in marriage and elsewhere is used deliberately. It does not always occur. Sometimes it occurs in marriage and but little with friends or fellow workers; sometimes the reverse. Thus one able man of 60 had lifelong difficulties in a series of companies in which others were happy; and he had troubles in his local business club and with other groups. But difficult as he was outside his home, he remained an excellent, even-tempered, devoted husband and father. His family suffered indirectly, however, for his frictions at work held back his advancement in position, income, and security.

Hostility, like other strong emotional forces such as dependence or competitiveness or envy, is so readily displaced (or in the terminology of the animal ethologists, redirected) that one sees all sorts of variations. A husband may be angry at work but take it out on his wife as a whipping boy, or he may take out at work the anger he feels at his wife. The same variations are seen in women. One wife is loving with her husband, but cannot hold domestic help; another is charming to everyone except her husband, who serves as a constant target for her stream of hostility.

That emotional reactions toward parents are transferred to others in life, including spouse and children, is not surprising if we recall that our needs for love from parents as children are never fully outgrown. Our childhood dependent-love needs continue with a power many times greater than we realize. Everyone deeply craves love, often with much dependence. These needs attach to anyone close. And it is these needs for love that motivate so many to go to parties to meet new people, hoping that the one who can satisfy them may be there. The childhood love needs seek satisfaction in adult life from a person of the opposite sex, and are reinforced by full sexual desire. Thus the need for love from parents is turned to husband or wife, but the need now includes sex and the whole mating instinct. And the adult's need for love carries along all or some of his reactions to his parents that were bound up with his need for love as a child.

How much of the childhood pattern is directly transferred to wife or husband, how much the person reacts in his marital home as he did in his parental home, varies from person to person. Most, I think, do transfer the larger part of these feelings. Some do not, and these people may have intense feelings toward their parents which may remain thus fixated on the parents themselves for life. There are intermediate cases in which only a part of the pattern is transferred to the marriage.

# 17 NOT TRANSFERRED: HAPPILY EVER AFTER

**The good feelings of childhood may be transferred to the wife, while the old feelings of rejection, clinging and rage remain fixed upon the original members of the family who generated this pattern of reaction.**

Childhood patterns live a life of their own, exerting their influence throughout a person's existence. Most of us are to some extent trapped by some amount of deleterious childhood conditioning but in some cases it does not enter the marriage directly.

Danny sat in my office giving an impression, quickly confirmed, of vitality, intelligence and maturity. What then did he wish to improve in himself?

Patient: I must adjust to my family's having rejected me—and I can't, and I am getting irritable with my good wife. Everything in my life is better than anyone could ask for. I have a wonderful, easy, mature, congenial wife. Our children have turned out to be decent, good, successful people with good marriages and fine children of their own. I am interested in my legal work and in reading, politics, art and music. And my wife, Dina, shares all these interests except the law, my profession.

In spite of all these blessings I cannot accept the rejection by my family. It is absurd. I am 61 years old and yet am getting more and more bitter and short-tempered, and this is threatening my marriage. I have four brothers and sisters, actually they are half brothers and sisters. My mother died when I was a year and a half old. My father remarried within a year. As the children came along

I grew up with them as their brother. But I was the outsider for Mum. She gave me good care, but she never let me forget what she was doing for me. If I was sick she reminded me of her sacrifices in coming up the stairs to see me or bring a tray. Yet she would be the last person in the world to think she contributed anything to this rejection. She is a hale 80 and I'll say she is a fine woman. Today, in spite of herself, she admires me. But she still shows the definite preference for her own children, all of whom are superior and exceptional.

Analyst: Please tell a little more about those earliest years—before age 6.

P.: Father's marriage to Mother had been a love match. It had been a wild romance. I was a truly loved child and my father was completely devoted to me. Mum, my stepmother, is a great woman but she has always had this aloofness to me. I was always falling, bumping my knee or arm, but she took any attention she had to pay me as a great nuisance. If I was sick, she would say, "Look at all I do for you, running up and down the stairs," and such remarks. Gradually I saw that she did not say these things to her own children. She always talked of "my brood"—and that definitely did not include me.

Today my wife and I are left out of all my family's affairs. This is especially clear and painful at the holidays. At Thanksgiving or Christmas there is never even a phone call to say, "See you after the holidays." If we invite any of them for dinner, they cancel at the last minute. Or they may just not come, and then phone two days later and say, "Oh, we forgot."

A.: What is your very first memory?

P.: All my early memories are about being with Father. My true mother died when I was a year and a half old, and I was with her parents until a year later when Father remarried. My first memory was, I think, before that. It was of being with Father and his saying to some people, "This is my son." Father died when I was 25. [This memory clearly confirms his longing for love, acceptance and the pride of his parents.]

Now here I am happily married, professionally successful, with lots of friends and interests, but I have this heartache. It is ridiculous to still make an issue of one tiny thing when everything else is as nearly perfect as life affords.

A.: How long have you made this an issue?

P.: Always. When my wife first noticed it, she was irked and said loudly and positively, "Just stop it—forget it." Later she completely refused to hear about it.

A.: But you come to see me only now in later life. Is it worse recently?

P.: I suppose I feel it more now. It's always been there, but the last six months or year I have not been coping with it. No one knows this. Everyone says, "Don't worry about Danny; he's made of stern stuff; he'll always land on his feet."

A.: Why are you coping less well in the past year?

P.: One sister and her husband who did keep some contact moved away some years ago. The two brothers and their families I sort of wrote off. In a way I don't even care that much about Mum any more. But we were very devoted to the other sister, Letty, and her family. A year ago her husband was about to do a very foolish thing in his business from a legal standpoint. I pointed this out. They both accused me of meddling. I spoke with them and we seemed to have it resolved. They couldn't have been nicer. But in fact we never got together again. That was the last straw. And from then on my preoccupation with this began to be unhealthy, and now it threatens my marriage. I am 61 and my wife and I don't have that much time left.

A.: Did you have a dream last night?

P.: No.

A.: Any recent dream?

P.: No. In childhood I used to dream of running and my feet would get heavier and heavier. You know that dream. Now I only dream bits of daily life.

[Did the dreams reflect trying to be free, to escape something, to reach something—love—and being blocked? We recall that he often bumped himself.]

A.: You know biology well enough to know that the course of development takes the young away from the parents and the whole parental family, in species that have families. But if a child feels that the mother is too cool, the child is apt to cling, to be excessively attached, to fight for what he lacks from the mother.

P.: Yes. Mum never kissed me, never put her arms around me. I used to weep about it. But as I grew a little older I developed a façade. I cried no more; I became perfectly groomed; all that sort of thing. And everyone thought I was unusually stable, a rock to whom others turned. "Don't worry about Danny; he's strong and solid." And now I cry over a book or play, but no longer over reality; for reality I just—shrug.

In this instance the childhood pattern has not developed directly toward the spouse. It has never been transferred from the parental family where it is still fixated. It affects the marriage only indirectly by generating bitterness, irritability, preoccupation with it, and a short temper.

Danny presented not only instructive dynamics but a therapeutic challenge, for as these notes indicate, he came with quite thorough insight, but needed the help of the analytic situation to outgrow his childhood pattern which, however circumscribed, had trapped him for a lifetime. It is not unusual for a person to have the most accurate, complete, and penetrating insight, and yet for the emotional core of the difficulty to be remote from the kind of conscious realization that can deal with it, resolve it and be rid of it.

As in Danny's childhood dream, he is trying to escape, but his legs are heavy and he cannot. Many people are correct when they say they need not go to an analyst for the kind of insight they have, but they may need him urgently to help them *use* this insight to solve their problem. And as this example shows, that problem can worsen even in the sixties, despite the most favorable life circumstances and despite unusual maturity in all the rest of the personality. Analytic treatment can be thought of as having two parts. The first is to *understand* the dynamics behind the difficulty. The second is to *use* this understanding curatively, to free the person from the difficulty. (In the process, the transference of the disturbing pattern to the analyst is usually of great importance.) This is as in the rest of medicine: rational treatment based upon thorough, accurate diagnostic understanding at all times.

Probably Danny's strengths, his ability to develop an effective façade, derived from the year and a half with his true mother, from his devoted father, and from what was good in the interrelations with Mum and the half siblings. As usual it is a matter of the balance of forces. The good relationships of his childhood gave him the soil for healthy maturation, but these drives toward maturity could only defend against but not adequately resolve the trauma of the discrimination and exclusion to which he was subjected from the age of two and a half. Apparently a sound base was laid during the first eighteen months, and the next year was also good, so the seedling was off to a good start and could withstand the injurious preference of Mum for her brood, with no greater harm to Danny's whole life than what he related.

It is interesting and encouraging that Danny did very well with analytic treatment at two visits per week, despite his having been partially fixed in his pathodynamic pattern for almost a lifetime. Some analysts will insist that meeting less than four times a week is psychoanalytically based therapy and not psychoanalysis. Many books and articles have been written about this. In my opinion the essential is to understand the emotional forces behind the problem and to do what is most effective and time saving to help the patient deal with these forces. The process, as Freud stated clearly, is one of "after-education" to correct the parental "blunders" (also his term).

Danny, through Mum's behavior, was conditioned by her treatment to think of himself as an outsider in the family. He grew up in that setting, and what we grow up with in attitudes and feelings during our earliest formative years continues. Danny needed help in changing this set way of thinking and feeling. I believe treatment would have succeeded with one visit a week, but his particular pace was such that it was more smooth and rapid with two visits. I did not start at four or five meetings a week because stirring up and working with one's feelings so intensively is not optimum for many people. The unfolding of the emotional forces, the development of the transference—in fact, every constructive feature of the psychoanalytic process—is present even at one meeting a week if the analyst is skilled in this. It is a matter of adjusting the procedure to what is best for the individual patient. It worked for Danny during the two and a half years before the war; and the result held, as I learned by letter and upon seeing him during his occasional business trips from Chicago.

In some cases a person vows that he will never treat his spouse and children as he was treated in childhood. He becomes a model mate and parent. But there is a risk, a chance, that these mature defenses might at some point weaken and the old childhood feelings erupt. This is one reason that some "pillars of strength" sometimes collapse. It is safer to have a good, secure, loving, easy 0 to 6 at the core of the personality. But even when this is not the case, the defenses and reactions may work well and permanently.

# 18 NOT TRANSFERRED: IN A WIFE

An excellent wife and mother, who has kept her difficulties with her parents confined to them.

Once after a strenuous, hectic spring we made arrangements, with all the innumerable details, to take off on a vacation. We arrived, unpacked, had a bit of supper, and at last stretched out to relax. Just then the phone rang. It was Julie. Julie was a tall, slender, violet-eyed young wife, with a son and two daughters. She was charming and yet down to earth and practical. She had been to see me a few times before her husband was transferred by his company to a western state in which there were no trained psychiatrists at that time. On the phone Julie was in a panic. In her considerate way she apologized for calling during my vacation. She had strong self-control but it was obviously now threatened by her agitation. "I am losing my mind," she said. "I am not just saying this. I am fighting against going crazy. You know how I feared moving here. Randy had to for his job, but we are only fifty miles from where I was born and where all my family are. Now I'm all mixed up with them. I'm going out of my mind. What shall I do?"

Since there was no analytic psychiatrist available anywhere near her, we handled the situation by phone, seven days a week. It worked. She gradually withdrew from the brink. The near-psychosis was indeed a reaction to her family, especially her parents. Her father had always been and still was the complete commander. When he entered the house all noise stopped, everything centered around his wishes and comforts, his whim was rigid law. Julie's mother was utterly dominated by him and kept the children under control, mostly with guilt and a sense of obligation to parents. To develop guilt and obligation in a child, to make a child guilty and ashamed is a poor method of helping him mature and form good feelings toward himself and others.

155

What saved Julie in childhood apparently was her escaping from her home to friends. This pattern continued into adult life. She had a good marriage in Chicago. Her upsets there were mainly reactions to letters or phone calls from her parents.

So many people throughout their lives, even as adults, react violently to their parents. Marilyn, who at 50 was a grandmother, began to have depressions. They were traceable to her mother's coming from Denver to Chicago to live. Marilyn lived on the South Side, her mother on the North Side, but her mother was solicitous, phoned and expected to be phoned almost daily, and gave gratuitous advice thus stirring up Marilyn's childhood pattern of the old submissiveness to her mother, which enraged her. But her rage was always repressed; it generated guilt and she became depressed.

The point about Julie is that throughout the three years of learning to handle her violent feelings toward her parents, she remained an excellent wife and mother in spite of her terrible anxiety about losing her mind. She never transferred to her husband and children any of the pattern toward her parents. Her marital family was affected only indirectly by her being upset by her parents. Gradually she disengaged her feelings from her parents sufficiently to be completely free of symptoms. She was for years free of anxiety and able to enjoy her family, friends and interests, although at the cost of some guilt for not seeing her parents. She found that it was impossible to see them without going all to pieces, without intense anxiety, which took every ounce of her strength to control, and which in the extreme threatened her with mental breakdown and almost entire incapacitation.

Analytically we had hoped that she would resolve her childhood pattern to the point of tolerating a reasonably friendly, adult relationship with her parents. But this was not achieved. Once she said, "I know they are elderly and I am now the young strong one. I know that bygones should be bygones. I know that to go and visit for a few hours should be nothing at all. When I see my father, or even talk with him on the phone, I tell myself all this, but I can't fight off memories of childhood—of his coldness and strictness and the ways he treated me. Then I rage inside, and I feel guilty and suddenly I'm in pieces and fear losing my mind again."

This is a cruel clash—between the parents and the husband and children; but the choice is obvious. The parents have little time left and, sadly, are only reaping what they sowed. A marriage is for more than half a lifetime, and the children have their whole lives ahead of them, including their own future marriages and those of their children, down through all the generations to come. The Bible tells the wife she must leave her parents and cleave to her husband. And it is the same for the husband. It is basic biology: The general rule in the animal kingdom is for the young after adolescence to leave the parents or to be pushed out or deserted by the parents; for the parents have taught the offspring all they can and have prepared them to survive on their own and to follow their instincts to mate and form their own families (or whatever the variation is for the given species).

Julie did not hesitate. Communication with her parents upset her so badly that it jeopardized her home, the well-being of her husband, and the emotional development of her children, with all its implications for *their* marriages and children. Therefore, defending her home like a tigress, she reluctantly cut off contact with her parents. Isolating herself from them returned her to her normal happy life in home and community.

After the war her father sent them a gift. She assumed that it was intended in a kindly way; but it was enough to arouse her old love needs for her parents, her old sense of obligation, and her rage and guilt. Again she became almost paralyzed with anxiety. Again she recovered at the price of withdrawal from her parents and became stabilized for the next few years.

After this period of happy stability, Julie began to feel secure enough to visit her father and mother, who were now getting old. Analytic help had achieved a happy life for her, but it had never resolved the feelings still stirred up by her parents. But visiting her parents seemed worth a trial. She went only for a day, but that did it. Again she fought against losing her mind and required some help to regain her stability in her own home, in her own life. Julie shows the enormous power of these childhood patterns toward parents and others, and how they may stay attached for life to the original persons who provoked these reactions. In this case they were not transferred to spouse and children at all apparently. In fact Julie has had one of the best marriages I know of.

# 19 PARTLY TRANSFERRED: FRIGIDITY

Let us now look at an example in which the childhood pattern had some direct effect on the marriage, but only in a limited, circumscribed fashion.

In many homes the father is so absorbed in his work that he is a rather peripheral figure, who most of all wants to relax and be left alone. But Laura's father was a vivid and important figure in her childhood. He was the sort of man who turned all his charm to the world. Outside his family he was all kindness and consideration and was universally popular. But in the home he was narrow and rigid, insisting that everything be done as he directed, that everyone conform completely to his crabbed, pinched little ways. He was controlling and dominating, always critical and ever ready to launch a withering verbal attack. Yet he loved Laura, and she received much love and support from her mother. The balance of these emotional influences on Laura was such that she was not crushed, but did develop fixed defenses against her father's domination, criticisms and attacks. These defenses formed one part of her inner make-up. On the surface she was friendly and well liked, and with her trim little figure and appealing face had no trouble attracting boys. She married a man who was quite the opposite of her father. They had three children and a marriage far more congenial and harmonious than most. Her husband, Mike, with his easygoing ways, was so different from her father in personality that the pattern to her father never developed toward Mike, except in one circumscribed area. In their sexual relationship Laura could not abandon her inner defense and let herself go. The result was desire without orgasm. This did not particularly bother Laura, however, and fortunately it did not bother Mike much either. For the rest, they had a fine marriage.

With Julie and Danny (Chapters 17 and 18) intensive analytic

159

work did not reveal any appreciable transference of the childhood patterns to the spouse. In Julie this seemed to be, as we have noted, because the marriage continued the early pattern of escape from parents to good relationships with friends. In Laura only a certain part of the pattern was transferred to the spouse. But most of the examples in this book describe marriages in which enough of the childhood pattern emerges to make more or less serious emotional difficulties.

*Jealousy is cruel as the grave: the coals thereof are coals of fire, which hath a most vehement flame.*

SONG OF SOLOMON, VIII; 6

# 20 CLOSELY TRANSFERRED: JEALOUSY AND PARANOID JEALOUSY

Jealousy is a terrible emotion, one of the extreme forms of psychological cruelty. In the vignettes in this book in which a person felt jealousy, I have felt totally inadequate to convey the poignancy of the pain, the mental anguish and the torment as I have seen it in the person talking in my office. The agitation, hand-wringing, head grasping, pacing as if caged, and weeping or frozen silence express an inner torment which is indescribable.

Why jealousy should have such power and cause such pain is quickly apparent. Ethology shows that animals tolerate other species in their own demarcated areas of feeding and nesting, but fight off their own species. For example, a bird will not mind too much, under ordinary conditions, if a bird of another species, running short of worms, berries, seeds, or other food on his own staked-out ground, trespasses somewhat and feeds. But he is apt to fight in deadly earnest if a bird of his own species appears—partly because, in all likelihood, this bird is able to mate with the female and thus might break up his home. In general, animals do a lot of growling and snarling for warning and bluffing in order to avoid serious fighting; but once they have mated, they will risk injury and death in battling to keep their families. And it has been noted that the animals defending their homes are usually much more valiant in combat than are the intruders, who have no such just cause.

Guy de Maupassant wrote a story called "Love." The following is an excerpt from its ending:

Two birds . . . glided rapidly over our heads. I fired and one of them fell almost at my feet . . . and then . . . above me I heard a voice, the voice of a bird. It was a short, repeated, heart-rending lament; and the bird, the little animal that had been spared began to turn round . . . over our heads, looking at its dead companion which I was holding in my hand. . . . "You have killed the duck," [Karl] said, "and the drake will not fly away."

161

He certainly did not fly away; he circled over our heads continually, and continued his cries. Never have any groans of suffering pained me so much as that desolate appeal, as that lamentable reproach of this poor bird which was lost in space.

Occasionally he took flight under the menace of the gun which followed his movements, and seemed ready to continue his flight alone, but as he could not make up his mind to this, he returned to find his mate.

"Leave her on the ground," Karl said, . . . "he will come within shot by and by." And he did indeed come near us, careless of danger, infatuated by his animal love, by his affection for his mate, which I had just killed. . . . Karl fired. . . . I saw something black descend . . . I put them . . . into the same game bag.

Only man's colossal egotism has kept him from recognizing what is known to every child with a pet, every animal trainer, every veterinarian, most farmers, and others familiar with animals: namely, that animals have needs and feelings and personalities just as humans have. The physiology and biochemistry of living processes are basically the same in animals and man, and modern medicine is based on this fact. Animals suffer from most of the same dire diseases as man: tuberculosis, heart disease, cancer, arthritis, and many, many others. We are built on the same anatomical, physiological and biochemical ground plan. We eat, eliminate, need shelter and exercise like most animals; we play as they do; we also are dependent as they are, need social cooperation, need to love and be loved, need to establish families, to reproduce, and to raise our young with affection, protection and much teaching.

Intellectually we are far superior. But brains do not produce happiness. We tend to worship sheer intellect, but intellect is only an amoral tool, like big muscles. It is a tool of the emotional life, which can be used for cruelty and destruction as well as to make a secure and satisfying life. Life is primarily of the heart, of the feelings. Whether or not we annihilate each other, with thermonuclear bombs or in other ways, will be dictated by our feelings: hate, power-seeking, love. The intellect only makes possible the application of atomic power; the ways and goals of its use are dictated by the heart, the feelings, the personality patterns—the identical kinds of motivations that make the rest of the animal kingdom feel and behave as they do. And they, although far inferior to us intellectually, are far superior to most of us morally and in mature, responsible, loving behavior to their own spouses,

children, friends, and all their own kind. Certainly we have much
to learn about our own nature from our animal cousins. They cannot talk but they often do better than man in making their feelings
known: they openly reveal their feelings by their mien and behavior. If we see jealousy in them, we can be sure that it is the
same deep, primitive form of response that we ourselves experience.

Besides seeing in animals the power of jealousy for their home,
mates and young, we can deduce it from our knowledge of psychodynamics. In all close attachments between adults there is a strong
residue of the child's dependent-love needs toward its mother, those
deep needs which the mother and father will, if mature, respond to
by giving the child what it craves. The child's very existence depends upon his needs for food, warmth, protection and cleanliness
being satisfied; and the assurance of satisfaction of these biological
needs lies in the feeling of being loved by the mother and father.
These needs, still present in the adult, attach normally to the mate.
This is part of the interdependence. The infant's needs are lessened
in intensity in adult life. The mate is a contemporary, another poor
suffering mortal like ourselves in equal need of tender loving care,
and cannot be such a mother or father as we had in childhood and
resent relinquishing—or such as we did not have, and therefore
still inordinately crave.

Jealousy signals a threat to one's mate and young and home,
and to the all powerful needs for love and dependence. And in addition, it is a terrible blow to the self-esteem. For as the dependent-
love needs are transferred to wife or husband, he or she comes to
stand in some degree for mother and father. To be rejected by the
parents, whether for oneself alone or in favor of another, is to be
held unworthy, insufficiently lovable by the all powerful parents
whose opinion of oneself one accepts. If they think us not worthy of
their love, whether or not they openly prefer a brother or sister,
then we take over in some degree this opinion of ourselves.

These few remarks about jealousy are only meant to indicate
some of its roots: how deep it is biologically and psychodynamically,
and hence what a terrible state to suffer from or to provoke in
another human being or animal.

Jealousy, like other painful feelings, can arise as a natural reaction to sufficient external provocation; it can also be generated
from within; and it can be caused by a combination of both external
circumstances and internal patterns. This combination of external

and internal causes seems to be portrayed in Shakespeare's *Othello*. If what Iago tells of Desdemona is true, Othello's jealousy is externally stimulated by her infidelity. But why is Othello so ready to believe Iago, rather than to trust his own true and loyal wife?

Even when confronted with betrayal, not all men and women react with equal intensity. It all depends, of course, on the individual's childhood emotional patterns. As we have seen in our discussion of infidelity, one mate may never think in terms of jealousy or suspect infidelity even when there is cause, while another experiences jealousy when there is no external cause whatever. Reading infidelity into a situation where it does not exist or exaggerating a simple, slight, natural interest in someone into proof of faithlessness is usually caused by projecting something in one's own emotional patterns onto the other person. When the exaggeration is extreme and especially when it is combined with a strong element of hostility, it is called paranoid.

In psychiatric practice it is often very hard to discern just what is internal and what external. Persons with strong paranoid streaks are usually among the master rationalizers. They can prove anything and they can pile up such arguments as to be very convincing. Often it takes a while before one realizes that they are weaving reality into their fantasies, into their emotional needs, and that it is useless to argue with them. One will never win a point or have any influence on their thinking, for their thinking and way of seeing reality lack almost all objectivity and are determined by childhood emotional needs and patterns.

They are tendentious. They select the facts and reasoning to prove their emotionally pre-established conclusions. But this can be tricky. Years ago I saw a man who was in a mental hospital for ten days' observation because he was suffering from the delusion that his wife was putting poison in the lunches she prepared for him. It turned out that it was no delusion—she really was. We obtained some of the sandwiches.

Another man who had escaped from a private mental hospital, was picked up by the police. It was in the 1930's. In the interview in the hospital, he "proved" that Hitler had gotten control of all the private sanatoriums in the country and was railroading people into them on false commitments for political motives. So logical and convincing was he that the policeman who was present saw no signs of delusion in this. But this man's idea was part of a whole delusional system that was entirely a product of his fantasy, and, except for his use of a few kernels of truth, built up beyond all reality.

When you see a husband or a wife in the office and hear one side of the picture, it is very hard to evaluate the total situation and often it still is difficult even after you hear the spouse's side. For as we have noted, one must discern not only the dynamics of each, but also the interplay of these dynamics between the two. Sometimes it helps greatly if one can get the opinion of fairly mature children or others who are in the home. But how they see it must also be evaluated: are they reasonably objective, or strongly identified with the husband or the wife?

One wife, Sonia, accused her husband, Steve, of being unconsciously mean to her, of little cutting remarks, of driving the car in ways that frightened her, of embarrassing her by being late when he escorted her, of coldness of manner. He, on the other hand, showed how justified all this was as reaction to his wife's underlying hostility to him. She admitted this hostility to him but said it was an unavoidable reaction to how he treated her. Was he hostile to her, and, if so, how much was a natural reaction to how she acted and how much arose from inner sources? To what extent did he have a streak of coldness, sullenness and hardness?

Both he and his wife had the highest love and regard for their son, Stanley, who was in his early twenties. He came to see me. I had hesitated to see him because I did not want to risk any influence on his alignment with one parent against the other. Even sympathetic listening can encourage hostilities and help consolidate attitudes and feelings. But my fears were groundless. He was quite mature and objective and loved both his parents devotedly. This made him secure enough to speak easily and freely. There was no question, in his view, of his father's unconscious hostility to his mother. Stanley had long recognized it; he had tried to discuss it with his father, but the father was truly not aware of what he was doing. The result of it all was that I felt much more secure in my understanding, for what the son said coincided with my own impression. His view came from a lifetime of living in the family, mine from a few professional hours with each parent in the office. If our views were the same, there probably was some reality in them.

Both parents accepted some analytic help—the mother by her own wish, the father reluctantly. But his resistance against it was discussed from the beginning. He gained insight into his feelings and attitudes toward his wife and the marriage began to improve. He had certain rigidities that made help very difficult, but once he was won over to acknowledging his part in the constant contention, the atmosphere improved markedly. Both understood better the vicious circle set up by the hostilities and the need to give a little more love and affection and patience and to settle for receiving a little less of these without anger.

Now we come to a man in whom the source of the problem was easily recognized and was definitely internal. He was more than willing to follow his wife's suggestion that he come for an opinion. Let us call them Charlie and Carole. The marriage, he said, was only six months old but fraught with bitter fights. He had other problems, but these, he said, were minor. What he came about was his marriage.

Patient: The trouble began almost as soon as we were married. This was strange, for we had lived together for some months before the ceremony and all went beautifully. We had no fights and were very happy. Then Carole had to go home to California because of an illness in her family, and we were separated for a few months. We could hardly wait to be together again and to be married. At the time of my vacation from my job—I'm an accountant—I went to California and we were married there. Almost at once, before we left on our honeymoon, a strange thing happened. I felt that Carole was being a little too friendly with an uncle of mine who was present. I was jealous. I'm still not sure but what she may have had some feelings for him. He was about 50, but youthful and attractive. It seemed that something changed in me after the ceremony.

The honeymoon lasted three weeks and we were pretty happy; but I was not at ease. When we got back we had people in, and they invited us to their house. I had old friends, married couples who had never met Carole. One of the couples were close friends of mine, though nearly twenty years older. Carole talked to the husband alone for what seemed to me too long a time. I became so jealous that I was in a rage at her. I tried to hide it but couldn't, and we had a big fight after we got home that evening.

Carole has a part-time job as secretary in a business firm. There are men around, of course, and you know how they feel about secretaries. There are one or two I'm suspicious of. They make me so jealous that Carole is going to give up the job, although we need the income until I'm a little better established and we start a family.

Recently we went on a vacation to the shore. We used to go before we were married. This time she eyed the good-looking men on the beach, and this enraged me. In the evening I took her out to dinner, but in the restaurant I could see her interest in other men. I got so mad I just walked out and left her there. We have our good times still, but more than half the time we fight, so that I'm afraid she will leave me. There is always a particular man that I think she is in love with in preference to me. I am getting to doubt whether she really loves me.

Analyst: Could this jealousy be all in your mind?

P.: I guess maybe it is, but I can't help feeling this way. I need your help with this. I know it is my problem, but I think she does have this interest in other men. I get so mad I call her all kinds of names, and it is hard to keep control of myself and not hit her.

A.: As you tell this it sounds rather unrealistic, if I follow you correctly. You are jealous of your wife's being in love with a man, but it seems to be a different man every day. If it's someone you know, it's usually a man who shows no interest in her, or sometimes it's even a total stranger. Do you seriously believe this?

P.: Well—I guess I believe it and I don't believe it. One moment I'm sure it's true and can't stand it. And then at another time I think it's foolish. Of course I'm here because I think it's my problem and I know I must learn to trust her.

Now it sounds as though this man's jealousy is mostly internally caused, that is, mostly delusional, and that he has partial insight into this fact. I have given only a small sample of the discussion of jealousy with him; the rest was of the same nature. He came for help because he sensed that it was his internal problem, but still he could not help believing his own delusion: that his wife was really rejecting him in favor of some other man with whom she was in love, but always in a quite unlikely, unrealistic way. But of course I would have to see his wife.

The interview continued.

A.: Please tell me a little about the highlights, the main features of the emotional relations in your home during your childhood, as far back as you can remember.

P.: So far as I know, my home was normal until my father was killed in an auto accident when I was about 4 years old. I do not remember him but I seem to have only good feelings about him. After that, everything changed. My mother had to get a job. My younger brother and I hardly ever saw her. She was in and out. She went out with other men, trying to find a second husband, and she did marry one. But after my father died, the main thing was that she was distracted; she lost her interest in my brother and me, and was always leaving us to find a job, to do her job, to go out on dates, to be interested in something or someone else.

About two years later, when I was about 6, she did remarry. This man had two children of his own, and then they had one together. This stepfather never talked to us. He acted as though we didn't exist. And Mother gave all her attention to him and the other children. When I was 9 years old I was sent away to boarding school. My mother hardly ever wrote and never came to see me. I had trouble with a teacher and with some other boys. I wrote her but she never did anything but tell me to be patient. When I got older and began to get jobs outside of school hours, she became interested in me; but then I gradually began to see that it was for the money I earned. Sometimes I hate her and hope I never see her again. But I think she loves me in her own selfish way, and I still hope that she will be good to me, write me a good letter, be interested in me rather than always in something or somebody else.

A.: What is your very first memory—one of those little scraps long before continuous memory?

P.: I was about 5. It was Mother's birthday. I went in to see her. She was not alone. A man was there talking with her. I was terribly embarrassed and did not know what to say. So I just left. I felt that this was the wrong thing, and I went to my room and cried.

[This expresses in one poignant scene the essentials of his childhood situation and his reactions to it.]

A.: Any other very early memory?

P.: I remember waking up at night and seeing something on a table that scared me. It turned out to be a glove of Mother's.

A.: Have you a recent dream—one last night?

P.: No, but I dream frequently. They are mostly nightmares: somebody is killing people and is going to kill me.

[This seems to indicate strong hostility, probably guilt, and certainly fear, as in the second memory where it is connected with his mother.]

A.: Any other kind?

P.: Well, lately I sometimes dream that Carole is with some other man. I had one crazy one. She was taking care of a little boy about 7 years old, and I had the idea that when he grew up she would be in love with him and have an affair with him, or leave me and marry him.

A.: How do you get on with people?

P.: Quite well. But I'm not easy with people. I have a few fairly close friends. But I guess I'm shy. I just can't be a "hail fellow." I go to parties and meet people, but I don't have much to say. I just don't make acquaintances easily.

Now these pieces fit together very well. The central pathodynamics, as seen in the early history and earliest memories and dreams, describe a pattern that accounts for the delusion of his wife's interest in and love for another man. Charlie's delusion is not really psychotic, for he knows, although he cannot fully believe it, that it is a product of his own mind. His grasp of reality is otherwise sound: The disturbance is circumscribed, confined to this one area in relation to his wife. Apart from this the marriage is excellent. Therefore we can consider this neurotic rather than psychotic.

This neurotic delusional jealousy is the simple, direct continuation of the childhood pattern toward his mother after the loss of his father. The mother was interested in other men and then fell in love with one and married him. Now he continues this pattern of feeling toward his wife. The rage at his mother for this rejection in favor of job and another man is repressed and projected. It appears in the dreams as nightmares of someone's killing others and threatening the patient. This killer is the representation of his own inner repressed rage at his mother, for whose love he still yearns, and at his innocent wife, toward whom he continues the childhood pattern.

Why did these ideas of Charlie's develop immediately after he married Carole, and not while they were going together and even living together out of wedlock? Our guess was confirmed by later material: The reason was that although he was rejected for another and unloved since he was about 5, his healthy core until then gave him the mental strength and maturity to stand this until his marriage. He was able, in other terms, to build defenses against his feelings. He withdrew somewhat from close *emotional* relations with anyone. He kept buried his love needs, his feelings of rejection and frustration, his jealousy and his rage. All was bottled up within him. He never dared give in, even in thought, to his deepest needs— the dependent-love needs for his mother—for if he did, he would suffer the pain and anguish of neglect, rejection, jealousy, and of the rage and hate that these aroused within him. He could not believe that any woman would really love him if his own mother did not and he did not dare to open his hopes and longings to one. Even when Carole lived with him, he could not believe it. But when the ceremony was over, when she had now ultimately given herself to him, the rejected child's deepest love needs could no longer be contained. They welled up and broke through his defenses against them. But with them came all the rest of the pattern: the feelings of neglect and rejection by his mother for another man, who gave nothing, but to whom his mother gave the love that he, the child, so needed and craved. This whole pattern erupted suddenly toward his wife, rather than emerging gradually over some months and years, as is probably more usual.

Lawyers who examine witnesses are reputed to develop over the years quite a sense for whether a person is lying or truthful. The analyst from his professional experience with many persons develops a similar sense for what is going on. Years of experience form a kind of baseline. This is, of course, only a guide. In this case the material seemed clear and convincing, rather than almost impenetrable or vague or only suggestive, as it is in others. But of course I talked with Carole, not once but several times, to get her view of Charlie. It would be dramatic, and a good story, to report that, as she saw it, the impression Charlie gave was false and misleading, but the opposite was true. There were serious difficulties, but not in perceiving the dynamics and the interplay between this husband and wife. What she told and what she related coincided with my impression of Charlie, derived from the first interview with him, and confirmed by many more. Carole herself had had a period of analytic work, and with her permission I talked with her former analyst, who added further corroboration. Of course I was eager to know something of her makeup and of how she may have played up to Charlie's problem. From her former analyst and from herself I learned the following.

Carole had been overprotected by her mother and overly attached to her. This heightened dependent-love need for mother, with an underlying repressed resentment against her, probably formed one of the strong common elements in the dynamics of both Carole and Charlie, made them understand each other, identify with each other, love and marry. I do not mean to oversimplify this. There were other features in the attraction. For example Carole, as a loved child, tried to satisfy her needs vicariously, by rescuing and mothering small animals, and now by rescuing Charlie, who in part was so appealing because of his insecurity about being loved or lovable. At any rate Charlie was completely a one-woman man, and had never gotten close enough to a woman other than Carole, nor risked a rebuff sufficiently, to have ever had any other sexual affair. And Carole was entirely a one-man woman. She had been firmly attached to her mother, but transferred this attachment to Charlie. Defiance or resentment in the form of sexual acting out was not part of her dynamics. She slept with Charlie before they were married only because she was positive in her own mind that they would marry. Or she never would have given him her virginity, which she prized and held for her true love and husband. Her analyst felt sure of this; her associations fully supported the truth of this and revealed no dynamics in behavior, fantasies, or dreams to the contrary. She was another example of fidelity and infidelity being mostly characteristics of the individual personality. Sexual acting out is a favored mechanism of some persons, while others do not have it in their makeups—they have other mechanisms.

Charlie suffered from his jealousy and the rages that went with it. The rage was projected, as we saw in his dream of the killer; and the anxiety in this nightmare and in the second memory was a symptom in real life. His anxiety was increased by the guilt he felt for his hostile outburst at his good, innocent and devoted wife. He attached this anxiety to all sorts of things—fear of thunderstorms, of flying in planes, of bugs; and typical of how irrational man's intellect, of which he is so overweeningly proud, can be, he immediately felt sure that every pain or ache or common cold was cancer, but this did not prevent him from smoking two packs of cigarettes a day.

It is hard not to think then that the human mind, nature's greatest achievement in the development of intellect, at least on this planet, is a biological failure emotionally. The very need for love, intensified because unsatisfied in childhood, led Charlie to do things for which he despised himself—things like suspecting his loyal wife, spying on her, flying into accusatory rages at her. Then he reviled himself for this, consciously in the self-recriminations, unconsciously during sleep in his nightmares and while awake in his depressions and irrational fears and anxieties, which built every minor occurrence into a portent of impending tragedy. His craving for love, his dire need, isolated, alienated and estranged him from others who would have given the love; thus the need, by its own excess, defeated itself. This is one of the greatest ironies of life—. that a wish, by being too strong, too importunate, can prevent its own gratification. Another irony is that the innocent child must pay throughout his entire adult existence for abuses visited upon him through no fault of his own by parents who themselves may have been well meaning.

The difficulty, mentioned above, was in treatment. This was an unusually clear case in many ways. One could hardly find a better example of a person's gaining sharp insight in the very first interview, confirmed by all later material from himself and other sources, but nevertheless reacting with rigid resistance against change. The stubborn fixed pattern only softened through hard analytic work at three meetings a week over a period of three years. Insight alone can be powerfully helpful in some persons but have little effect in others. However, insight is the *sine qua non*, the essential base, for any rational treatment designed to relieve symptoms permanently by changing the underlying pathologic childhood patterns that caused them and by helping the person outgrow these patterns. So the dynamics were clear but the treatment difficult, because Charlie was so fixed for so long in these attitudes and reactions. But gradually he learned to discriminate between what was an appropriate response in childhood to his mother's treatment of him, and what was a proper response in the present situation to his wife.

# V  Some Types of Persons and Circumstances

# 21 FEMME FATALE AND DON JUAN

**Strong feelings, shaped into patterns by how the child is treated, can intensify as well as inhibit or pervert sexuality, as shown in two famous types.**

Sometimes the most charming, alluring, irresistible girls make the most difficult wives. This is apt to be the case when the girl's dependent-love needs have been intensified by her childhood experiences and seek gratification through her feminine sexuality when her needs for parental love take the form of cravings for romantic sexual love. The childish dependent-receptive love needs conflict strongly with the masculine strivings and ideals of aggressiveness, drive and accomplishment.

Edith's father died and her mother had little time for her. The child repressed the pain of rejection and she repressed anger, and the guilt for the anger as well. As she grew up, the full force of her repressed, internally frustrated craving for love was channeled into her feminine desires for love from a man. Thereby she became incredibly appealing—a femme fatale, attaching to her any man she cared to attract. But when she married, the whole pattern emerged toward her husband, as is usual. Within months he became, in her mind, in large part the depriving mother of her childhood. Her mature wifely love was vitiated by the unsatiated demands and rages of her childhood, repressed but never outgrown.

Often the quality of a child, of a little girl, in a woman is itself especially appealing—for various reasons, depending upon the make-up of the man. It often stimulates normal parental protectiveness and the masculine sense of power and mastery. If the girl has much guilt and longing for punishment channeled into her femininity, then male sadism is aroused also. Thus the disturbed childhood patterns, depending on their nature and on the other influences, affect in different ways the sexuality, as well as all other aspects of the personality—inhibiting, warping, deflecting, intensifying.

Besides heightening femininity and masculinity, one of the many other results is the particular exaggeration and distortion that we recognize, usually with mixed feelings, as infatuation. We have mentioned a man, Art (see Chapter 5), whose relations with women repeated his absorption in his mother and his underlying hostile rebellion, resulting in a series of infatuations and escapes. He became infatuated with a girl, but then felt trapped and felt that he must escape from her to preserve his reason. Love and responsibility for a wife were overwhelmed by the childhood pattern—and so he oscillated.

Edith and Art both sought to gratify their hypertrophied dependent-love needs through closeness to the opposite sex. This increased their sexual tension to a bursting point, which made them unusually attractive sexually. Such exaggerations (boy-craziness, or nymphomania, and girl-craziness, or satyriasis) may arise from reinforcement of sexual desire by other emotions also, very often hostility. (We have already remarked that most compulsions express, in some part at least, the pressure of underlying, frequently unconscious, hostility.)

A common result, in the man, is Don Juanism. The particular dynamics that one Don Juan showed was a simple manifestation of the "give-get" interplay. An unattained woman meant to him "get"—the promise of all the closeness he still craved from his mother, now enhanced by full adult sexual desires for the girl. But when she yielded and fell in love with him and looked to *him* for love, sex, affection, responsibility, for the gratification of her own needs—when he was to "give"—then she no longer was all that his childish desires demanded. She now was no longer the giver but the getter. Hence he lost interest and soon felt coldness, even repulsion, for her and felt that she was only a drain upon him, trying somehow to exploit him. And so he would turn to a new girl, seeing in her the old promise, only to go through the same process of disillusionment.

Sometimes he would look backward to one of his earlier, discarded flames who had withdrawn her love from him and, in proportion to her unattainability, would feel increasingly that he had made a terrible mistake in leaving her, that she was, after all, the true love he had been seeking. If he returned to her, and, being tempted, she yielded again, then to her sorrow the pattern would be repeated. Some men with this "give-get" conflict do, however, mature enough to handle the giving and responsibilities of marriage, although sometimes only after disillusionment, irritability, hostility and varying degrees of depression.

*A child may have too much of mother's blessing.*

RAY

# 22 A BACHELOR

A kind of man who is the despair of women, especially in areas where desirable males are outnumbered by females.

One outcome among many of resisted overattachment to the mother is the perennial bachelor. It is probably entirely a matter of the quantitative balance of emotional forces whether the result is this or something quite different. And of course permanent bachelorhood, like everything else, can be a result of many different backgrounds and dynamics. It is a final, common path of various motivations. Art, the man referred to in "Double Bind," who could not bear to be married or to be alone, who could not live with a woman or without one, who was powerfully, irresistably impelled toward one woman, and then equally compelled to escape from her to save his sanity, was a kind of bachelor, an unsuccessful bachelor and an unsuccessful husband, caught between Scylla and Charybdis, caught between magnetic poles of excessive attraction and repulsion.

In contrast was a man we will call Tony. He was attracted to women, to one in particular, but weakly. Far from feeling that living alone was driving him out of his mind, that being alone in an apartment was not to be borne, that to eat dinner alone evenings was torment, Tony relished this life for its peace and freedom. His small apartment was his castle, his retreat, his haven. When I asked him about eating alone in restaurants each evening, he said, "But I am not alone. I have the best of company—the books that I most enjoy reading." Tony was the despair of the nubile beauties. One in particular began an all-out affair with him a few years back, but as mating it progressed no further. Tony felt unwilling and unable to marry her and felt guilty about continuing their relationship. But she clung, still hoping, and he never insisted on breaking off, probably could not quite do so. He feared marriage, feared being

179

tied down, feared being committed forever; he liked the freedom and serenity of his own life. His feelings of loneliness were not strong. His urge toward women in general, toward this woman in particular, and toward living in a marriage were weak. Why?

His central dynamics were these: He was an only child. Upon him was vented the full force of his strong mother's maternal drives. She was a powerful personality, dominating her husband, her home, her only chick. She was controlling and anxious (a common combination). For example, she worried so about his eating that she tried to control it almost to the mouthful. The child reacted against this by losing his appetite, being almost unable to eat at all. Only when he was left alone did he come to enjoy a reasonably normal intake. Small wonder with this conditioning that he continued, though nearing 40 years of age, to prefer dinner alone, with a good book. His mother's satisfaction in his school work was not aggressive and therefore did not cause him to react against it. It "took." He enjoyed intellectual pursuits because they provided an escape.

When I first saw him and inquired about his conflict over marrying the girl (call her Tess), he said he hesitated to marry her because he was not sure of what people would think, whether they would approve of her. I tested him with "How can you care what people think or say? The only question is whether she is right for you. If so, let others think what they will. 'To thine own self be true,' and they will respect you for it." This was enough to start tracing back the "they," which, as anticipated, led to his mother. He was not sure his mother would approve of his choice. His father played almost no part. All paths back from his various current patterns, whether being alone, liking books, being overanxious about his health, taking care about food, preferring solitary restaurant dinners, needing approval for his choice of girls, all led back to Mother.

He had a dream of a man of about his own age marrying a woman in her late sixties. His first thought was, "Does this mean I want to marry my mother? That is strange. I still think of her, though she has been dead ten years. I do want to please her. I fear to go against all she told me. But I always fought with her."

"Why?" I asked.

"I never really knew. But from the time I thought of coming to see you, I've thought quite a bit about my childhood. And I think it

was because of her constant domination and her anxiety about me
—my looks, my health, my food—everything I'm anxious about
now."

This theme led to his defenses against his mother and his wishes
to escape from her orbit, which he failed to realize until he finished
college and started work, that is, until he was out of it enough to
see it. And this lead to his dynamics vis à vis Tess.

She was a girl with a similar unsuccessful masochistic rebellion
against her mother. This similarity was the positive element in
their attraction. Her rebellion had hurt her: the repressed anger
and the guilt had kept her from a good marriage and from a job
worthy of her looks, personality and ability. This corresponded to
the first memory Tony had: he hurt himself on a toy his mother
had given him.

The negative elements in his attraction to Tess lay in those
qualities of hers that appealed to his repressed rebellion against his
mother. Tess was so unlike his mother that his mother would
surely disapprove. She was of different socio-economic and religious
background. But he could not marry her, for she represented defiance of his mother—a defiance of his internalization of her training, her imperatives during his childhood. The mother herself was
dead, but he could not go against her, against his partial identification with her. But equally, his rebellion would not let him marry a
girl who signified giving in to his mother.

Further, he did not really want to marry Tess wholeheartedly
anyway, or any other girl. He liked her because she was totally
apart from his mother, she was weak and needed him, and to his
mind she was not at all a mother figure; she appealed to his
strength and not to his submissiveness. He was attracted in an
adult, masculine, sexual way to her, because she was so novel, so
different from his mother, from all his mother stood for, and from
his own attitudes toward his mother.

But as was indicated by the dream of marrying the elderly
woman (only a small sample of the evidence), part of him had not
relinquished his childhood need for the strong older woman. Tess's
appeal was in being so unlike his mother, but she could not win
against the other part that felt that she was somehow imperfect
and inadequate—because she was *not* the strong mother (and because she did not embody that perfection that his mother wanted
for him, her only child). Such a man usually feels that the strong

woman who represents his mother has no sex appeal whatever. If he tried sex with such a woman, one stronger than himself, he would be impotent in some degree. The weak girl, dependent and submissive to him, arouses his masculinity, including some normal sadism. She is the weaker one; he can do as he will with her sexually; therefore with her he is potent. But she does not satisfy the need for the mother which has not been outgrown.

So Tony was not torn almost asunder like Art, but was almost in balance on dead center. No girl could move him, for she fought an unseen adversary in his own unconscious, the living memories and aftereffects of his deceased mother. In Tony the balance of forces was in equilibrium, so that motivation for change by analytic therapy was insufficient for resolution. He felt no real urge to marry.

*Let me not to the marriage of true minds*
*Admit impediments.*

SHAKESPEARE

*"I know what you are getting married for . . . But are you friends with her? . . . talking and so forth? . . . does she laugh at what you think is funny? . . . you will be young and high-spirited only a little while. How will you get along unless you are friends and like the same kind of jokes?"*

SCOGGINS

# 23 DIFFERENCES IN BACKGROUND: THE "UNSUITABLE" MARRIAGE

Innumerable stories deal with Cinderellas and princes, with waifs and heiresses. Here we seek the part played by the childhood emotional pattern, which has proved so useful a key to feelings between people.

Let us turn to a young man and his sister, three years younger, whose father was from Beacon Hill and whose mother was from Chestnut Hill. They came to Chicago because of business and lived on the North Shore. The family was more than comfortable financially and ranked high socially. The children went to the best private schools. When they were grown, they met leaders in every field and thus had wide connections and many opportunities for good careers.

The son, Lou, started off in a large industrial company and did brilliantly, but resigned. He repeated this in another position. He then got a job on a ranch doing manual work, where he met the daughter of a Mexican laborer. He fell in love and brought her to his home to meet his parents. They were horrified by her manners, her faulty English, her lack of money, her different religion, her background or, in their view, lack of it. A battle ensued, but Lou stood up even to the threat of disinheritance. He thought that his parents' objections to Lillian were to superficialities. To him she was a lovely and a loved child; he thought her natural, genuine, and free—close to the real feelings of people and animals. Not that

183

he could have understood it and put it just that way at the time. He became a Catholic and married her. He served in the war. When I last heard from him he was running a ranch. He and Lillian were extremely happy and had five apparently happy children.

His sister Marian never married and was isolated and lonely. She had been the favorite child, although the parents had loved both children deeply. But the mother, especially, was too protective and restricting and always expected the children to behave perfectly. The children lapped up all the love from the parents and were addicted to it, but to be assured of it they had to be perfect. The children could never express the least anger at their mother or dissatisfaction or withdrawal because she would take this as meaning they hated her. Lou, the less favored one, was able to express some spontaneous feelings in childhood, some self-assertiveness, some hostility. But Marian, being so doted on, needed to keep her parents' adoration, and to do so had to be faultless. When grown she felt totally inadequate for she felt that she had no personality of her own. She lived by subservience, by trying to please everyone, through suppressing her own feelings. She hated this, and therefore she hated herself and she hated everyone. Life, she said, was torment.

Few persons, I think, can survive without breakdown if they have no human relationships. Marian clung to a tenuous stability by working with those on the fringes of society, those on skid row. Marian's hostility came out more masochistically, more toward her own self, than did her brother's, whose rebellion was sufficiently effective and free from guilt for him to achieve a gratifying life. Marian was "loved" more; she felt that to keep this love she must conform more. Hence she could express herself less, and felt more guilty about the natural aggressiveness and hostilities of childhood, about the normal drives to activity, and about the ordinary angers that any child would feel at the inevitable frustrations. (Guilt is in part a product of anger at someone whose love one craves.) Therefore her rebellion was more subterranean; she hurt her parents only through damaging her own life.

But the main dynamics were the same in both brother and sister: To keep their mother's love they had to be flawless and excessively virtuous. This was too extreme for them to tolerate. Without realizing it, they turned against their mother and all the standards to which, with the best of intentions, she tried to mold them. Persons of the same social class and background, such as those with successful businesses, all reminded them of the parental mold and they fled from these in fear and resentment, seeking a life of their own, on their own, seeking their own identity. Whether this can eventuate from a childhood in which the mother (or father or both) was not also in some way hostilely controlling, I do not know. But this outcome in some form or degree is frequent. In another family, for example, a daughter refused an inheritance of some millions, went off on her own, married a teacher of a different background, and had a good life. Her brother stayed close to his parents and repressed his rebellion until he was in his forties when, to the grief of his wife and children, he took to wine and women, in the company of immature companions of dubious probity.

There are several morals to be drawn from this. The chief one for our present concern is that similarities in social, financial, religious, cultural, educational and other areas are not the fundamentals for a happy marriage. True, they can make a marriage—or break it— or prevent it entirely. But differences in background can be the essentials for two persons complementing each other. These factors are not rock bottom—they merely operate in accordance with each person's underlying dynamics.

# VI    Some Hazards of
       Marriage and
       Their Prevention

*Love is to the moral nature exactly what the sun is to the earth.*
                                                        BALZAC

*Deceive not thyself by over-expecting happiness in the married state.*
                                                         FULLER

Adolescent seeking, pregnancy, children and divorce, while not central to our topic of marriage, are so germane to it as to require a few illustrations of several relevant points.

# 24 THE PREMARITAL PERIOD

Something of what can occur while one is young and free and seeking a mate.

Humans are forever caught in a biological instinctual dilemma, being on the one hand promiscuous in the sexual urges but on the other having to fuse these urges with permanent mating to one spouse. Before having to make a commitment to mate and family, can the adolescent not freely enjoy and indulge in sex, or is sex so involved with mature mating that it cannot be for pleasure alone, even in adolescence? If an adolescent is relatively mature, sex will involve urges to find a mate and will not be free; but if there is a lack of maturity, a predominance of disturbed childhood patterns, then these will make trouble in the personal relationship with the partner and thus interfere with the sexual freedom and enjoyment. Although we may want to enjoy sex for itself, it seems that this is impossible because sex is too involved with other instincts and forces in the personality.

Adolescence can be a difficult time. The human organism at about 12 to 14 years of age suddenly feels the full force of the sexual urge. Yet the adolescent has not yet reached full growth or strength and is not yet mature, physically, mentally or emotionally. If this period from the burgeoning of the sex and mating drives until maturity and establishment in career and marriage lasted two or three or four years, it would be difficult enough. In a pioneering or agricultural community a boy of 18 or 19, if mature enough emotionally, could work his own land and provide for a wife and young. But the increasing duration of education means that a boy is 21 before graduating from college, with another three to six more years added if he studies for the professions. This makes him 25 or more before he has even begun his experience in life, before he has even been tested by the responsibilities of the world and of supporting himself and others. Many, as we know, collapse under the first real responsibilities and regress in different ways and degrees, some even so far as to require hospitalization.

What then should adolescents do in the meantime? Some guide to the answers must lie in what they *do* do and in the consequences.

First, as to the boys. We have a double standard. A young man is thought to lack masculinity if he does not have sexual experience, say by about age 21. Some start at 14. But with whom? Experience with a prostitute does not seem a proper initiation into what will be his most valued relationship—that with his wife. But if it is a girl of as high a caliber as he wants his wife to be, will they not become emotionally involved? And, if there is mutual orgasm, will not the full force of the girl's love-needs, mating instincts and maternal urges be aroused? Will she not want marriage? And then will the young man either marry her although not in love with her, or knowing that from the beginning he wanted sex with her but not marriage, will he reject her? And will this rejection not only hurt her, frustrate her deepest instincts, but permanently injure her self-respect and self-esteem? And if the young man is mature, will he not feel this, feel that he has "used" a fine girl, and generate a guilt that may lead him to punish himself, subtly but surely, for a long time? This is in fact a common story.

But between the prostitute and a girl of this sort is there not another type of girl, who will gladly have sexual affairs but with no strings attached? Yes, there is, but the ones I have seen are neurotic, for their sex is split off from their love, mating, reproductive and maternal instincts. A friend of mine once jokingly said he would like to meet a nice masochistic girl, that is, one who would give and suffer. So here we are again. The girl who is available is neurotic, she suffers from a disturbance in development that is not promising for her to achieve a happy marriage.

But cannot sex somehow be freely enjoyed in a setting of friendly companionship without the involvement of the mating instinct, until the right time and the right person comes for this involvement as marriage? A few words are in order in connection with May, whom we met in Chapter 11 as Mel's inamorata.

May was a young woman of average good looks and with all the attractiveness of youth. What made her embroil herself emotionally with a man, who, however interesting, was twice her age and had a wife, five children, and a home that had been established and apparently stable for nearly twenty-five years? Why would she forgo young love and the freshness of starting life with her own man, a man who, like herself, came to marriage unused? This pattern is not, however, unusual. I have seen it in college girls and have followed the later lives of some of them.

One sophomore had a rather half-hearted interest in finding out why, when she wanted so much to marry and have a family as soon as possible after graduation, she should be having heavy affairs now with a series of boys and be sleeping with them. A healthy young junior thought life quite simple: a girl should have her fun while young. Maybe she was right. My own view may be grossly slanted because it is only the people with problems who come to my attention. This girl, so frank, direct, honest and out-going at that time, phoned me from St. Louis some eight years later. She was in a panic—pregnant by a married man and shaken by the realization that, now 28, she was having a continuous series of dead-end affairs, with no marriage in sight. She sensed that somehow her sexuality had broken loose from her mating instincts and she wanted help.

Another college girl went through a period as a freshman when she was so attracted in every way to much older men, between the ages of 40 and 60, that she turned away from them as a defense, as an opposite reaction, when they were friendly to her. Her dynamics showed (among other interplays of motivation) suppressed rebellion against her parents, chiefly her mother.

Then there was an apparently quite normal, controlled girl, Andrea, who also had a penchant for older men. She later moved to another city, but when she was 28 she came back to see me. She had just broken off a clandestine affair with a man of about 45 who had a wife and three children, and now was attracted to a man less than ten years her senior, about whom she had grave doubts. We will call him Al. I referred her to an excellent analyst in Milwaukee, where she lived. Her doubts were justified: Al was a sadist. His ex-wife had not been able to get away; she had felt that her life was in some danger, and would be more acutely so if she made any move. So she took advantage of a visit to the pediatrician as an excuse and left her husband and abandoned her child. Of course Al raised a furor but in the end she was free legally. He pursued her and threatened her until she moved to Canada. The analyst suspected this ex-wife of being paranoid and Andrea also, but it turned out that their fears were realistic.

The girl's material showed a strong masochistic, or self-punishing, tendency. In childhood her hostility was strongly repressed. All was love, yet she had dreams of all sorts of bad things happening to herself. These dreams involved her younger brother. As nearly as could be discerned, the issue reflected an overindulgence, overprotection and overcontrol by her parents, especially her mother, during the first year or two, generating an overstrong dependence on her mother. The arrival of a brother when Andrea was two and the turning of the parental attention toward him therefore caused an intensified hostility in Andrea. But the family's standard of never expressing hostility, only love, caused Andrea's hostility to be repressed. This she was able to do, but at the cost of turning it against herself down underneath.

The psychiatrist did his best to analyze this masochism, but Andrea persisted in acting it out. She married Al despite all she knew about him. The psychiatrist told me that her parents had taken the opportunity to phone him to blast him for trying to prevent their daughter's marriage to the man of her choice, although she had told them her fears soon after the one time they had met him. (If parents can understand and advise after one or two meetings, I admire and applaud their insight and sagacity.) Six months after the marriage Andrea called her psychiatrist again. Her husband's pattern toward his first wife was repeating itself with her. It included physical sadism. She told her psychiatrist this, thanked him for his past efforts to forewarn her, but said she could not come to see him because of fear of her husband. After the war when I saw the psychiatrist, I asked about them, but he had heard nothing further.

In different personalities hostility and guilt take different forms and involve sex in varied ways. Since those people with problems are the only ones who contact me, perhaps other girls whom I do not see find happiness in a series of sexual relations before marriage, or outside it, or in these affairs with older married men. Statistics on this would be interesting. The only generalization I could make, very broadly, from the situations like Andrea's that I have seen or have known about is that a strong sado-masochistic component is the common element, a strong tendency for the love and sex and mating to be deflected into a path that causes suffering, sometimes extreme suffering, to others—to the man, his wife and his children —and punishment to the girl herself. To her, at the time, it is "true love," an infatuation from which nothing can dissuade her. But the truth is that one must use one's head in guiding one's heart because often one's heart is largely directed by darker forces, infantile patterns full of hate and sadism and destructiveness directed to others and to oneself. The head, the ego, the highest powers of reason and judgment must be aware of these or one will, as Wilde wrote, "kill the thing he loves," and himself also.

How sexual freedom before marriage works out is a very complicated matter, and it is just because it is so complex that the outcomes are so individual. This complexity arises from the involvement of sex with other major forces in the total personality.

In the first place sex is a physiological reaction of body to body, but neither body exists without a personality. Sexual intercourse is not, as is often said, a simple bodily function like urination or defecation or eating a meal (anyway, who enjoys eating alone?). It always involves the two personalities. When one's most secret, most utterly egocentric sexual fantasies come to reality, they are always altered by the interplay of the personalities. At least this is true except probably for criminals or schizophrenics, who are incapable of identifying with, feeling with, another person. Putting it most conservatively, it is very difficult to keep personality out of the purely physical act. Sex involves another person; it is part of an interpersonal relation.

This is not surprising, because sex is part of reproduction; further, it is part of the mating instinct. In many species, this is a cooperative undertaking between male and female—building the nest and rearing the young. Whatever the exact underlying instincts for mating may be in human beings, there is no doubt that human children do not mature normally to emotional health unless reared in a secure home by both a father and a mother. I do not mean to say that some excellent adults have not come out of broken homes or orphanages. (In these, good fortune has provided adequate substitutes for the parents.) I am speaking of the base—the complete, loving secure home—and not the exceptional situations. Sexual intercourse is part of the mating instinct, and hence cannot be dealt with as though it were an isolated act. It is sometimes split off, as we have seen, but perhaps this is always or usually pathological in some degree.

In our examples, the problems that arise from trying to satisfy sexual desire as though it were an isolated, independent function emphasize how involved it is with the mating instincts and the total personality. The adult personality is the result of a long development which follows the emotional attachments and reactions of earliest childhood. Thus sexual indulgence is intimately involved with mating and all the other forces in the personality, both the infantile and the mature.

One of the chief of these forces is of course the young child's consuming need for love and care from his mother. And in adults these dependent-love needs usually seek satisfaction from the person who is desired sexually. As we have noted, sexual desire usually follows the original path of the childhood attachment (imprinting, Chapter 2). This is clearly seen in adolescents who normally leave home, but then feel lonely and crave love. This craving is combined with sexual desire, so that their needs for love now include both forces and draw in other motivations as well. If enough of these desires and motivations are drawn in, then they experience the feeling of "being in love." If the infantile forces predominate over the mature ones, then their feeling is an infatuation, implying a certain deficiency in their sense of reality and responsibility and a disregard for the welfare of the "loved" one for that person's own sake.

Some relatively mature personalities do not handle their sexual relations or even their feeling and behavior toward the opposite sex in a mature fashion. This is most clearly seen when sex is used for neurotic "acting out," that is, for following childhood patterns of behavior toward others, rather than sex and mating being expressions of the mature motivations of the healthy adult. Hence sex can express hate (as in lust–murder) or infantile dependence ("clinging vines" or passive, dependent men), grasping ("gold-diggers"), or any other feeling, as well as mature love and responsibility. Sex has "content"; it serves as an outlet, pathway, channel, or drain for every kind of feeling and tension, mature and immature. It is also the great consolation and diversion. Between couples who deeply attract each other it is one of life's culminations. But because of the intrusion of powerful, often disordered, infantile desires into the mature motivations and mating instincts, parents, schools, churches, and others concerned have justified fears lest the adolescent who rides these wild horses may unconsciously and unintentionally cause serious harm to himself or to others.

We mentioned before a college girl who said, "Isn't it strange that I have all these affairs when what I really want is a good marriage and children." A woman may be promiscuous although she wants more than anything else to be a faithful wife and mother. How this can occur is illustrated by a young woman of considerable beauty whom we will give the name of Beryl. The key was expressed in a poignant dream: "In the distance I see my mother; I run toward her. She waves to me and I am overjoyed. But when I get near her, feeling so happy, she looks at me and says, 'Oh, it's *you.*' Then I realize that she had thought that I was my brother."

Beryl longed for marriage, for a husband to love and be loved by, for children and a stable home. Yet, in her mid-twenties, she could say with hyperbole, "I must have gone through a thousand men." She would meet a man and long to be close; soon she would be dating him, sleeping with him and perhaps living with him. But she would want to be *so* close to him that he would feel uneasy and begin to withdraw. This would threaten her and enrage her; she would storm at him in a temper tantrum. He would feel threatened and defensive. Soon she would pick a fight and in a matter of weeks the affair would break up in anger. She was beginning to see this pattern in her own behavior and to see the instability and neuroticism of her various men. Her own pattern was readily traced back through the wreckage of her passionate, turbulent, explosive affairs to the emotional suffering of her childhood. She had a brother, Bart, two years older, who was openly adored by her mother in shameless preference to Beryl. In preadolescence Beryl mentioned this to her mother who confessed that she had always felt something special for Bart. He could do no wrong, Beryl no right. Her father was only a peripheral figure, absorbed in his work. But he had feelings of love for Beryl as a child, and this saved her.

As is so often the case, the partially rejected child becomes overclinging and fights desperately for what is deficient, like a half-starved animal for the succulent food which is so close yet denied. And the constant, unsatiated, emotional hunger sustains a ceaseless underlying resentment, ever ready for bursts of rage. Longing for her mother's love, combined with resentment, produced guilt and the feeling that she deserved punishment. If you must have someone's love and are dependent on him or her, how can you burst out in rage at that intimate person? Hence Beryl's anger stayed subterranean and was mostly vented on herself (like stumbling and hurting oneself when in a rage at another person).

Toward her brother Beryl felt the adoration of the younger

sister, and her longings for his love and affection were increased by her mother's rejection. But she also felt hatred toward him out of envy and jealousy of his being preferred by her mother. All these feelings were eroticized, colored by sexual tones. From an early age Beryl took every opportunity to go nude in front of her brother. Only once however was there any physical contact: when she was about 13 she entered his room nude when he was undressing. They got on the bed but at the first touch panicked. That was the end of any overt eroticism between them and the incident was never mentioned thereafter. But her patterns toward both her mother and her brother underlay Beryl's relations with boys, and they came into the open when she was in her early twenties and went all the way sexually. Then appeared the too intense love needs, the feelings of rejection and frustration, the rage, the picking of fights exactly as with her brother, the final breakup, the intolerable loneliness, the longings for marriage, the new man, and the old cycle. Through it all, however, she was able to work steadily and support herself. If the balance of forces and the choice of analyst are propitious, even problems such as Beryl's can be helped and the girl, despite her wild oats, may find the right man for herself and make a go of the marriage she so deeply wants.

Whether or not there are girls who just have their fun and then, when ready and when they meet the right man, settle down, I know that there are boys like this. Their sexual adventures satisfy a curiosity prior to marriage, and then they are better able to settle down with the wife of their choice. Men are always ready sexually and, willy-nilly, with a woman or not, by wet-dreams or masturbation, will have their emissions with orgastic overflow about three times a week, whether they wish it or fight it. Some who have been embroiled with girls have concluded that it is best to rely on this safety valve and marry as early as possible.

In a way it seems a great loss that youth, as yet uncommitted to the weightier responsibilities of career and family, cannot freely enjoy something which exceeds all other immediate pleasures and culminations as does sex. But humans have many built-in conflicts. Why indeed should sex come in full force before the child is yet an adult? Why should the emotional development be so readily warped by parental influences? Why the hair-trigger readiness to become hostile? Why is sex so detachable from the other instincts that go into mating, reproduction, family life and rearing of young?

On the other hand children raised with good relationships to their parents achieve adequate emotional maturity and become stable, healthy spouses, parents and citizens. Adolescents who play with sex are apt to find that sex and the other potent instincts are playing with them. They are apt to get caught in the grip of their instincts as these forces are handled by their particular individual dynamics.

These dynamics (it seems to me from such observations as have been presented here) are the strongest factor in the long run, assuming a reasonably stable environment. A still young and charming mother feared for her two daughters who were nearing puberty. She feared for their sexual behavior when the urge hit them. In anticipation she was imposing strict moral training in the religious setting of their church. This was fine—if it was done in a way the girls could accept and did not produce the opposite effect by antagonizing them and inciting them to revolt.

Actually the most effective and reliable control over adolescents lies in mutual love, in good feelings between parents and child. This is the great, central fact. Given this, there is little cause to worry about girls or boys injuring themselves or others by their sexual behavior. A teenage girl (let us call her Nina) who always had excellent relations with her parents talked to me easily and freely, in a friendly, social (not professional) relationship. She told me of a girl at her school who had a reputation for sexual looseness and another who was leaving because she was illegitimately pregnant. I said, "Something must be very wrong in those families, in the feelings between those girls and their parents." She replied, "Of course. My friends and I have known that and expected something like this. The girl who is pregnant has a brute for a father. Now he will blame her, but he is the one who should be blamed; he made her like this."

There was no need to worry about this teenager. She knew the physiological facts of life; far more important, she knew the emotional facts, as seen in her remark. And the essential, the real base, was her good relationship with her parents. "Sex education," in the form of explaining to the adolescent where babies come from, is of course almost pointless. Their questions should be answered as soon as they are old enough to ask them; but the parents' tone and attitude are more important than the content. And this tone and attitude will reflect the only real essential: the mutual love and trust that make mutual frankness natural and easy. So long as the girl or boy loves his parents and is sure of their love and can communicate freely with them, talking over any subject with no holds barred, being direct and open about all relations, including those with the opposite sex, because of mutual trust—so long as this kind of child-parent feeling exists, there need not be any worry about the child. That child has no hostility of any consequence toward his parents to deflect toward others to hurt them or toward himself to cause self-injurious masochistic behavior.

Contrariwise, if this mutual love and trust, this free communication between parent and child (and this is a two-way channel) is lacking, then there is no possible way that the parents can control a teenager. A teenager cannot be chaperoned permanently. If he is driven into a feeling of hostility and guilt, he can always surreptitiously find ways for acting out sexually, and in other ways, to the harm of his parents, himself and others he involves.

Nina, the girl just mentioned, controlled her sexuality without difficulty until she graduated from college and married at the age of 21, with all the components of marriage unified and fused, giving herself to the man of her choice with a clear conscience and no apologies, and entering with him into a rich and satisfying love life, resulting, when they were settled, in wanted, loved children. Perhaps other girls freely have all-out sexual affairs but afterwards re-integrate their sexuality with the other components of matrimony and settle down equally well into a stable home life. I do not know what the statistics would show. But I am sure that in the long run the major "destiny which shapes our ends" consists, barring unusual circumstances, in the essential dynamics of the individual personality, the continuation of the earliest emotional reactions to the parents.

*The good can be won; all that we dread can be conquered.*
EPICURUS

# 25 PREMARITAL INTERVIEWS

## Some experience with what can be done clinically to help make better marriages.

The author has found premarital interviews with young men and women to be helpful, particularly in making clear certain points. Many, if not most, young couples, although they may have definitely made up their minds to marry and would let nothing stop them, nevertheless also have certain anxieties and insecurities about taking this step. Sometimes they are not quite clear in their own minds as to what the sources of these doubts are. A few interviews should give them a chance to verbalize some of these anxieties and should help them define them and discover something about their sources.

Many couples do not realize the difficulties of marital adjustment. I would follow those who point out the discrepancy between the Hollywood version of marriage—the glamorous girl and man who live happily ever after—and the actual statistics, which show that for every four marriages in a given year there is one divorce. Obviously brutal destruction of illusions would serve no good purpose; gentle leading to a realistic view is the only safe ground for making the difficult adjustment necessary for marriage. Certainly the differences between fantasy and reality should be clarified and emphasized. The distinction is of vital practical importance. Only a portion of one's fantasies can ever be realized. But if that is known and accepted, then one can pine less for the fantasied potentials and enjoy more fully the actual realities.

It is difficult for youth to have an appreciation of the demands that marriage makes upon one's capacity for giving love, interest and attention and for taking responsibilities within the home. The *New Yorker* cartoon of the young couple standing at the altar, each one thinking of the other one bringing breakfast in bed, is all too typical.

It might be a good idea for the couple to understand the limitation of anyone else's capacity for judging who is a good mate for another person. Harmony is, of course, very largely a matter of how two personalities fit each other. Often it is a matter of how two neuroses fit each other. How the dynamics mesh may be seen frequently in those who seek premarital psychiatric evaluation, exactly as they do a physical examination, even before their engagement. This is, of course, a much better time than after the couple have been engaged for a long period and are on the very brink of marriage.

There are certain possibilities for predicting the success of a marriage. It is well established that the basis of the emotional relationships of adult life is laid in childhood. As we have reiterated, each person follows in his marriage, usually with uncanny precision, the patterns of emotional reactions that he had in early childhood toward members of his own family. Therefore a boy or girl who has had basically good, close relationships with both his parents and with his brothers and sisters can generally be counted upon to have the capacity for a good relationship with his spouse and children. Conversely, a young person who has had disturbed relationships with his parents during his earliest days, weeks, months or years is usually not a good risk. It may be that the balance of forces is such that this person may still turn out to be a good spouse and parent, but there is definite risk involved.

One great difficulty here lies in the fact that a person may have relationships with his parents that appear superficially to be good, but there may be important tensions underneath the surface. One must take into account the fact that every person operates on two levels, and one must try to discover the true deeper feelings and motivations. The years from conception to five or six are the most crucial and of course usually the hardest to find out about. It is then that the core of the personality is laid down. The child who has had excellent relationships within his own family until that age has a healthy base to his personality which is apt to make him good marriage material even though things may have gone wrong after that age.

Electronic computers may yet be very helpful, but they will have to be asked the pertinent questions. My own experience with this is negligible, but the questions I have seen asked of computers were far too superficial and remote from the basic dynamics of a good marriage to be of any real value.

Another difficulty is in the premarital interview itself. Here there is not the same motivation to reveal oneself as there is in treatment. Here there is not the urge to relieve suffering. Instead one or both of the pair may have reason to hide the truth in order to make a good impression.

Perhaps all couples should know the usual course of emotional development in marriage. Most couples are brought together because of identification. This is generally taken to mean similarity of interests but in reality it usually goes much deeper than that. The similarity usually is in the basic emotional needs and drives. Two people may be brought together because they were both deprived, or because they are both hostile to their fathers, or because both of them have an older brother or sister with whom they had problems of competition. Often the more intense the emotion toward the members of their own family (for example, the greater the deprivation each has suffered) the more the couple are brought together, the more they understand each other. So far so good. After marriage, however, the underlying patterns to the parents begin to assert themselves. Now the feelings of deprivation (or other troublesome feelings) begin to be directed toward each other. Each one feels that the other is not doing his part, not giving enough; and keeping to this particular example, the very sense of deprivation in both, which led to their falling in love, now leads to marital disorder.

Couples should be aware of the tendency, often more transparent in girls than in men, of an individual to get into a position that brings suffering. This is seen clearly in the many girls who get themselves involved, sexually or otherwise, with men who never marry them or give them happiness. Often they damage their reputations because of the relationship. If marriage is achieved it is very often with a man who is in some way sadistic, usually unconsciously so. One hears again and again of cases in which the husband treats his wife shabbily and drives her into a nervous breakdown or to the verge of it, or else makes her life miserable. Not infrequently, however, this is the responsibility of the wife in that she picked this particular kind of a man to marry because of a masochistic trend within herself. In addition to that she sometimes, by her own behavior, brings the man's sadism out by subtly provoking him. Of course men have this tendency also. The important point here is that neither one of the couple should make a neurotic, especially a masochistic, choice of a partner.

Another point, often closely related to this is the matter of ulterior motives. Sometimes there is more of an element of winning prestige or money through a marriage than the young person may be conscious of. Sometimes, particularly in girls, there is an element of escaping from an unhappy home. If these motives can be frankly expressed and discussed, the marriage starts off on a much better basis and a great deal of the undercurrent of guilt is obviated. This is of first importance because the tendency to make oneself unhappy stems largely from feelings of guilt—deep-lying guilt toward one's parents and also currently generated guilt within a marriage.

It usually seems to be healthy if each individual of the couple is able to discuss in a private interview something of his whole philosophy of sexual relations and his past experiences. This is borne out by the Kinsey report, which shows that without treatment sexual patterns seem to change not at all in the course of people's lives.

The "helpability" of emotional problems should be pointed out. The psychiatrist sees many couples who come to him after years of strife and who are on the verge of divorce, or after divorce has already occurred to the detriment of themselves and the futures of their children. Yet the basic emotional difficulties are frequently found to be perfectly solvable problems, and much of their suffering could have been prevented if they had sought help earlier. They should know that if things do not go well, it does not mean that the marriage has been basically a mistake and a failure. Sometimes the difficulty is rather deep-seated, and considerable treatment is necessary (as in most of the marriages described in this book). But in many others the main point can be reached in a relatively short time and sometimes simply a few interviews with a good person or treatment over a few weeks or a few months can be of appreciable help. Many young people are astounded to learn that the personality and motivations of an individual are not utterly fixed and unalterable and that with help significant steps can often be achieved toward adjustment and maturity. It is, as we have stressed, a matter of the balance of forces, within each individual and between the two persons.

# 26 AN INCIDENT OF PREGNANCY

The meaning of "reactive" in a situation that unbalances the "give-get" equilibrium.

This book is primarily about husbands and wives, but we cannot neglect mention, however brief, of the great biological upshot of it all.

We distinguish *internal* disorders from ones that are chiefly *reactive* to forces of external circumstances. Some persons are or become disturbed, may even break down, under the most favorable conditions of life, no matter how kindly fate has treated them. Others remain stable in the face of outrageous fortune.

I had known Rosamond, as we will call her, since her girlhood. She had a fine figure and a pretty face. She was especially attractive in her healthiness, wholesomeness and good sense. She found her man—one of similar qualities—and they married and had three children in rapid succession. Roland was a good husband and father. He provided a small house and car and whatever the children needed, but never earned enough for Rosamond to have help with the house or children. Together they did everything, being skillful with maintenance of all kinds—painting, upholstering and the like. The children thrived and were healthy, bright and athletic. As they grew older Rosamond had a little time for her friends. One thing that I could tell she missed was vacations, just getting away from the same old show. Summertime was better, because then she could get in some tennis at the neighborhood courts. So their lives passed in a routine way that some might consider humdrum.

In the midst of my dinner one evening Roland phoned and told me that Rosamond was weeping uncontrollably and was wild. I asked if she would speak to me on the phone. She did. I listened for a few minutes, told her I would be free after dinner, and asked her to come over with Roland in about three-quarters of an hour. This was deliberate on my part. I had judged that nothing dire would happen at the moment, and conveyed this reassurance by asking her to come a little later rather than immediately.

They arrived. I asked Roland to wait while I talked privately with Rosamond. She was upset all right. She was wild. She was not uncontrolled but was too near it for comfort. I knew her as a stable person and could not believe all this upset was from inner reasons; but human nature is full of surprises. By now the reader will have guessed the answer. This extreme hysterical state, which her husband thought was rather psychotic and was indeed so unlike her usual self that it could be called "out of her mind," was a violent reaction to the fact that her menstrual period had not occurred. The core of the reaction was unmitigated fear and rage—in general and at Roland in particular, whom she blamed for this.

Their children were now 14, 12, and 10. Rosamond had been a good mother and wife and for sixteen years had discharged all her responsibilities, effectively but without relief and with very little time or legitimate indulgence for herself. It had been a simple life, a good life, but her "give-get" equilibrium had been out of balance —too much unremitting give, too little appropriate get. She had been strong, stable, loving, uncomplaining. But she had been incubating her plans. With the youngest now 10, she felt she could get out of the house some at last. She had found a position in an active small business. Here she felt unchained from the kitchen; she felt free; she had an outside interest. She saw new faces and was immersed in a larger interplay of relationships with varied persons. She had found hard-earned partial freedom, variety, interest, change. For her, life was beginning at 40.

And then the thunderclap. Was she to lose all this and go back to the unrelieved restrictions and demands of pregnancy, home and a small baby all over again? Her new life, for which she had worked long and hard and which was in all ways deserved and proper, suddenly at one stroke was threatened with destruction. If she lost it, she would be 50 years old before she would again have an opportunity for this sweet and precious share of partial freedom. She felt trapped. And in truth she *was* trapped—by the crude physiology of reproduction and the prospective years of mothering.

She gave me permission to have a few words with Roland. He could not believe that Rosamond could be so upset over being pregnant, because he thought that women were delighted to have children. Of course I suggested a laboratory test as soon as the result would be significant. It came back negative, as is not infrequent in such cases. Thus the problem was resolved, and they returned peacefully to their fourth decade of life and are now well into their sixth.

In this instance I have not given Rosamond's "nuclear emotional pattern," her main dynamics and the "specific emotional vulnerability" which her missed menstrual period and supposed pregnancy struck. The reason is that it was not indicated to explore this in the emergency interview with her, in fact it was strongly contraindicated. To go into it would have gained little at that point and probably would only have upset her even more, by shaking her self-confidence and distracting her from the external situation that so upset her. It was far better to treat this as a normal, intelligible reaction to a difficult situation which could be dealt with. In such cases it is a matter of looking into the externals before thinking of changing the patient to help her handle them. Can life be changed to fit the patient or must the patient change to fit an unalterable situation? Is the problem chiefly reactive to external difficulties or is it mostly internal? These questions are always among the first in the mind of the psychiatrist.

# 27 THE CHILDREN

"Whatever happens, it is the children who suffer."

Often it is through the children that I see the parents and their problems. Almost invariably a child's symptoms are in reaction to pressures, conflicts and tensions of some kind in the home. There are unmistakable, sometimes dramatic, exceptions. Pressures from outside the home affected the emotional equilibrium of one boy so seriously that sending him to a hospital was under consideration. This was a baffling problem, for the marriage and the home were in all ways far too sound, healthy and harmonious for a reaction of such severity. This I told the parents, but I insisted that there simply had to be something traumatic enough to cause this gross upset. It was discovered, after a rather assiduous search, that he had been beaten up, since the age of about two years, by a neighbor's child, only a year older but much bigger and stronger. Once we detected the cause, and separated the boy from his "friend," his improvement was, fortunately, dramatic and complete, and has held ever since. But he still becomes upset when he has any contact with the other boy. The parents themselves gradually were able to discuss with their son the whole situation, so that he had the protection of insight into it.

The wholesome home life won out. The principle of investigation was the same: exploration of the problem with one parent or both. Sometimes the mistreatment is at the hand of a nurse or someone else close to or responsible for the child. But most often the trail leads to strain and contention within the home. This may be because of others in the home, like one or both grandparents or other relatives; but in the majority of cases it is the treatment of the child by one or both parents or the emotional situation between the parents.

Jimmie and Janet were conscientious parents. Their oldest child, Jill, about 9, was beginning to have nightmares and was somewhat anxious; her *joie de vivre* was diminished; she was less outgoing, even a little withdrawn; and eventually her grades in school began to drop alarmingly from their usual high level. The parents called me. Rather than seeing the child, I asked them to come in first to tell me how it all looked to them.

By the time I met Jill, what she was reacting to had become pretty clear from my talks with her parents. As in most cases, it is much more important to remove, correct or at least diminish the source and cause of the trouble—conflict between the parents—than it is to treat the child. It was a fascinating experience to run a clinic for children, in which I met and got to know each child a little, but in which the basic treatment was only with the parents. The results were most gratifying. Sometimes, as with Jill, it is mostly a matter of reducing the contention between the parents. In other cases it involves dealing with the mother's or father's feelings, attitudes and treatment of the children. Sometimes one parent or both are merely misguided and require some education. At the other extreme, one parent is incorrigible, and more must be done therapeutically with the child to help him understand what he is reacting to, and how to use his insights in order to develop properly in spite of the particular situation with the parent.

For some years I was puzzled as to just why children seem to react with such upset to conflict and hostility between their parents, even if the parents both unquestionably love the child dearly and the child has good relations with both of them. Now it seems to me that most generally this is because of the child's conflict of identifications. As we have mentioned, we relate to other persons as objects (of dependence, love, hate, sex and so on) or by identification (feeling with them, imitating them, taking over their attitudes, empathizing with them, introjecting or taking them into one's own mind). If the parents are in serious conflict, if there is much hostility between them, the child is torn. His dependent-love needs are satisfied well enough, if the parents both love him, as Jimmie and Janet loved Jill. But Jill could not use the usual paths of identification in her emotional maturing; she could not use them as patterns of adult maturity for her to grow into. For if she identified with one parent she was hostile to the other. In order to avoid taking sides, she withdrew from identifying; thus she lost much of this very important way of relating to her parents and of following this line of *being like* them as a road to maturation.

A further deleterious effect on the child is the view of marriage he obtains from the friction between the parents. Here again if this occurs early enough in his life and is sufficiently severe and prolonged, then, as from all strong early influences, an emotionally-based concept of each parent and of marriage is formed in the child's mind; and these early "imagoes" of the parents and of others important to the child and the concepts of their emotional relations, once formed, are probably never erased. The child may thus grow up with a view that marriage is frustrating and hostile rather than loving and harmonious. And if the child does identify with one or both parents in this relationship, then the child to this extent brings feelings of frustration and hostility to his own spouse.

In view of such considerations, I was eager to meet Jill but not to advise treatment unless the interview very strongly indicated it. It is good for a child to have a psychiatrist as an understanding friend, but only provided he is exactly the right psychiatrist. At least as much as in the rest of medicine, the motto is *primum non nocere*, the first duty of treatment is to do no harm. We would much rather see problems within the family resolved within the family. We want to keep the parents as the main confidants and supports of the child. They are there all the time, through most of the child's life. And it is more natural for the child to solve his problems with his parents.

This need not deny the child any insights that psychiatry* can contribute, but the insights mostly can be imparted by the parents. The parents will achieve them by working with the psychiatrist on

* The term psychiatry, as used here, always refers to dynamic psychiatry, that is, to psychological understanding and treatment based upon psychodynamics. Psychodynamics is the embryonic science of emotional motivation and reaction—the understanding of a person, his childish and mature impulses, in adjustment and maladjustment, in emotional health and in disorder. Freud made the great breakthrough in his discoveries, and now there are further contributions from all the sciences of the personality and behavior. Because of these further developments and contributions and because many analysts strongly prefer to use the term psychoanalysis in its narrow sense, restricted not only by theory but by the mechanics of treatment (for example, frequency of meetings, use of a couch), it seems less controversial and more correct to use here the broad terms dynamic psychiatry and psychodynamics. Our purpose is insight, understanding and treatment that is based upon the dynamics of the individual.

their own difficulties, and also by direct discussions of the child with the psychiatrist, who can suggest the insights and how to convey them to the child. This usually improves parent-child relations in an effective and natural way and helps the emotional growth of all concerned. Usually the parents will not give insights as the psychiatrist would; they will mostly work them into dinner table or bedtime conversations, and often they will do it indirectly by discussing some other person or a character on television or in the comic strips. By such natural methods even the smallest children can be reached, with the parents always biding their time and waiting for the proper moments.

Of course I mean all this as realistically and flexibly as possible but shall not go into detail, because our purpose is not a treatise on technique. Sometimes it is best for one psychiatrist alone to handle a marital problem, but more often the complications of so doing outweigh the advantages. Sometimes occasional visits of the child to the psychiatrist are indicated—to the psychiatrist of both parents, or, when they have different psychiatrists, to one or to the other. Sometimes it is best for the child to see a psychiatrist of his own. The child's visits, to whomever, are sometimes best kept few and far between, but in other instances systematic treatment for the child is indicated. In these cases the psychiatrist should determine whether or not the parents are to some extent trying to unload onto him their own responsibilities for the child. The basic principle in all treatment is clear: *Understand the patient.* In dealing with family problems it is a matter of understanding each of the personalities and the emotional interactions between them.

*Everything that dies dies by its own corruption; all that injures is within.*

MENANDER

*It is not marriage that fails, it is people that fail. All that marriage does is to show people up.*

FOSDICK

# 28 A DIVORCE AND THE CHOICE OF MATE

## A marital failure raises the question of whether age and experience help appreciably in selecting a wife or husband.

It is a commonplace to say that we must make the most important decision of our lives, the choice of a mate, when we are too inexperienced and too suffused with sex and other feelings to have good judgment. That is certainly true. But I am not at all sure that after many more years of living one would choose any better. This is reflected in the well-known recognition that when people remarry, their second mate usually turns out to be remarkably similar to the first. However this is by no means always so. It probably depends on the strength and fixity of the underlying disturbed childhood pattern.

One girl, Eve, tall, willowy and shy, was from a home in which the father disdained the mother, and the mother was so masochistically submissive to him, so doormatish, that the girl could not respect her. When a senior in college, Eve fell in love with a superior young man, Reed, who was starting off well with a large firm. Passionately attracted to each other, they slept together for some months before they married. But sex is as sensitive as it is powerful. Since their meeting, he had been irresistible to her. Now, the instant they were married, she lost her desire for him.

However, in time her sexual feelings returned and the whole relationship settled down into a happier marriage than the average. They were especially happy with their two sons. Reed was killed in the last months of the war. Eve continued to live in Chicago, but once when she was in this area she came in to see me and told the rest of her story.

"Two years after Reed's death I married. Clarence [as we will call the new husband] seemed stable and devoted to me and the boys. But in a matter of months marriage with him turned out to be impossible. Clarence was just a complainer. We agreed in a friendly way on a divorce. Of course I know that any friendly agreement is against the law. It is collusion, and no ethical lawyer will touch the case. The law in this area apparently is not designed to keep the peace. It insists that divorce must be a hostile, antagonistic, punitive process. But Clarence and I decided to remain friendly and just leave the law to the lawyers."

Eve was right, of course. The only criterion for divorce in all states is *guilt*. The form of the guilt is called grounds. A new approach is gaining acceptance: to handle delinquent spouses much as delinquent children are handled—not by examining the guilt of the defendant, but by seeking the basic causative factors and trying to remove them by the use of all necessary specialists from all disciplines. The criteria of the juvenile courts, set by law and philosophy, are not guilt and punishment but what protects society and is best for the child. That of the divorce court would be what protects society and is best for the family and each of its members.

"I don't think it was the lawyers," Eve continued, "but Clarence's own make-up that turned it into a contest. But the lawyers helped. I don't blame them too much; each was honestly trying to guard his own client's interest. Anyway, somehow Clarence felt I was holding out on him, insulting him or something. I wanted nothing—no money—only freedom for myself and the boys, just to correct a mistake. But he took it personally. He gradually changed his mind about our friendly agreement and decided to contest the divorce. It made me physically nauseated to line up every complaint I could think of against him, but I had to do it. Before we married my lawyer had insisted on a prenuptial agreement to protect what I had from Reed. I told him at that time I just couldn't ask that of a man I was about to marry, a man I thought loved me and the boys and whom I loved. But fortunately the lawyer insisted and Clarence quite willingly signed.

"Once I said to him in the midst of all this, 'We've been married less than a year. We know it was a mistake. Why do you oppose this divorce? You prevent yourself from being free, and it is a terrible situation for me and the boys. You get no advantage. Why do you contest it?'

"He said, 'Because I get the satisfaction of hurting you and preventing you from ever marrying anyone else.' I guess he was a psychological sadist. I guess this was what you call 'passive aggression.' "

In the end it was a dirty business because of Clarence's make-up and because of the archaic divorce laws. At last Eve was free, after much ordeal and expense. Her years of living had not enabled her to make a better choice than when she was a young protected college girl. Is this not true of almost everyone? Of course her judgment of Clarence was no doubt influenced by her eagerness to marry—to have a husband, a father for the children, increased financial security, and everything else that a man gives a home. But then is not almost everyone's judgment strongly colored by something, if only strong emotions, when it comes down to choice of mate?

Three years later Eve wrote me as follows:

"The two years after the divorce were hell. But now I'm married again—to a good guy. I've waited for a year to write you just to be sure this one was for keeps. It's not perfect, but neither was it so with Reed. It's good though, and I'm lucky and happy. It surprises me, because Eric is ten years older than I am, and I thought he was a confirmed bachelor and that something was wrong with him because he'd never married. But he is okay sexually and is not only devoted but thrilled with suddenly having a wife and two grown sons. I just hope his burst of family enthusiasm doesn't lead him to insist on a baby."

*You get love by giving it—not by demanding it.*

# 29 MATURE LOVE

One may be called on to protect one's mate, not from external dangers, but against something within.

When someone asks me what kinds of people and problems I see professionally, I usually say, "I have an office practice, not a hospital practice. I see the everyday problems of everyday people—like you and me." Those I am privileged to see and help are by and large quite superior persons. Whatever beneath the surface is causing trouble, in their egos they have maturity, compassion, courage, emotional honesty and other fine attributes. I do not like the term "patient," although we are in a patient-doctor relationship, for mostly we are not dealing with "sickness" in the usual sense of the word. We deal with human beings, whose problems have mostly arisen from childhood patterns generated by their parents, as they interact with the circumstances that fate and they (consciously or unconsciously) have gotten themselves into.

These people are helped by insight, by a largely educational procedure that exposes the more or less hidden roots of their problems and enables them to help themselves. Most problems are basically in human relations, in feelings toward others. The relation to the analyst is a sample human relation. Childhood patterns are transferred to him, along with the mature, realistic feelings and judgment. This is the transference. What is solved in miniature in analysis is like a vaccination that protects the *analysand* from life's more trying emotional burdens (the term "analysand" is in many ways a more suitable appellation than the term "patient"). Insofar as the disturbing elements can be "analyzed out" of the relation with the analyst, so that only good, free, easy, friendly mature feelings remain, then the analysand has a workable model and experience for use in his relations with other people in his life. Basically analysis is simply emotional honesty, and very often requires a certain nobility.

214

A man with some feelings of insecurity, inferiority and anxiety, despite his outward success, was telling me about his home life. "I recognize," he said, "my wife's very fine qualities, but something in her make-up makes her charming to everyone except me. People all praise her. Besides charm, they tell me of her maturity of judgment and her realism, how efficient and practical she is, and how kind, considerate and thoughtful she is. But toward me she shows none of these feelings. We used to have a loving relationship. But in the past few years she has shown, more and more, only criticism and anger toward me. It's gotten to where nothing I do is right. She sarcastically twists my kindest words around. If I am quiet with the children, she tells me I am neglecting them; if I play with them, she scoffs, 'Just another child.'

"For years I've tried to overcome her hostility to me by giving her so much attention, consideration and affection that she would be forced to soften. This worked for a little while only. Recently she has wanted a divorce. I myself have now come to feel, 'Get it and good riddance.' But I can't go through with it. For I know that she is a child underneath. She acts so independent, but I do not believe she could survive without me. What you said is so true: People usually hate a person they are dependent on. And I think she is a masochist. I think a divorce would destroy her and all she has in life in her present position.

"As I visualize such a future, I could not let her do that to herself. I live in a constant stream of hostility from her; but as I see it I have no choice but to be strong and stand it, for if I reacted as she wants me to, she would ruin her life. It is not easy for me, for I need much love. I had a lot in childhood, as I told you, and also a lot since. But I could not cause her the pain of jealousy or deal her such a blow, nor can I let her isolate and destroy herself. You once mentioned a Norse god who was a god because he could live without love. I can understand that now, unfortunately."

Perhaps this man was wrong in his judgment. Perhaps his wife would have thrived and prospered after a divorce. I think, though, from other information I had, that he was right. But even if he misread his wife's behavior, can we not take heart about human beings from this kind of mature love for another? Of course, when faced with such a marriage, the analyst also thinks about this man's own possible masochism, thinks that perhaps he kept himself unconsciously in a deprived position, the butt of hostility out of inner needs for punishment, some unknown guilt perhaps. But masochism has never been evident in his previous life with his wife or with others, or in his dreams. From all that could be learned, he did what he did out of mature love.

# VII    Some Rapid Resolutions

Fascinating as are the processes and problems of treatment, they concern us only insofar as they illuminate the dynamics of marriage. Three examples at different ages show that when the emotional forces are in favorable balance they can tilt very quickly toward improvement in a person or in a marriage.

# 30 IN ADOLESCENCE

A blitz-analysis in which one burst of insight enabled masculine pride in independence to conquer dependence on a girl.

A young college man, Ray, had felt so fatigued for two weeks that he could hardly move. Although he was an athlete, he could now hardly walk for more than a few minutes. College had begun but he felt unable to leave home to attend. Nothing in the routine of the interview provided any clue to the trouble. Asked about present relationships he said these were fine. Girls? Fine, too. But I noticed a slight hesitation. He tried to pass it off, but I insisted. I had to force his response. Finally he blurted out, "I had my first sexual affair with a girl this summer. She ended it a few weeks ago. One day I met her in a store. I just saw her, but I could tell somehow or other that she had slept with an older man she had told me about—a man of about 40 who is married and is very successful. I asked her and she admitted it." I let him pour out the details for a bit. Apparently his need for a woman, including all-out sexual relations, was intense. But he doubted seriously that any other girl would have an affair with him. Losing her, he thought he would have no girl for sex. He was not ready or financially able to marry, nor would he have married this girl anyway. "Where does the girl live?" I asked. "Just a few blocks from me," he said, and then he started—almost jumped. "What!" he exclaimed, "You aren't saying that all this is because I want to be near *her!*" That was sufficient. His pride was strong. To think that he was still dependent on a girl who met his devotion by tossing him over for a middle-aged man, or for anybody! It was unbearable, unthinkable. Shocked at himself, he was jolted back to his usual self. He left, told his parents he was straightened out, and shot back to college without delay.

Of course what had happened was that he had been in the midst of an adolescent rebellion against his own submissive dependence upon his parents, especially his mother. Intensely conscious only of the powerful sexual attraction to the girl, he had, all unconsciously, developed the same dependence on her. When the interview made him aware of it, it hurt his pride painfully and mobilized the full force of his rebellion and assertion of independence. It was a successful "blitz-analysis." The result held, but after graduation he returned to go into the whole conflict more thoroughly and did very well in outgrowing the tendencies to become submissive and dependent on others. He no longer needed to show his independence only by fighting his tendency to be dependent. As he genuinely grew to be more independent, his hostilities diminished and he could relax and enjoy life more and more.

# 31 IN MIDSTREAM

How a shaft of insight, in a person who is ready to use it, can rout an alarming symptom and start the person resolving his personal and marital problems.

It has frequently been remarked that the deeper working of the human mind only becomes comprehensible through its struggles with suffering. Certainly if one but listens openly, with relative freedom from preconceptions and clichés, to patients who come for relief from psychic pain, one hears many fundamentals clearly and directly stated with but little disguise. Certainly one quickly grasps the meaning of feeling and thoughts being unconscious or more or less unconscious.

Sylvia was an attractive woman of 40, married, with two sons, 10 and 12. When she came to see me with the common complaints of anxiety and depression, I wanted to hear her story as she would spontaneously present it; and I had in mind supplementing what she told me with the usual data used for dynamic understanding: a picture of her present life, recent dreams, early childhood (0 to 6) emotional pattern in her family, earliest memories and the course her life had taken. But the main point was quickly reached.

Patient: I have been tense for some time—really some years I guess, but worse in the last six months. I've come to see you because now I've been snapping at the children, and I can't stand the thought of hurting them. I know the most sensitive time is before the age of 6, but I can't believe it won't hurt them at this age too, to have a grouchy, ill-tempered mother. I notice my feelings in the rest of my life also, but do my best not to show them. We have many friends, including a few good close ones. I do a lot of things in our church and community. We play tennis regularly. We are in perfect health and have a good life. It seems silly to feel this way.

Analyst: Will you tell a little more about your relationship with your husband?

P.: He is a fine person, devoted to me and the children. There is some tension there though. I feel I can never entirely please him. He is always somewhat dissatisfied, no matter what. He comes home in a reasonable mood but pretty soon he acts cranky and critical. He may even flare up some and then apologize. His apology is sincere enough, but this goes on and on. [She seems angrier and angrier as she talks.] He is a lawyer, and makes occasional out-of-town trips. . . .

A.: Why do you stop?

P.: [Hesitatingly] I can hardly believe what I'm saying—that I'm really glad when he goes; it's a relief. But I miss him when he's gone. I want him back, but when he comes, I get tense and wrought up again. . . .

A.: Again you are silent. Is this hard to tell?

P.: Yes. It is awful. I feel so disloyal. And I feel I'm invading his privacy and mine.

A.: We might pay a little attention to why you feel this way about what really amounts to simply being honest about your feelings. But I can easily understand your hesitation about this in a new situation, and will try to make it as easy as I can for you.

P.: I guess you're interested in dreams.

A.: Very much so. [Not infrequently in approaching feelings which are difficult to face, a person goes to a dream. And this dream usually reveals in disguised form what is being held back. Therefore I am glad to digress to the dream.]

P.: In a dream I had about two weeks ago the boys and I were at the tennis court, chatting and happy. Then we noticed a log there. But it turned out to be a big dog. It seemed to be friendly, but then I thought it was dangerous and might attack us.

A.: What does the dog make you think of?

P.: About a year ago we had a dog. He was quite a problem in the house—house-breaking, worms, ticks, everything. It was more than Myron, my husband, could take. He tried so hard to be patient, but he lost his temper and I lost mine. I shouldn't blame him, but he makes me so tense. We really have a very good marriage but. . . .

A.: Again you are silent. The associations to the dog lead again right to anger at your husband. Could it be that you have not quite wanted to face the truth about this? Is it possible that his making you tense really means that he makes you angry, and that your anxiety and depression are the result of bottled up anger at him, which you have not fully acknowledged and which just simmers?

P.: [Here is one of those significant expressions and pauses which are difficult to depict, but which show that a psychic reality has been touched, often show it more clearly than the words that follow.] Maybe it could be. Maybe I've sort of sensed something like this for some time.

A.: If it is so, then we should discuss it further in another visit. And also, should I not meet your husband? Would he come?

P.: I think so. He is really a fine person. He is away on a trip now. As soon as he returns I'll ask him to phone you.

[It is always interesting to see this more or less conscious awareness. In this case it is awareness of the anger at the husband. One might see it the other way round, as more or less unconscious. Technically, it would be called preconscious. In ordinary language, Sylvia dimly sensed but did not fully recognize her anger at Myron, and she had no realization of its intensity, which must have been strong in order to produce her symptoms of tension, anxiety and depression.]

When he came to see me, Myron, of middle height, stocky and pleasant, began the interview with no reluctance.

P.: I am really very anxious to talk with you. I wanted to do so anyway, because I've had an experience that has really scared me. I haven't told my wife because I haven't wanted to upset her, but I thought I had a heart attack. A week ago I suddenly felt my heart pound and was short of breath. I took my pulse and it was about 120. I went to see my doctor. He examined me and said there was nothing wrong with my heart and that he thought there was nothing wrong physically at all, but that this was from nervous tension. I haven't had it since then.

A.: What was going on when it occurred?

P.: Nothing. I was dressing for dinner after a board meeting.

A.: What was that?

P.: You know I'm a lawyer. I do mostly corporation law. I have to do with mergers, reorganizations and the like. As a result, I'm on the boards of some companies.

A.: And?

P.: This was an important meeting. I had an important part in it. There was a lot of hostility and aggressive talk. I got quite a lot of it and was pretty strongly attacked, but not all openly and directly. I tried to relax and forget it when I returned to the hotel to get ready for dinner. That's when this attack came.

A.: Were you aware of being irritated or angry yourself?

P.: I was aware of being tense. Actually I've been tense ever since my mother died six months ago. I've always been rather tense, but it's been much worse for these six months.

A.: What kind of feeling do you think is causing this tenseness?

P.: I don't know, but it may be irritability. I must admit I've been awfully irritable, mostly with my family. I try to control it, but find myself snapping at my wife and even at the children. I feel very bad about it, but I find myself being critical and irritable, and sometimes I flare up without meaning to. When I come home after work I'm so tired I can hardly move. When I feel nervous I'm a little short of breath. But I had a complete physical, with X-rays, electrocardiogram and blood tests, and everything is normal.

A.: Have you any more ideas about the tension? How do you get on in all aspects of your life?

P.: I get on fine. Basically we have an excellent marriage. We have good friends. And I get along fine in my law firm. We enjoy the theater and tennis and have a good life. I work hard but not too much and I thoroughly enjoy it. I have a front row seat in American business. As to tension, I only know I've been more tense since my mother died.

A.: Please tell about that relationship, including earliest childhood.

P.: My father was killed in a car accident when I was 12. My sister was 20 at that time and she married a year later. I lived with my mother. Mother did some work in the home and for the rest we got by on my father's insurance. Mother was extremely dependent on me, especially when I got a little older. She did nothing without me. She was very strict. I always tried to please her but it was a struggle. She acted as though her life depended on me. I got engaged to a girl but I was so irritable because of living with Mother that I broke it off. Finally I did marry Sylvia. Mother did not approve. She never got along with Sylvia or even with the children. But Mother felt that *they* did not like *her,* and felt very unhappy about this. I tried my best. I did everything I could to make Mother happy and comfortable, but it was never enough. She would only have been happy if I had left my wife and children and come back to live with her, but this she did not really want.

A.: Go on.

P.: I always have some fear of not being competent enough, although I know that in actuality I am. And I am really very happily married and have fine youngsters. But I am tense.

A.: Tell a little of the emotional relations in your earliest years, before 6.

P. My sister was eight years older than I. Father was with a very large company and worked almost all the time. So I was close to Mother—very close. Father was swell, so warm, so friendly and understanding; but Mother was the power in the house. She made all the decisions. She worked hard. She was bossy and very strict and directing. But she was very kind and I was very fond of her. She wanted me to be proper, to be a fine man, to look right, speak right, do right, and I wanted to also, and did. I would have paid quite a price if I hadn't. Father was fine and easy, never a cross word to me. We got on perfectly, really loved each other. But Mother was never happy. She was helpful to others, but strict and critical. As I tell you this I can see that one of the strains in my marriage is because I tend to be like Mother in being too strict with my children. The children's real warmth goes to my wife much more than to me. It's the same with our friends. They are loyal to me and respect me, but their warmth goes to Sylvia.

A.: What are your very first memories?

P.: The earliest is of being carried or taken along by the hand, by Mother. Then I have one of doing something for Father and being very happy.

[Here the two themes are clearly portrayed—with Mother, but directed by her; with Father, but doing something for him and happy in the relationship.]

A.: Did you dream last night?

P.: I do remember a dream of a few nights ago. In it I was living with my mother. It was a beautiful place. I was wandering in the garden and had to be careful of the flowers. Meanwhile Mother was cooking dinner for us.

A.: Does this make you think of anything?

P.: No. Well, it's not my home. That's all.

A.: What do you mean?

P.: I think of being irritable in my home. That's all.

A.: About what do you think you are irritable there?

P.: It just occurred to—maybe—hm! I'll be damned—maybe—maybe because people are not treating me the way Mother used to.

[With this tears flow. He must use his handkerchief. A sensitive area has certainly been touched.]

If the house is not picked up, neat and in order, or if someone is thoughtless, or if they don't look after me as Mother did—yes—then I get tense and irritable. And in the office too. There's always a little tension. If all is smooth I don't notice it; but if anything goes wrong then I feel it. I try to build a tolerance of others.

A.: Because you cannot expect others to behave toward you as your mother did?

P.: True. I was the only son and felt the pressure as though I were an only child. I used to pray for a little brother or sister. I was critical of Mother, but she did so very much for me. Even as I tell you about her I feel I should not be critical because she did so much for me.

A.: I guess you see the identification with your mother—tending to be like her and her model of how you and others should be. You said you are like her at home and in the office. And also your feeling of guilt toward her because of your hostility to her, a resentment that, however, has mostly been repressed. And your anger when people do not mother you as she did.

P.: Yes, I see. But I don't want to be like Mother. She was respected, but she was not happy, and she did not make her family happy. She did so much for us but would not leave my father or my sister or me alone to live our own lives [tears]. My wife is so different; she will have no part of mothering me. She sends out my clothes to be cleaned and mended. She refuses to mother me.

A.: You must become fully aware of your anger and what makes it. Like your wife's refusal to mother you, which may be the very best thing in the world for you.

P.: Yes, I see your point. I'm sure it's true. If she let me slip into the same feelings toward her that I had toward my mother—I just don't want to contemplate it.

A.: That is one of the central secrets of maturing and of psychotherapy—to avoid entrapment by your childhood patterns, so that you feel as a mature adult would toward others, in a realistic way, and not as you did as a child toward your mother, or toward whomever the disturbed pattern developed. I think you will solve this well because through it all there was also real love between your mother and yourself and because your relationship with your father was so easy, warm and secure. I feel pretty sure your episode of a fast heart beat was nothing more than repressed anger because the others in the board meeting did not treat you as your mother did, and because they did not behave as your mother, and now you, expected. And your tension is anger because you miss your mother and all the solicitude she represented. With your wife's personality as it is, I think you can outgrow the expectations toward her that you had to your mother. As you do that, she will be more responsive, warm and giving to you, and you will be less and less irritable. The vicious circle will stop; there will be less undercurrent of anger, and more giving, tolerance and warmth.

In this fortunate instance improvement did indeed start after this single interview in which it was possible to uncover the essential dynamics. Of course such insight alone is only effective where the balance of forces in both husband and wife is thus favorable. Sometimes one can see clearly in an hour a pattern that takes years to resolve. But here the wholesome and mature impulses preponderated; the exacerbation of demands and resentment by the mother's death were alleviated. And Myron was on the way out—out of that part of his feelings toward his mother that caused tension and irritability when transferred to his family and business associates.

Usually it is unwise for husbands and wives to discuss their unconsciouses with each other. But there are no rigid rules, only guiding principles. Myron did tell Sylvia of his tendency to want her to mother him and his anger when she didn't; and of his recognition of his being like his mother in strictness and criticalness although he did not want to be this way. This helped, for it only made explicit what Sylvia sensed anyway; it might not have helped if Myron himself had not been eager to reduce this component in his marriage. With all the love from and toward his mother, and so unambivalently toward his father, and toward his sister as well (although she was not a prominent figure in his life), he had the base for good relationships. He was not psychoanalyzed in the sense that he did not go through a "transference neurosis," that is, the living through toward the analyst of the disturbed pattern toward his mother.

This transference was apparently not necessary; the good feelings predominated. Although older than I at the time, he related to me warmly, openly, and with confidence, following the pattern toward his father. We had twelve meetings—weekly at first, then fortnightly, then monthly. The anxiety attack did not recur. His relations to his wife and children had their ups and downs but improved steadily; his tension in his profession diminished.

He could use the insight to spot his tendency to want others to behave like his mother toward him or in line with the standards of behavior she set for him and for everyone. But the unconscious is treacherous and I thought the time might come when he would find it advisable to return for more intensive work. But he continued to improve. Perhaps the friendly relationship with me helped, at least over the first few years. We continued to correspond for eight years after the war and to meet occasionally when he came east. Then he moved to southern California and we lost touch. The quick collapse of the neurotic structure was most gratifying, in contrast to instances of equally clear and simple dynamics in which the balance of healthy mature forces and disturbed infantile ones is such as to be very stubborn and resistant therapeutically.

*Let us cherish and love old age, for it is full of pleasure, if one knows how to use it.*

SENECA

*A time to love, and a time to wed, and a time to seek rest.*

DIONYSIUS

# 33 IN THE DECLINE

Age is not the obstacle to help with emotional problems it was once thought to be—the essential is still the balance of emotional forces. But there is no cure for waning charms and powers except graceful acceptance of nature, of the life cycle we are all born to, and making the most of our pleasure in the mature pursuits.

A successful business executive of 56, Owen, came for consultation because of anxiety. The suspicion, created by his story, that there was an undercurrent of rage at his wife was quickly confirmed by his report of a dream of riding into a slum area in which a man attacked a woman. The slum area turned out to be his unconscious; the attacker, his own hostility to his wife. He had been close to his mother, he said, but not really close, not the way he wished, and he had repressed resentment against her. His father had died when Owen was 5 years old. It was soon evident that Owen was overly dependent on his wife, following the pattern toward his mother.

His wife was threatening to leave him, or at least to have a sexual affair with some as yet unchosen man. She was enraged at Owen because he did not function well sexually. He no longer had the interest, she complained, nor gave the performance. First she thought he had a mistress. Then he thought something was wrong physically; he saw a urologist, then an endocrinologist, and tried hormones. All to no avail. Now he had developed anxiety about his sexual ability and thought that the problem was psychological, that he had developed some sexual inhibition. He had never had this

229

problem before, except once or twice in youth when he did not function well sexually—but then it was only a transient problem under unusual circumstances.

Of course he had thought of the fact that he was 56 and his wife 52. They were grandparents. This, in my opinion, was a matter for graceful acceptance of the inevitable, after a lifetime to be grateful for. Battling against the course of the life cycle could only add struggle and frustration. It was, as usual, a matter of making the most of what existed, not raging against the reality. He saw this and talked it over with his wife. She was well preserved but long past the menopause. He would arouse her without being able to follow through adequately. On her side, her own desires would arouse those in her husband. He would try or not try, and either way would more often than not leave her urges unsatisfied.

After some recognition of the facts of life, she adjusted reasonably well by having a bedroom to herself, thus being separated from the temptations of the conjugal bed. With her anger and her threats of infidelity removed, and with insight into his own rage at her because of this, Owen's anxiety diminished rapidly. Then he too had to face the years of adjustment to waning desire and potency. They reached a good *modus vivendi,* with mutual understanding of these tribulations of decline.

There was one untoward but revealing incident about two years after this. Owen was reading in bed in his room. The weather was hot. He was seminude. His hand wandered idly to his genitals. His wife suddenly entered. She went into a rage because she said he showed more evidence of potency there alone than he had the few times that they succeeded in having relations.

Such a case is typical. Certainly the gradual decline of desire has its problems no less than the sudden onslaught of the sexual urge in adolescence. Of course, a few men remain fully active sexually well into their seventies, and some probably longer. But most go through the decline in their late fifties, and for many it begins in the forties. Wet dreams and masturbation show the physiology to be intact still, but lust and potency no longer power effective performance.

*Give me other mothers [and fathers] and I will give you an-
other world.*

St. Augustine

*Over the unborn our power is that of God and our responsi-
bility like His toward us. As we acquit ourselves toward them,
so let Him deal with us.*

Bellamy

## A CONCLUSION AND PERSPECTIVE: MARRIAGE, HOSTILITY, AND HISTORY

Science, to put it oversimply, is a repeating method of drawing key formulations from factual observations and testing these formulations with further observations.

A recapitulation of what our examples have shown and a look beyond the marriages for consequences to society at large, and for what may reduce the suffering human beings cause each other.

It takes human beings so many years to mature that one might think we would do a thorough job of it. Perhaps we do, on the average, physically and intellectually; but emotionally it seems to work the other way—we are children for so long that we never get over it.

The emotional patterns with which children react to treatment by parents and others responsible for and close to them continue for life. Of course in adult life these patterns come out toward other persons, are transferred to them—not only to spouse and children but also to friends, acquaintances, associates, various groups in society, country and humanity. One's feelings toward his parents repeat themselves toward the world. Hence *each person behaves in society about as he did in his childhood home. The home shapes the citizen. Thereby the home shapes history.*

If the child was given love and security and respect for his personality from conception through the early days, weeks,

231

months and years (from 0 to 6), then he continues to feel loved and respected and secure with people in adult life and in his own mind with himself. With this basic condition met for adequately maturing emotionally, he or she becomes a good, responsible spouse, parent, friend and citizen. However if the child's needs for love, security and respect are not met, then the two opposite effects ensue: (1) he feels unloved, insecure, not respected by others and by himself, and (2) he does not adequately mature emotionally.

The reason for the latter is that the child naturally tends to grow from his initial parasitic helplessness at birth into his adult responsibility for himself and others. If he is unloved, insecure, unrespected, he cannot grow satisfactorily into the responsibility for others that is the basis for being a loving, respecting husband or wife, parent, friend and citizen. Instead, since frustration of fundamental needs threatens the child, he reacts with a tendency to fight and to escape—fight and flight. Little and helpless, he can do neither openly but frustrations accumulate beneath the surface, making an adult who is hostile or withdrawn or both.

The path to maturity is apparent if one observes a good mother or father with a loved child. This relationship is strong and clear throughout the animal kingdom; we use the expression accurately when we speak of fighting like a tigress to protect one's cubs.

Just visualize the baby or small child, utterly helpless, entirely dependent for his life on the parents. Weak and helpless as he is, if he is left without parents or substitutes of course he panics. He feels weak and inadequate and inferior to the big adults; he is so competitive, fighting for his position, because being loved is his only guarantee of survival. Being helpless the child is insecure and anxious, readily threatened and frustrated, and therefore angry. His hostilities are constantly restrained by his parents (or substitutes) and so usually are his sexual desires, which can only be used for play and not for mating or reproduction. As he reaches his full size and strength, the child becomes able to mate and reproduce, and this reverses the attitudes: the child now as an adult must be responsible for himself and for his spouse and children.

Hence *responsibility* is such a big word in the dictionary of the emotional life. We grow *out* of intense needs *for* love and dependence, which cause insecurity, anxiety, frustration, competitiveness, and the consequent tendencies of hostility and withdrawal, which lead to guilt and shame. We grow *toward* increasing capacity for independence, giving love, responsibility, and for living and letting live in a friendly, cooperative way.

Harmony and satisfaction in marriage are difficult to achieve even at best. This is because marriage is a complex interaction of feelings. In simplest terms, the husband is part mature, part still the child he was. So is the wife. The mature part drives the husband to find a wife, enjoy sex (which is easy), rear the young (which is a strenuous lifetime job), and support the family. But he may not relish all this to the full because the childhood part resents the responsibilities and makes him feel resentful and impels him to escape them in various ways. The conflict between the mature and the childish parts of his make-up tend to frustrate both. The same is true for the wife. She may maturely want marriage but childishly reject its responsibilities. Both husband and wife may want to give less and get more. If both husband and wife had childhoods with good, loving relationships, they work out their conflicts between childishness and maturity to a reasonably satisfying, happy solution. But if their childhood patterns of feelings toward others are full of frustration and anger, then this is an added source of difficulty.

In addition to the maturity, childishness, and patterns of feelings toward others, there are the sexual urges, tastes, inhibitions, and exaggerations; the physical health; and the habits and rhythms of living, such as activeness, amounts of sleep, and hours of retiring and rising. All these in each partner must jibe reasonably with those in the other. No wonder marriage takes a lot of maturity and adjustment, and no wonder the reality is often different from the dream. A lot of capacity for taking responsibility, giving love, and tolerating hostility and frustration is required. It is difficult to give up *having* a parent in order to *be* a parent. We all look for some—sometimes too much—of the parent in our spouse.

Improper child rearing, by not meeting the child's basic biological needs, prevents its maturing to these capacities. Hence all the neurosis, psychosis, addiction, crime and war. Hence all the marital misery and the transmission of all this pathology, all this emotional disorder, from generation to generation. Hence marriage and history are what they are.

The more one sees and learns of how children are treated from conception on, the less surprised he must be at the state of the world with all its hostility and suffering. In fact considering what children are subjected to, the surprise lies in the world's holding together as well as it does. There is even a possibility that self-preservation will nose out hostility and the need to suffer, so that we do not destroy others and ourselves.

Of course I am aware of being judged too optimistic for concluding that wanted children, reared from conception with love and with reasonably mature parents as examples, develop into adults of good will; and that if all, or most, adults were of good will, we could solve most of the world's problems by reason, in an attitude of social cooperation. Some ethologists will deem my conclusion naive, in light of the powerful instincts that they are observing in so many species. I do not mean to undervalue the strength of these, including those that analytic psychiatry has not studied explicitly, such as intergroup fighting for territory, or has known by different names—drives for status, for example, being known as narcissism, competitiveness and masculine protest. On the contrary, the findings of ethologists are deeply gratifying to anyone who has long known that instinct theory could never be adequately developed by clinical observation alone, without the study of instincts in animals. Study of animal behavior is a relatively new science, burgeoning with observations, ideas and unresolved problems. But a review is not necessary. If the systematic clinical observations of the practicing analyst are also descriptions of reality, then they must stand on their own as fact. The problem then is only in uniting the psychological clinical findings in people with the findings of the other human behavioral sciences and with those of ethology. As we noted earlier, the importance of man's long childhood seems to be this: the effects of this early period, of imprinting, conditioning and other learning, is to mold to a large degree and more or less permanently the many powerful innate instincts. Thus checks are formed against hostile aggression by love, by identification with kind parents, and by training; and such forces strengthen the social cooperation seen in all animals and described by Allee in *Cooperation Among Animals*. These early experiences thus shape the over-all pattern of thought, feeling and behavior, that is, the personality in each human for life. Hence the vast range from the psychotic lust murderer through every variation to the man or woman of genuine, responsible good will.

It is glaringly obvious that the disease that wreaks such havoc upon humanity, imposing enormous burdens when latent, and killing and maiming by the millions when active, is not heart disease or cancer or any other nonhuman agent—it is man's hostility to man. This hostility of members of a species to their own kind is unique in the animal kingdom. This exaggerated, destructive hostility goes beyond the normal, useful fight-flight response of other species. It is a symptom of emotional disorder, of failure to mature into a responsible adult of good will. This cancerous hostility is the essential step in all psychopathology, from internal psychological suffering through to acting out as violence.

One important cause of this disease, this exaggerated hostility, is no longer a mystery. It lies in faulty child rearing by omission and commission. This cause lies in such mistreatment as underprotection or overprotection, deprivation or spoiling, domination or premature responsibility, dotingness or hostility, over-discipline or absence of socialization. Such are the things that stunt and warp development, making hostile emotional cripples instead of mature, loving, responsible husbands and wives, parents, friends and citizens. The contrast between such mature adults of good will and those of cruelty and violence is dramatic, despite all the intermediate mixtures. By making every child a wanted child, by assuring every child of the love, security and respect that he needs as much as he needs food and shelter, we can prevent tormented marriages, mental illness, crime and war. "If we had one generation of properly reared children we might have utopia itself."

# REFERENCES

Since this book presents clinical material and is not a theoretical study based upon the vast literature on sex, love, and marriage, only a few immediately pertinent references are given.

1. Ackerman, Nathan, *The Psychodynamics of Family Life*, N.Y., Basic Books, 1958.
   A scholarly, pioneering presentation. It is interesting to read this study which comes nearly forty years after Flügel. Focus is on family inter-relations rather than directly on the dynamics of marriage and what lies behind them, but it gives a broad perspective.
2. Alexander, Judge Paul W., American Bar Assn. *Journal*, Feb. 1950.
3. Allee, Warder C., *Cooperation Among Animals, with Human Implications*, N.Y., Schuman, 1951.
4. Ardrey, Robert, *African Genesis*, N.Y., Dell Publishing Co., 1963.
5. Ardrey, Robert, *The Territorial Imperative*, N.Y., Atheneum, 1966.
   His books contain many questionable points, but are intriguingly written and thought provoking.
6. Ashley Montagu, M. F., "Marriage—A Cultural Perspective," in *Neurotic Interaction in Marriage* (V. W. Eisenstein, ed.), N.Y., Basic Books, 1956.
7. Ashley Montagu, M. F., *The Meaning of Love*, N.Y., Julian Press, 1955.
8. Bell, Norman W., and Vogel, Ezra F., eds., *A Modern Introduction to the Family*, N.Y., The Free Press, 1960.
9. Bergler, Edmund, *Unhappy Marriage and Divorce*, N.Y., International Universities Press, Inc., 1946.
10. Blood, Robert O., Jr., *Marriage*, N.Y., The Free Press, 1962.
11. Bossard, James J. S., and Boll, Eleanor S., *Why Marriages Go Wrong*, N.Y., The Ronald Press Co., 1958.
12. Bowlby, John, *Child Care and the Growth of Love*, Baltimore, Penguin Books, 1953. (Based on *Maternal Care and Mental Health*, N.Y., Columbia Univ. Press, 1951.)
    The subject is not marriage, only a related topic; but the thinking is dynamic and scientific.
13. Carrighar, Sally, *Wild Heritage*, Boston, Houghton Mifflin, 1965.
    An excellent, indispensable must as background for all students of human motivation, personality and behavior. Digests much of the recent ethological literature. Describes the behavior of animals in nature clearly and interestingly.
14. Chance, Erika, *Families in Treatment*, N.Y., Basic Books, Inc., 1959.
15. Clay, George R., "We're All Guests," *New World Writing #8*, New Ameri-

can Library of World Literature, Inc. Reprinted in *The Best American Short Stories of 1965* (Martha Foley, ed.), Boston, Houghton Mifflin Co., 1956.

16. Durant, Will, *The Story of Civilization*, N.Y., Simon & Schuster, 1935–.
17. Ehrenwald, Jan, *Neurosis in the Family and Patterns of Psychosocial Defense* (Hoeber, ed.), N.Y., Harper & Row, 1963.
18. Eisenberg, Leon, "The Family in the Mid-Twentieth Century," *Social Welfare Forum*, N.Y., Columbia University Press, 1960.
19. Eisenstein, Victor W., ed., *Neurotic Interaction in Marriage*, N.Y., Basic Books, 1956.
    Not the same focus on dynamics, but some relevance, particularly the chapter by L. Kubie on "Psychoanalysis and Marriage" and R. H. Wel's chapter, "Psychiatry and the Law in Separation and Divorce," a clear statement on this subject.
20. Flügel, J. C., *The Psycho-analytic Study of the Family*, London, Hogarth Press, 1929.
    An early classic that is still valuable and contains the germinal concepts of many later developments; however, it deals hardly at all with marriage itself.
21. Ford, C. S. and Beach, F. A., *Patterns of Sexual Behavior*, N.Y., Harper & Bros., 1951.
22. Freud, S., *A General Introduction to Psychoanalysis*, Garden City, N.Y., Garden City Pub. Co., Inc., 1938.
23. Freud, S., *New Introductory Lectures*, N.Y., Norton, 1933.
24. Galdson, Iago, ed., *The Family in Contemporary Society*, N.Y., International Universities Press, 1958.
25. Goldstein, J. and Katz, Joseph, *The Family and the Law*, Glencoe, Ill., Free Press of Glencoe, 1965.
26. Greene, Bernard L., ed., *The Psychotherapies of Marital Disharmony*, N.Y., The Free Press, 1965.
27. Grotjahn, Martin, *Psychoanalysis and the Family Neurosis*, N.Y., W. W. Norton & Co., Inc., 1960.
28. Hess, Robert D. and Handel, Gerald, *Family Worlds*, Chicago, University of Chicago Press, 1963.
29. Josselyn, Irene M., "The Family as a Psychological Unit," *Social Casework*, 34, 1953, pp. 336–43.
30. Kinsey, Alfred C., et al., *Sexual Behavior in the Human Female*, Phila., Saunders, 1953.
31. Kinsey, Alfred C., et al., *Sexual Behavior in the Human Male*, Phila., Saunders, 1948.
32. Kluckhohn, Florence R. and Spiegel, John P., *Integration and Conflict in Family Behavior*, Topeka, Kansas, Report No. 27, Group for the Advancement of Psychiatry, 1954.
33. Kohut, Nestor C., *A Manual on Marital Reconciliations*, Chicago, Adams Press, 1964.
34. Lorenz, Konrad, *King Solomon's Ring*, N.Y., Crowell, 1952.
35. Lorenz, Konrad, *On Aggression*, N.Y., Harcourt, Brace & World, 1966.
    Authoritative descriptions of a range of animal behavior bearing on the

problem of hostile aggression. Applications to human war are not convincing, but are a beginning. They do not take into account the effect of early conditioning and the differences between humans of violence and those of good will.

36. Masserman, Jules H., ed., *Science and Psychoanalysis* II *Individual and Familial Dynamics*, N.Y., Grune & Stratton, Inc., 1958.
37. Mudd, E., Mitchell, H., Taubin, S., *Success in Family Living*, N.Y., Assoc. Press, 1965.
    An interesting and illuminating systematic study of 100 "successful" families in the various aspects of their relationships and functioning. Each chapter has an extensive bibliography.
38. Mudd, Emily and Kirch, Aron, eds., *Man and Wife*, N.Y., Norton, 1957.
    A concise, multi-authored discussion of many aspects of marriage.
39. Parsons, T. and Bales, R. F., *Family, Socialization and Interaction Process*, N.Y., The Free Press, 1960.
40. Saul, L. J., *Bases of Human Behavior*, Phila., Lippincott, 1951.
41. Saul, L. J., and Wenar, Solvieg, "Early Influences on Development and Disorders of Personality," *Psychoanalytic Quarterly*, Vol. 34, 327–389, 1965.
42. Saul, L. J., *Emotional Maturity*, 2nd edition, Phila., Lippincott, 1960.
43. Saul, L. J., *The Hostile Mind*, N.Y., Random House, 1956.
44. Saul, L. J., "Othello: Projection in Art," *Journal of the American Medical Association*, Vol. 200, No. 1, pp. 39–40.
45. Saul, L. J., "Sudden Death at Impasse," *Psychoanalytic Forum*, Vol. 1, No. 1, 1966.
46. Saul, L. J., *Technic and Practice of Psychoanalysis*, Phila., Lippincott, 1958.
47. Waddington, C. H., *The Ethical Animal*, N.Y., Atheneum, 1961.
48. Winch, Robert F. and McGinnis, Robert, eds., *Selected Studies in Marriage and the Family*, N.Y., Holt, Rinehart & Winston, Inc., 1953.
49. *The World Almanac*, N.Y., N.Y. World-Telegram and The Sun, 1966.

# INDEX

disturbances in, 21
and independence, 73, 75
in marriage, 13–14, 15, 21, 51
and proper child rearing, 106
and responsibility, 73
*See also* Love, mature
Moral law, 17–19, 21

Neurosis, 37, 51, 97, 233
infatuation as, 103
Nymphomania, 176

Object relation, 12, 46, 208
*On Aggression*, 22

Parental treatment, *see* Child rearing
Parenthood, 13, 15, 18–21, 192, 193, 197
Parents
as confidants, 24, 209–10
"Generations don't mix," 83
and identification, 208, 234
object relations with, 208
and sex education, 197–98
Physiology of gratification, 68
Potency, 230
Promiscuity, 194–96
rejection a cause of, 195
Prostitution, 190
Psychiatrist, *see* Analyst
Psychiatry, 209n.
Psychoanalysis, *see* Analytic Treatment
Psychoanalyst, *see* Analyst
Psychodynamics, 39, 49, 85, 163
defined, *vi*, 209n.
how to discern, 36–37
in fiction, 144
Psychosomatic symptoms, 126
Psychotherapy, *see* Analytic treatment

Quarrels, *see* Conflict

Regression
in analytic treatment, 110–11, 119
at birth of child, 94
family as victim of, 95, 121

and masochism, 122
vs. progressive forces, 119
recovery from, 94–95
severe, 77, 79, 121, 123, 138, 190
and sex, 94
in successful men, 120
war as, 115
"Repetition compulsion," 56
Responsibility, 73, 76, 78–79, 95, 106, 232
avoidance of, 77, 84, 93–94
family, 12, 13, 51, 73, 233
financial, 12, 13, 15, 87, 120, 125
for the home, 87, 125
individual, *vi*
in marriage, 199
Romance, 12, 13, 70

Sadism, 10, 12, 18, 43, 106, 182, 192–93, 201
Satyriasis, 176
Sex, 15, 19, 192–94
in animals, 23
and conditioning, 8
as drain of feelings, 23, 29, 43, 68, 81, 192, 194
education, 24, 197–98
as expression of love, 12, 70
extramarital, *see* Infidelity
hostility in, 96, 192
impersonal, 29, 31, 43, 96, 190, 193
importance in marriage, 13, 96, 114
and imprinting, 7
and mating, 8
need for wooing in, 23–24, 65–66
and personality, 7, 193
perversions, 76, 106
premarital, 189–90, 192–94, 196, 198
and regression, 94
and reproduction, 12
and youth, 12, 189–90, 194, 196, 232
Sibling rivalry, 128–29
Smoking, 82
Social cooperation, 9, 17–18